EXETER
BURNING

The Exeter Blitz Illustrated

PETER THOMAS

HALSGROVE

First published in Great Britain in 1992
Second revised edition 2002

Copyright © Peter Thomas 1992

British Library Cataloguing-in-Publication Data
A CIP record for this title is available from the British Library

ISBN 1 84114 157 7

HALSGROVE
Halsgrove House
Lower Moor Way
Tiverton, Devon EX16 6SS
Tel: 01884 243242
Fax: 01884 243325
email sales@halsgrove.com
website www.halsgrove.com

Printed and bound in Great Britain by Bookcraft Ltd, Midsomer Norton

INTRODUCTION

To mark the 50th anniversary of the bombing of Exeter in May 1942 I produced, in 1992, the book *Fire on the Wind*. It was based on the official wartime records for the City of Exeter that had never before been made available for publication. The records were produced in conjunction with 150 wartime photographs from my private archive The Isca Historical Photographic Collection, many of which also had never before been published. The combination of official records and historic images produced the most important reference to wartime Exeter that has ever been published, although only 1000 copies were printed to mark the 50th anniversary.

The written records had lain unnoticed with the police authority until they were brought to my attention by a friend and colleague, Mr Brian Estill, the curator of the Police Museum. After expressing to him my disappointment at not turning up any official information I was elated when shortly after our conversation he deposited with me a number of metal boxes, stating 'I think this may interest you' and promptly left me to it. On opening them I was astounded by documents marked 'secret' along with other conspicuous official headings. Here was the information that Exeter people had spoken about for nearly fifty years and the stories I had heard throughout my life started to unravel. It was extraordinary handling important historical documents that had involved local people whose lives had been radically changed by the major events the documents described. It was an awe-inspiring feeling, mixed with excitement, handling such records. I resolved that a determined effort would have to be made to publish these and, later, due permission was given by the Chief Constable.

Upon publishing, the first edition was soon sold and has not been reproduced since, although there have been constant requests for the book over the past ten years. The relevance of this information grows even more important as each generation passes, taking with them memories we shall never have the opportunity to hear again. For younger people it is often a revelation to hear and read of the circumstances their parents or grandparents endured, and of course their family name often appears in the official documentation.

One factor above all has come to the forefront for many people who were either very young or who came to Exeter after the war – the extent of the devastation. The evidence is revealed in the 150 photographs that graphically portray this aspect. Time and time again people are surprised and often unaware of the extent of damage that occurred, particularly the loss of major historic buildings and streets. The wholesale destruction of the city was to be a major turning point in relation to the change of character that was to ensue with post-war building. The destruction continued under the city's own hand right up to the 1980s. For historians, researchers, planners and others this book is an invaluable aid to understanding Exeter at this period and charts the reasons why the central areas of the city look as they do today.

I am delighted that Halsgrove have taken the opportunity to reprint this book, now called *Exeter Burning* as it will once again make available a most valuable record.

Peter Thomas
Abbey Road
Exeter

ABOUT THE AUTHOR

Exeter born local historian, photographer, author and lecturer Peter Thomas has been involved with Exeter's local history for nearly thirty years. He is the owner of The Isca Historical Photographic Collection that he established in 1974 to protect the city's visual heritage. The Collection is now recognised as being of local, regional and national interest and is estimated to contain up to 60,000 images.

As a local author Peter is well known for a number of history publications, having produced 13 books designed to heighten public awareness of historic Exeter and to promote The Isca Collection. Two commercial videos have also been made, 'Old Exeter' and 'The Exeter Blitz'. The latter was produced to mark the 50th anniversary of the Exeter Blitz in May 1942.

As a photographer Peter started taking photographs at the age of eleven and for thirteen years worked in a photographic retail outlet in Exeter where he gained an interest in the history of photography and was a collector of photographic antiques. Latterly his role changed to The Tourism Promotion Officer for The City of Exeter during which time, he created the city's guided tour service, Exeter Guided Tours, and the famous Exeter Redcoat Guides. Under his management approximately 450,000 people came to Exeter to undertake guided tours and to discover the history of the city. In 1987 he produced, instigated and managed the largest historical exhibition ever held in the city 'The Great Exeter Exhibition' that attracted 10,000 people in one week. To heighten the city's profile in the tourism stakes he also created 'The Exeter Historical Pageant' and 'The Exeter Heritage Weekend' that also attracted thousands of people to the city.

Peter Thomas has lectured for many years on many aspects of Exeter and latterly has been undertaking significant presentations at the Northcott Theatre attracting audiences of up to 500 people. Major presentations include 'The bombing of Exeter in Sight and Sound', 'The Rebuilding of Post-war Exeter' and 'Pre-War Exeter'. Hundreds of images are used for these productions.

Peter has frequently been called upon to assist with television productions and has been interviewed both on TV and radio on a number of occasions. He is currently seeking to create a major heritage attraction for Exeter utilising The Isca Historical Photographic Collection and has staged a major exhibition on 'The Bombing of Exeter' to mark the 60th anniversary of the city's destruction in May 1942.

He is a regular contributor to the county magazine *Devon Today*.

ACKNOWLEDGEMENTS

I should like to thank the following people and organisations for their help in the production of this book.

Firstly I am indebted to the Chief Constable for official permission to publish the official war time documents. Very special thanks are given to Police Constable Estill of the Devon and Cornwall Police Museum for his invaluable assistance without which this book would not have been published. As always thanks are given to The West Country Studies Library. Thanks are also due to the Exeter Fire Services. I am most grateful to Mr Bert Baker who has been so very supportive and informative about the City during the war time period. To Arthur Curtis, for his fascinating account on siren alerts and other information, my thanks. I should also like to acknowledge the late Ernest Fraser and his wife for giving time to talk of his experiences. For permission to use archive photographs The Museum of Arts and Culture, Lübeck, Germany, and to Mr Hans Peter Asmus for his assistance. For valuable help and assistance Mrs L. Till, Mr K. Lark and Mrs M. Wilmer. A special acknowledgement to Mr and Mrs Sprague for permission to use their photographs. Also to Mr G. Cornish, Mr S. Salter. Mr K. Maun, Mr E.A. Evans, Mr R.W. Bray, Mr W. Dymond, Mr M. McGahey. To the educational unit of Exeter Cathedral and Mr Henderson. To Mr Paul Cleave for a number of interesting items and also to Mrs J. Kemp, Mr B. Brewer, Mr H. Bennett and Mr T. Barrell. It is also appropriate to acknowledge the late Reverend R. Langhorne for his photographs and all those photographers whose work from this period was used. I should like to thank the late Mrs J. Venning for giving permission to use her husband's maps of bombed Exeter. Finally to all the citizens of Exeter who have in some way helped towards this production my sincere thanks.

DEDICATION

To my father, the late Walter Charles Thomas

LIST OF ILLUSTRATIONS

THE ISCA COLLECTION

The Isca Collection was first started in 1974 by the author after discovering that a huge collection of photographic plates and negatives were liable to be disposed of. The resource was the work of Henry Wykes and his assistant Marjorie Hockmuth. Following the closure of the Wykes Studio in Northernhay Place, Exeter, in 1974, the author obtained the complete collection of some 42,000 half-plate negatives. Examination of these records revealed that they showed Exeter as it had been from around 1910 up to 1970. It was obvious that the work was of vital importance to the history of Exeter and started the author's passion for collecting photographic records of the City of Exeter. To date the Collection includes negatives, prints, slides, albums, books and other items of interest.

In the following years numerous exhibitions have been undertaken, assistance given to TV documentary makers, along with radio interviews and press coverage. The Collection has been responsible for a number of publications to date including *Old Exeter*, *Aspects of Exeter* (co-author Jacqueline Warren), *The House That Moved*, *Exeter in Old Postcards*, and *Exeter in Old Photographs*. It has also assisted with illustrations for a variety of other publications. The Collection is the largest private carchive of Exeter records and is registered with The Royal Photographic Society in the British Photographic Record, a directory of historical photographic collections.

An aerial view of the city of Exeter showing the central areas dominated by the great Cathedral of St Peter and Bedford Circus, c.1930.

THE CHARACTER OF EXETERS
PRE-WAR STREETS AND AREAS

Central High Street showing the church of St Lawrence.

Sidwell Street.

High Street from the Guildhall upwards.

The entrance to Dix's Field.

The interior of St Mary Arches Church showing its Norman columns.

The Globe Hotel, Cathedral Yard.

PRE-WAR BUILDINGS, STREETS AND FEATURES OF HISTORICAL AND ARCHITECTURAL INTEREST

Upper High Street. Eastgate Arcade shown left.

Bedford Circus.

The Honiton Inn and lower Paris Street.

Central High Street, upper section.

London Inn Square.

Central High Street showing Commercial Union and Brufords.

MANY DESTROYED DURING WORLD WAR II

Fore Street. The Universal Stores once stood at the top of the street.

The corner of Sidwell Street and Paris Street.

Southernhay. The Gaslight and Coke company near Dix's Field.

Southernhay Congregational Church.

Plaza Cinema, London Inn Square.

High Street. Statue of Henry VII on Mark Rowe Building.

GAS MASKS

Gas Masks: Protection from the possible use of poisonous gas became a priority resulting in an awesome appearance when in use.

THIS IS THE WAY TO DEAL WITH INCENDIARIES!

12

THE AIR RAID SHELTER – THE ANDERSON

The Anderson shelter. Many domestic back gardens in the city had their own Anderson shelter buried in the ground. They were often cold, damp and filled with water.

Life could revolve around the Anderson Shelter.

AIR RAID 4TH MAY 1942

A PREMONITION

Many families spent hours underground or in basements.

A mother's instinct

On that night, my mother went upstairs to the bedroom but refused to undress. She said to my father "The German planes are on their way". After several requests from my father to "Get into bed and not be silly as it was now 1.30 a.m." she still refused and ignored his requests. Suddenly the alert siren sounded, my mother was fully dressed and looking out of the window. Within seconds she had myself and two sisters downstairs and in the Morrison table shelter. Shortly after a bomb fell which collapsed the ceiling onto the beds where we had been sleeping. Father rushed to put on his uniform over his pyjamas, left the house and we never saw him for another 48 hours.

THE MORRISON TABLE SHELTER

The enemy's present policy of attacking the residential areas of medium and small sized towns makes imperative the immediate provision of all readily available forms of air-raid shelter.

The "Morrison" table shelter is described in pamphlets issued by the Ministry of Home Security entitled "How to put up your Morrison Shelter" and "Shelter at Home". The efficiency of this type of shelter has been proved abundantly by experience in recent enemy raids, notably at Exeter and Bath, to mention only towns in the South West Region.

The number of Morrison Shelters issued to the public in Exeter up to May 2nd 1942 [just before the heaviest enemy attack on the city, May 4th] was 5918. Since that date many more have been distributed and erected, the total number up to August 8th being 9469. This is indicative of the favour in which this type of shelter is held in Exeter.

The following particulars taken from official reports, made by Regional bomb investigation and technical officers immediately after the enemy attack in every case, show conclusively the satisfactory behaviour of the Morrison table shelter in resisting the impact of debris falling upon it and shock following the detonation of H.E. bombs in close proximity.

Case 1. Wonford Street, Exeter, April 1942.
H.E. bomb exploded 15ft from the shelter. Crater about 43ft diameter and 15ft deep. House totally collapsed. Two people in the Morrison shelter on ground floor were dug out uninjured. The table shelter was found to be substantially undamaged.

Case 2. Wonford St. Exeter, April 1942.
The house adjoins case 1 and received a direct hit. H.E bomb struck about 5ft from edge of the Morrison shelter. Crater about 43ft diameter and 15ft deep. The house [two storeys] of "cob" and brickwork was completely destroyed. The shelter lifted in the air by blast. Damage to shelter was unknown at the time of the inspection as it was still partly buried under debris but the *five* occupants had been dug out all uninjured. The occupants had not been pinned down by any collapse of the shelter which stood on a concrete floor in a scullery.

Case 3. Regent Park, Exeter, April 1942.
H.E. bomb detonated about 30ft from the Morrison shelter. Crater about 48ft diameter by 15ft deep. The house [two storeys] was completely demolished but the shelter does not appear to have moved. The shelter contained two adults and four children, none of whom was injured.

Case 4. Roseland Ave., Exeter, May 1942.
A house of two storeys was completely destroyed by a direct hit by an H.E. bomb. There were six occupants of a Morrison table shelter on the ground floor of the house, none of whom was hurt. The shelter was tilted sideways [see photograph].

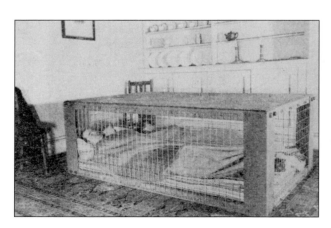

*The Monk's Road Incident. View to Beacon Avenue and
Exmouth Junction Railway Yard Raid, 4 May 1942.*

Case 5. Monk's Road, Exeter.

This is the most extraordinary of all the cases of recorded behaviour of "Morrisons" in the region. An H.E. bomb exploded forming a crater of 34ft diameter and 12ft deep. It completely destroyed a house in Monk's Road containing a woman and two children on the ground floor. The Morrison shelter was blown over a communal shelter (brick) in the street and landed on the bedroom floor of a house on the opposite side of the street. The table shelter was still more or less intact, the top plate of the table still being attached to the framework [see photograph]. The woman and one child were hospital cases but the second child was uninjured and running about the street on the day following the raid. Unfortunately the injured child has since died.

The four enemy raids on Exeter in April and May 1942 resulted in the death of 271 persons. Of this total two only can be associated with Morrison table shelters. One of these was the child who was injured in the Monk's Road incident [Case 5] who died later in hospital. No less than 293 Morrison shelters have been recovered from properties at Exeter destroyed by enemy action. Nearly all of these, excepting some damaged by fire after the inhabitants had evacuated the houses, are in serviceable condition.

It should be noted that all the photographs were taken when some of the debris above and/or surrounding the table shelter had been removed to enable the occupants to be got out.

Royal Commissioner's Office,
17 the Avenue, Clifton, Bristol.
15 August 1942.

THE BOMBING OF LUBECK, GERMANY

On the night of 28/29 March 1941 234 aircraft were despatched from England to bomb the North German city of Lubeck. It compared favourably with Exeter being of moderate size and of ancient origin. Its streets were narrow and contained many older buildings which would provide an excellent source for destruction by fire. It was said that Lubeck was not considered to be a vital target. The raid resulted in 144 tons of incendiaries and 160 tons of high explosives being dropped on the city.

This raid instigated the fury of Hitler who then ordered a series of reprisal raids to take place across England. These were to become known as 'The Baedecker Raids". One of those targets was to be Exeter.

Lubeck, spire on fire during a bombing raid.

Lubeck, Northern Germany, a devasted street.

Lubeck, central area after severe damage.

THE EXETER BLITZ 3RD/4TH MAY 1942

STATEMENT MADE BY ONE OF THE GERMAN PILOTS
Ernst Von Kugel

"It was a night of terror for the Exeter people. When I approached this town the bright reflections guided me.

Over the town I saw whole streets of houses on fire, flames burst out of windows and doors, devouring the roofs.

People were running everywhere and firemen were frantically trying to deal with the flames. It was a fantastic sight - no one who saw it will forget the greatness of this disaster.

We thought of the thousands of men, women and children, the victims of our deadly visit, but we thought of our Fuhrer and the command he gave 'Revenge'.

With cold calculation we carried out our orders."

NAZIS GLOATING

"Beautiful Picture Of Blazing Town"

ERNST VON KUGEL, claiming to be one of the German pilots who bombed Exeter on Sunday, broadcast to the German people yesterday in these terms:

"It was a night of horror for the people of Exeter. When I approached this town, the bright reflection of fires on the horizon guided me.

"Over the town itself I saw whole streets of houses on fire, flames bursting out of the windows and doors and devouring the roofs.

"People were running everywhere, and firemen were frantically trying to deal with the fires.

"It was a fantastic, fascinating sight. No one who saw it will forget the greatness of this disaster.

"While we circled the target of streets, my commander sighted a big, stately house on the fringe of the sea of fire. At that he aimed —and hit it with a high-explosive bomb.

"The bomb burst and debris flew towards the sky, the force of the explosion rocking our plane. What destruction!

"We thought of the thousands of men, women and children, the victims of our deadly visit. But we thought, too, of our Feuhrer, and the word of command he gave: 'Revenge!' With cool calculation we carried out our orders."

"ATTRACTIVE TARGETS."

Other German broadcasters are gloating over the work of the Luftwaffe in the South-West of England.

Here is one version of a raid on "one of the English cities which succumbed under the retaliatory blows of the Luftwaffe executing the promise given to the German nation by the Fuehrer."—

"The horridly beautiful picture of an inferno of flames devouring the centre of the town punished by the Luftwaffe will for ever linger in our minds.

"We flew many times over the place in search of most attractive targets. Our eye caught a small house with a picturesque tower adjoining a large building.

"Down went our bombs and we observed with fascination how the entire scene was transformed into a furnace of fire, of collapsing walls and roofs and of a sea of sparks glowing sky high.

"We knew that this night of terror meant grave misfortune and grief for hundreds of people, for thousands probably. But we flew in and accomplished our task with true airmen-like enthusiasm."

Another broadcaster described photographs taken of Bath and said with pride: "You can see that we completely erased from the surface of the ground the heart of Bath. Such were our orders and this is the result."

Express & Echo *cutting.*

Broadcast on German radio to England on 4 May 1942:

"Exeter was the jewel of the West... We have destroyed that jewel, and the Luftwaffe will return to finish the job."

Opposite page: *The bombing of Exeter, 4 May 1942. This unique photograph was taken from the top floor of the Rougemont Hotel, Queen Street. It shows the Cathedral with St Mary Majors Church illuminated by incendiaries and high explosives.*

Above: *View across the roof tops from Guinea Street to the Cathedral. As dawn broke on 4 May 1942 the City of Exeter was to be seen in a state of devastation.*

Opposite page: *Central High Street as seen from the General Post Office building. Destroyed buildings had collapsed into the street blocking access. The air was filled with choking acrid smoke which severely hampered rescuers. A tremendous temperature had been created by the fire, making the city feel like a warm summer's day. Workers stripped to the waist to be able to carry out their tasks while the sweat ran down their bodies.*

High Street showing Lloyds Bank (left) and Commercial Union (right).

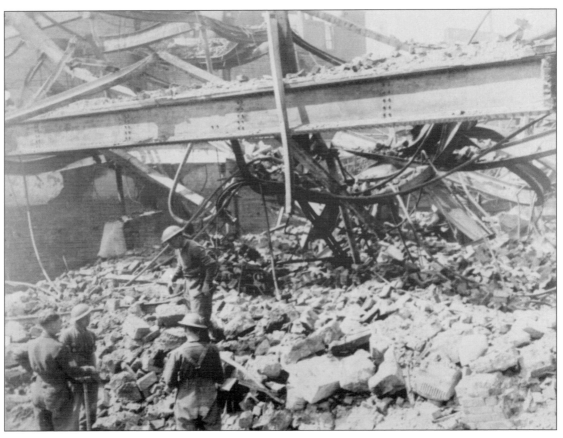

Wardens search the rubble for any signs of life.

Upper High Street. The General Post Office is seen in ruins. Workers were lucky to escape with their lives. The gap, left, is where the East Arcade once stood. It was totally destroyed.

High Street showing St Stephen's Bow. The ancient arch
belonging to St Stephen's Church narrowly escapes destruction.

Looking through St Stephen's Bow to Catherine Street. The arch
was later restored and still remains a unique feature of High Street.

Opposite page: *The centre of High Street looking towards Castle Street.*

High Street. Cooling down of Colson's premises.

High Street. Turntables in action at Colson's.

The Quay. Pre-war initiatives were taken to draw water from the River Exe by hosepipes which were relayed up into the City. This was to be a major factor in saving the City.

*Sidwell Street/Paris Street junction. Residents
wander stunned through a city hardly recognisable.*

The Red Cross helps out in Newtown.

Junction of High Street, Paris Street and Southernhay.   The steel framed building which contained L.H. Fearis and the Bude Cafe escaped total destruction.   Old Paris Street is seen left and the entrance to Southernhay right.

Paris Street.   Fire fighters battle to save the Palladium Cinema.

Paris Street. Wrecked shops after the raid of 24 April 1942.
South side (top) *and North side* (bottom).

*Paris Street. Police inspection. The Bude Cafe is seen
top left and the Savoy Cinema in the background.*

Newtown. The effect of the raid of 4 May 1942 on Portland Street.

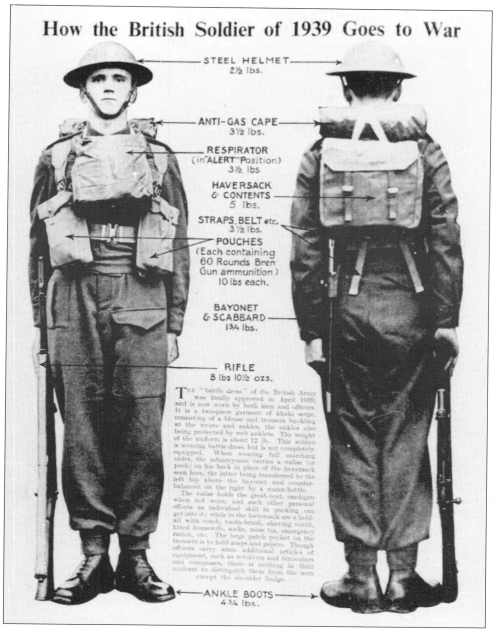

How the British Soldier of 1939 Goes to War

STEEL HELMET
2½ lbs.

ANTI-GAS CAPE
3½ lbs.

RESPIRATOR
(in "ALERT" Position)
3½ lbs

HAVERSACK
& CONTENTS
5 lbs.

STRAPS, BELT etc.
3½ lbs.

POUCHES
(Each containing
60 Rounds Bren
Gun ammunition)
10 lbs each.

BAYONET
& SCABBARD
1¾ lbs.

RIFLE
8 lbs 10½ ozs.

ANKLE BOOTS
4¾ lbs.

Many children who watched their fathers dress for war would never see them again.

Opposite page: Newtown. The pre-war area of Newtown and Sidwell Street were particularly dense in housing and business premises. This was to be the first area to sustain heavy raids. The Triangle can be seen in the centre of the photograph.

Prospect Park. Heavy damage was sustained by houses in this area during the raid on 24 April 1942. Buildings were turned white after having dust blasted into the brickwork.

St Thomas, Regent Street. Properties were totally destroyed by high explosive bombs on 24 April 1942.

Normandy Road. On 6 September a high explosive bomb penetrated the roof of 48 Normandy Road blowing the front of the property into the street.

Newtown. Damage in Portland Street after 4 May 1942.

A crater and damaged houses are all that remain at Comrie Crescent (above) following the night raid of 24 April 1942. An ancient building in King Street known as the 'Norman House' was exposed during the same raid and is seen to the left of the photograph below. The community have come to view the damage.

Okehampton Road. View of Okehampton Street from Exe Bridge after the night raid of 23 April 1942.

Wonford Street. A bomb crater and wrecked houses resulting from the night raid of 24 April 1942. People were trapped in two Morrison Shelters under debris for over an hour. They were rescued and found uninjured.

Paris Street and New North Road. The destruction of this corner site opened up new vistas of the Theatre Royal.

Sidwell Street. A further section of lower Sidwell Street was destroyed by communicating fires from a garage after inflammable material caught fire. Fire fighters were able to save the rest of the street.

Sidwell Street. The remaining half of the church tower stood in place defiantly until its demolition.

St Sidwell's Church received a direct hit during the raid of 4 May 1942. It cut the church in half. The bomb landed with such force that a section of granite weighing a quarter of a ton was hurled a quarter of a mile and landed through the roof of a house.

The clearing of Summerland Street and adjacent areas left vast ugly spaces.

St Lukes College. The well known teachers training college had a number of its substantial buildings gutted.

Dellers Cafe, Bedford Street. This prominent corner site was one of the most famous cafes in the south west of England. Built in conjunction with Lloyds Bank it was opened in 1916. It was the city's most prestigious venue for socialising and all manner of functions could be catered for. It was one of the city's greatest losses.

Deller's Cafe following its devastation on 4 May 1942.

High Street, the gutted premises of Lloyds Bank and Dellers Cafe showing Barclays Bank on the opposite corner of Bedford Street.

The site of Dellers Cafe on Bedford Street showing the public conveniences in the centre of Bedford Street. They were underground.

High Street to Bedford Street, the ornate entrance of Dellers would welcome no more guests.

Bedford Street corner. The property of Barclays Bank was gutted in the raid on 4th May 1942. It was the last premises to be demolished in High Street following the war.

The lavish interior of Dellers Cafe was destroyed.

*On High Street Dellers Cafe and Lloyds Bank proved difficult
to demolish due to the quality of their substantial construction.*

*The demolition of properties on High Street opened up views of the city that will never be seen
again. This photograph shows the site where Dellers Cafe and Lloyds Bank once stood. Bedford
Street is seen to the left and High Street in the foreground.*

Catherine Street is an ancient back street which runs parallel to High Street. It sustained severe damge during the war. The St Catherine's Almshouses survived as ruins and were kept as a memorial.

This scarred townscape was all that remained of Bedford Street following the bombing raids.

*On Catherine Street contemporary buildings
belonging to Bobby and Co. were to be demolished.*

The Abbotts Lodge and its partner, The Choristers School, stood behind Number 10, The Close. Both were splendid buildings and were destroyed on 4 May 1942 with loss of life.

The bombing of the Abbotts Lodge created an enormous crater. The hole was so large that it could have held a double-decker bus.

An extraordinary view from Catherine Street across to the Cathedral.

THE BOMBING OF EXETER CATHEDRAL

On 4 May 1942 a high explosive bomb was dropped on Exeter which landed beside the huge South tower of Exeter Cathedral. It crashed down through the Muniment Room and into the crypt where it exploded and totally destroyed St James Chapel. The bomb also removed two buttresses which support the great Exeter Cathedral and destroyed three bays of the Quire. As daylight filtered into the building in the early morning a scene of devastation faced Mr W. Dymond, the Cathedral Cross Bearer, and a number of other members of staff. Organ pipes were scattered over the floor, carved woodwork was blown into a thousand pieces, the pulpit was smashed and masonry lay all around. The air was filled with choking dust. With foresight, The Dean and Chapter had removed the ancient glass from the East window. It was stored together with the canopy of the Bishop's Throne in Mamhead House. Restoration work was carried out by Mr Herbert Read who completely restored the wooden screen in the South Aisle and St James Chapel was rebuilt. The tail fin of the bomb can still be seen today.

An incendiary bomb that fell on Exeter on 4 May 1942.

Cathedral Cross Bearer, Mr W. Dymond.

Opposite page: Exeter Cathedral as seen from the site of The Choristers School.

The majesty of Exeter Cathedral remained to dominate the City, as seen here from South Street. This photograph shows the ruins of the Vicars Choral at the base of the Cathedral.

A high explosive bomb completely destroyed St James Chapel. Hundreds of tons of masonry came crashing to the ground, in this photograph the figure of a man is dwarfed by the sheer scale of the rubble and the Cathedral behind him. Destruction of a further buttress could have seen the total collapse of a significant section of the Cathedral.

The damage caused to the south side of the Cathedral was phenomenal.

A view from the interior of the Cathedral out to the Bishops Palace prior to the rebuilding of St James Chapel.

A view from the interior of the Cathedral showing damage to external buildings.

A young boy searches the rubble of The Choristers School.

Damage to the south aisle of the Cathedral.

Reconstruction of St James Chapel begins.

Opposite page: *The King and Queen visit Exeter Cathedral to inspect the damage. The Queen is seen here with Mr Herbert Read who was in charge of the restoration of much of the fabric of the Cathedral. The visit was made on 8 May and was followed by a tour of the City.*

The Reverend Richard Langhorne (left) was headmaster of the Cathedral Choristers School. He recorded the destruction of his school on a simple Folding Kodak Rollfilm camera. The negatives were found only recently and are a valuable addition to Exeter's records.

The Cathedral Choristers School in ruins.

The front elevation of the Choristers School.

Choristers explore the ruins of their famous school.

Above: *The front elevation of the Choristers School.*

Below: *Although the majority of Exeter's beautiful Cathedral Close escaped destruction, numbers 11 and 12 were totally destroyed. Post-war both buildings were reinstated. The quality of the new buildings is so impressive that a visitor to the Close would be unaware of any change.*

The ancient church of Mary Arches was confined, pre-war, in a narrow cobbled street. The bombing of adjacent areas left the building exposed. The most remarkable feature of the church is its namesake Norman arches, thankfully these were not destroyed although the building did lose its roof (above). An American wooden landing barge was used to restore the roof after it had been ditched at Topsham.

The church of St Lawrence in High Street was gutted on 4 May 1942. Its famous porch, which held the statue of Elizabeth I survived. The statue was retained but the rest of the building was demolished.

Despite its difficulties, Exeter maintained its civic duties. The Sheriff's Coach is seen passing the ruins of St Lawrence Church in High Street.

The facade of the Commercial Union building and the church of St Lawrence in High Street were both still standing when this photograph was taken. Demolition contractors were soon to be put to work dismantling structures that had been partially damaged and were deemed dangerous. Both of these buildings were later removed.

The classical frontage of the Commercial Union was adorned with a full size statue of King Alfred.

The size of the Commercial Union property and the extent of the damage caused to it is visible in this war time photograph.

The most notable architectural feature in Exeter, after the Cathedral, was a Georgian Crescent of houses which contained a chapel. It was called 'Bedford Circus'. Although approximately two-thirds of the structure was destroyed by fire on 4 May 1942, a substantial portion remained. Bedford Circus was regarded as a highly important piece of English architecture and, although rebuilding was suggested, the structure was entirely removed.

Bampfylde Street connected High Street to Catherine Street. At its junction was a fine sixteenth-century house which at one time was property of the Bampfylde family. In later years it became a museum. It was one of Exeters most splendid buildings. The building was totally gutted during the raid on 4 May 1942. Only its Heavitree stone facade was left standing and this too was later removed.

St John's Hospital School occupied a site right in the heart of the city. The heavy bombing on 4 May 1942 totally destroyed the school and adjoining premises.

St John's School held a large prime location to the south side of High Street. There was an archway which provided access into the playground from the central thoroughfare. The photograph above illustrates the variety of buildings found close to the school many of which were destroyed. Premises on the north side of the playground were also lost.

St John's was known as the Bluecoat School due to the distinctive uniform worn by the children. Although the buildings were lost during the war, two statues were salvaged which show pupils wearing the uniform. One statue is found in Princesshay, which now occupies the school site, and the other in the Royal Albert Museum. The roof of the East Gate Arcade is visible in the background of the photograph.

The Globe Hotel was a fine building situated on South Street and Cathedral Yard. It was lost due to a combination of communicating fires and a lack of manpower. The totally gutted building was demolished. Originally access to South Street could be gained through either the hotel or Little Stile, a small alley to the left of the Globe. Today the site provides an open walkway from Cathedral Yard to South Street.

Uncontrollable fires from High Street, and in particular the East Gate, destroyed the fine Regency terrace at the top of Southernhay. Following post-war development, the area became a large open car park flanked by the City wall. The destruction of buildings opened up the ancient city wall and in consequence it has gained far more more significance as one of Exeter's most historical features.

View across to High Street from the back of the General Post Office building.

The lovely terraces of fine regency houses in Dix's Field were mostly destroyed yet the shells of the buildings stood for some time following the war. One of the houses was the headquarters for the Exeter YMCA. Recent redevelopment on the Dix's Field site has adopted a style similar to the original houses. Remains of former buildings have been completely restored.

Dix's Field.

The large and commodious Lower Market was a prize-winning design by Charles Fowler. It was built after a decision in 1833 to have two covered markets in the City. Its Italian style added to Exeter's prestige for architectural design. Although the outer walls survived the bombing on 4 May 1942, the market was later demolished thus creating another open space at the top of Fore Street. The new St George's Hall was built on the site.

The interior of the Market after bombing.

South Street, which was a narrow street pre-war, suffered badly owing to the older properties in the area. Whole sides of the street collapsed into the road and the area was substantially cleared. Some of Exeter's ancient roads disappeared in the post-war rebuilding.

Adjacent to the Lower Market was an old road named "Milk Street". It joined George Street which led to South Street. At the junction of these narrow thoroughfares was a small square, in the centre of which stood a large obelisk. It marked the site of an original water conduit. The photograph shows the obelisk exposed as never before. It remained in situ while all else was demolished around it until, after a period of standing alone, it too was demolished.

A view of South Street, looking towards Mermaid Yard across Sun Street.

Heavy bombing and extensive fires destroyed some fine buildings at the top of Fore Street including the famous Chevalier Inn (above). Fortunately, Cornish's, one of Exeter's most famous business premises, escaped major damage (below).

The remains of a window in a wall provided an appropriate frame for this record taken by the Reverend Langhorne, headmaster of the Cathedral Choristers School. It shows the rear of South Street still smouldering heavily after the raid on 4 May 1942. In the background to the left is the rear of the Lower Market.

A view from the centre of South Street looking towards
High Street. The buildings had toppled into the road.

On 24 April 1942 the West Quarter was bombed. On King Street a building of
historic importance called "The Norman House" was almost entirely destroyed and
its sad remains pulled down.

The church of St Mary Major stands miraculously amid the ruins in front of the Cathedral on Guinea Street and Sun Street. At the base of the church is the Vicars Choral in South Street. This magnificent hall was the last remaining structure relating to a complex of early dwellings and communal accommodation for priests attached to the Cathedral. The ruin of which has been maintained as a memorial.

On 30 December 1942 the Holloway Street area received six high explosive bombs, the result of a hit and run raid.

A view down Fore Street after the raids on 4 May 1942. A number of deaths resulted as staff were trapped in business premises. The facade of the Lower Market can be seen still standing on the left of the street.

Clearance operations begin in Market Street. Many of the old city streets were very narrow making it difficult for those people trying to contain fires. Old properties constructed from timber, plaster and lath were a rich fuel source as fires raged. The Lower Market is shown gutted.

As the buildings were cleared away so the centre of Exeter became a vast open wasteland. The photograph above shows South Street once a number of ruined buildings had been removed. These empty areas were a familiar sight for many years until the gradual redevelopment of the City centre. The rebuilding of Exeter was a controversial matter as many historic and architecturally important buildings had been lost. The shape of the City today is radically different to its pre-war image.

This extraordinary view is Catherine Street. The Cathedral in the background dwarfs the broken roofs of the devastated buildings.

Burnt, blackened and gutted the delightful St Catherine's Almshouses were to be retained in their ruined state as a memorial. Sadly, neither the almshouses nor the Vicar's Choral are signed as being Memorials to the Exeter Blitz.

THE HOME GUARD

In May 1940 the Prime Minister, Neville Chamberlain, asked the country for volunteers to help protect the country. The result was a volunteer movement of men which would later be named, by Winston Churchill, as "The Home Guard". This title brought much approval. In Exeter the initial response consisted of 2000 men joining the Home Guard. Many of those to come forward were ex-soldiers and those not quite fit enough for normal service.

Some of the members might never before have held a gun. Their duties included patrols, guards and observation. The headquarters and a training area were found in Pancras Lane. There was also an internal training area at the Higher Market in Queen Street for use in bad weather and facilities at the school house in Paul Street. The Home Guard was fondly named "Dad's Army" and finally stood down on 31 December 1944.

These two pages are dedicated to all the men who joined Exeter's Home Guard and fought to retain the city.

THE FIRE SERVICE

Despite their extensive training and enthusiasm for the undertaking, the Exeter fire services were to find themselves in a dangerous position beyond anything they had trained for on the night of 4 May 1942. Exeter was divided into fire zones, each of which was controlled by a senior officer. This organisation and preparation was soon put to the test by the 100 fires that soon raged across the City after the bombing raids began. The narrow alleyways and main streets became blocked with debris from collapsing buildings which made it almost impossible for crews to reach the fires. The use of further reinforcing pumps was also prevented by the rubble. The scale of the fires was enormous, they rapidly grew from small blazes to raging infernos and as fires communicated with one another the damage increased. Many of the crews had no idea where their colleagues were working as they all fought desperately to save some of their City's fine buildings. Fortunately the supply of water remained reasonably constant and some blazes were soon put under control. Nonetheless the face of the city was changed irreparably.

In Recognition of Services Rendered: Divisional Officer Willey (MBE); Leading Fireman W.M. Hall (BEM). *Commendation for brave conduct to the following firemen:* L.J. Gould; F.W. Wilson; A.W. Matthews.

This page is dedicated to all the men of the Fire Services who attempted to retain the fires that swept through the City during the air raids and risked their lives on behalf of Exeter.

The General Post Office, High Street, 1938. The Exeter Telegraph Instrument Room was situated on the top floor of the Post Office. Communication systems were of vital importance to the people of Exeter especially during the war years. The Telephone Exchange in Castle Street, which dealt with all the communications for the city, was threatened by fire on 4 May 1942. A call was sent out to "at all costs save the Exchange". The workers would often put their lives at risk to maintain Exeter's services. This page is dedicated to those who maintained the telephone exchange.

Left: *Mr Bert Baker was in charge of the Air Raid Precautions Centre. He entered the centre on 4 May 1942, when he stepped outside he was greeted by a city which was totally unrecognisable.*

Centre right: *Air Raid Precautions Badge as issued.*

Bottom: *The Central Library on Castle Street was utilised as the headquarters for Air Raid Precautions. The ARP was situated in the basement, entry to which was down a flight of sand bagged steps. It was the Exeter nerve centre for communication relating to war time operations. The contents of the Library, an estimated one million books and other valuable records, were lost. The remains smouldered for more than three days.*

GOLDSMITH STREET

A delightful Victorian building once stood in Goldsmith Street. It was built in 1887 as a police station. It became an important centre in Exeter for war-time activities. The police station was demolished in the early 1960s and now only a foundation stone remains to mark its existence.

Police Sergeant Ernest Fraser was on duty in the city during Exeter's blitz on 4 May 1942. Ernest Fraser died in 1992 shortly after meeting to talk about his war time experiences. A modest man, he made comment that many others had performed similar duties during the war. It was later discovered through many newspaper cuttings that he had been awarded a number of honours relating to merit including the highest honour for bravery.

By the KING'S Order the name of
Ernest Fraser,
Police Sergeant, Exeter City Police,

was published in the London Gazette on
9 October, 1942,
as commended for brave conduct in
Civil Defence.
I am charged to record His Majesty's
high appreciation of the service rendered.

Winston S. Churchill

Prime Minister and First Lord
of the Treasury

This page is dedicated to all members of the police force who served Exeter during the war.

FIGHTING FIRES

*This page is dedicated to all those who fought to save the City of Exeter
from destruction by bombing and fires.*

Many properties in the city were equipped with walkways at roof top level (left). Staff in business premises were on rotas for fire watching duty and would often have to sleep in their shops if it was too far to go home. As the incendiaries hurled down, individuals would use a long handled scoop to remove them from the roof before they caught fire. Unfortunately, the incendiaries were often accompanied by high explosive bombs leaving the employee with little hope of saving the building.

The pre-war city had taken centuries to develop its character. It was a patchwork of narrow roads, alleyways and courtyards (right). Many of the buildings were of part wooden construction, lath and plaster. The close proximity of the buildings to one another combined with the materials from which they were built made it incredibly difficult to prevent fires from spreading widely.

MESSENGER BOYS

A remarkable group of young boys were brought together in Exeter to act as messengers. The boys were issued with bicycles and as communications broke down they would cycle around the city passing messages from one centre to another. The city streets were blocked with debris which meant that their task was often difficult.

EVACUEES

MAYOR'S MESSAGE TO BLITZED CITIZENS: "DO NOT FLINCH"

"To citizens generally I can only say, I can only say 'Do not flinch.'"—This is the Message from the Mayor (Mr. R. Glave Saunders) to Exonians in their ordeal. "The superficial, emphemeral Exeter which we all knew and loved has been partly destroyed; a newer, better and greater Exeter has to be built in the years to come," the message goes on.

In a tribute to the citizens' courage, the Mayor says: "Our people from the highest to the humblest, stood this supreme test of their courage as Englishmen have done and always will do."

Places throughout Devon were allocated evacuee children from London and the Home Counties. In the photograph, children are being given some good Devon fare!

With the end of war services were held in the open in the Cathedral Close.

An American Bomber over the destroyed city of Exeter, 1945.

The remnants of Exeter's buildings in High Street stand awaiting demolition. Work has begun on Dellers Cafe and is looked over by King Alfred on top of the Commercial Union building. The church of St Lawrence is in the background. This devastation marks the end of an era for Exeter.

From the massive towers of the Cathedral the historic city of Exeter lies smashed. The horror of war becomes apparent and man's inhumanity to man. The message from this photograph is clear, it must never be allowed to happen again.

This photograph is the most often published image used to show the effects of war on Exeter. Once the demolition contractors had finished their work the cityscape was open and desolate. It is important to remember when looking at this picture that this shows "The city after the demolition of buildings affected by wartime damage."

A broken city seen from the towers of the Cathedral.

City and County of the City of Exeter
AIR-RAID PRECAUTIONS

Location of A.R.P. Services and Executive Officers in charge.

A.R.P. Report and Control Centre: CITY LIBRARY BASEMENT, CASTLE STREET (Telephone 54941 4 lines).

Alternative ditto: "SOUTHBROOK," TOPSHAM ROAD, (near Country House Inn). (Telephone 55471-2).

		Telephone Nos.: Administrative	Operational
A.R.P. Controller:	The Town Clerk, 10, Southernhay West	(4956)	
A.R.P. Officer, Air Raid Wardens, Messenger Services:	Chief Constable, Court House	(5364) (2224)	(55537)
Casualty Services:	Medical Officer of Health, 5, Southernhay West	(2572)	(55512)
Rescue Parties, Decontamination Squads, Road Repair Parties, Sewer Repair Parties, Water Repair Parties, Sandbag Parties, Mortuary Van Parties, Salvage, Removal and Storage of Furniture, Strutting, Shoring or Demolition of Buildings:	City Engineer and Surveyor — Also Co-ordinating Officer for Gas, Electricity, and other Services where road repairs are required to be undertaken.	(5032)	(55513)
Fire Service:	Chief Officer of the Fire Brigade, Danes Castle	(2222)	(2222)
Transport Officer:	Transport Manager, Corporation Transport Depot, Paris Street	(54905-6)	(54906)
Food and Shelter Scheme:	Deputy Public Assistance Officer, 46, Southernhay West	(54908)	(54908)
Information Centre:	Deputy City Treasurer, 3, Southernhay West	(55425)	

1

		Telephone Nos.: Administrative	Operational
Emergency Feeding:	Secretary for Education, 39, Southernhay West	(55435)	
Fire Prevention:	*8 Waterbeer Street* Fire Prevention Officer, 49, Southernhay West	(55565)	(55565)
Gas Precautions:	Gas Precautions Officer, 1, Waterbeer Street	(5131)	(5131)
Electricity Services:	Engineer and Manager, Electricity House, Fore Street	(4171)	(55514)
Gas Mains:	Engineer & General Manager, Exeter Gaslight & Coke Co., Southernhay East	(5151)	(55516)

N.B.—Telephone numbers are shown in brackets but it is emphasised that all reports relating to Air Raid Damage must be submitted through either (in the case of reports of fire) the Fire Control Room (Telephone 2222); or the A.R.P. Report and Control Centre (Telephone 54941).

AIR RAID WARDENS.

		Telephone Nos.: Administrative	Operational
Executive Officers:	Chief Constable	(2224)	(55521)
	Chief Warden, 1, Waterbeer Street	(5364)	(55537)

GROUP "A"—SECTORS 1 to 8.

Wardens Posts:		Tel. No.
No. 1.	A.R.P. Training Centre, Friernhay Street	(4702)
No. 2.	St. Sidwell's Methodist Church (Siren Post)	(3747)
No. 3.	... ...	
No. 4.	8, Northernhay Place	(3257)

GROUP "B"—SECTORS 9 to 20.

Wardens Posts:		
No. 5.	21, Southernhay West ...	(55394)
No. 6.	Norman House, King Street ...	(3253)
No. 8.	Salvation Army Hall, The Friars ...	(3208)
No. 10.	Roberts Road School - ...	(55307)

GROUP "C"—SECTORS 21 to 28 and 44.

Wardens Posts:		
No. 11.	48, St. Leonard's Road ...	(55629)
No. 12.	11, Lyndhurst Road ...	(2337)
No. 13.	Children's Home, Heavitree Road ...	(2887)
No. 14.	"Feltrim," Topsham Road ...	(3267)

2

GROUP "K"—SECTORS 109 to 124.

Wardens Posts:

		Telephone No.
No. 46.	Exwick Vicarage (Siren Post) ...	√ (54325)
No. 47.	1, Limegrove Road ...	√ (5304)
No. 45.	138, Cowick Street	√ (54086)

GROUP "L"—SECTORS 37 to 43 and 127 to 130.

Wardens Posts:

No. 15.	Salvation Army Hall, Burnthouse Lane ...	√ (3577)
No. 20.	68, Burnthouse Lane ...	√ (55329)
No. 19.	"Red-a-ven," Topsham Road ...	X (8184)

Head Wardens Post in Black Type.

CASUALTY SERVICES.

Executive Officers:

		Telephone Nos.:	
		Administrative,	Operational.
Medical Officer of Health	...	Office (2572)	(55512)
		Home (2848)	—
Deputy ditto		Office (2572)	(55512)
		Home (67333)	
Commandant of Casualty Services	...	...	(3464)
Deputy ditto		...	(2560)
Supervisor of First Aid Parties	...	(2572)	54685

First Aid Posts (including Cleansing Centres for Personnel):

		Tel. No.
No. 1.	Alice Vlieland Hall, Bull Meadow Road	(54685)
No. 2.	Wrentham Hall, Old Tiverton Road	(54147)
No. 4.	Shakespeare Road Community Centre	(4983)
No. 5.	Buddle Lane Community Centre	(5335)

Mobile First Aid Posts:

Nos. 3 and 6.	Corporation Transport Depot, Paris Street	(54906)
Duty Vehicle during "Alerts"	City Hospital ...	(55054)

First Aid Point: Countess Wear Hotel ... (809411)

First Aid Parties: All based on First Aid Posts

Ambulance Depots:

Corporation Transport Depot, Paris Street	(54906)
Motor Mecca, Magdalen Road ...	(55393)

4

GROUP "D"—SECTORS 29 to 36 ; 126 and 131.

Wardens Posts:

		Telephone No.
No. 16.	2, Stafford Terrace (Siren Post) ...	√ (2016)
No. 17.	Baptist Chapel, Hope Road ...	√ (3235)
No. 31.	Glico Filling Station, The Gallows	√ (67175)

GROUP "E"—SECTORS 45 to 75 and 125.

Wardens Posts:

No. 21.	Whipton Infants' School (Siren Post)	√ (67613)
No. 22.	145, Pinhoe Road ...	√ (5195)
No. 23.	St. James Park ...	√ (3859)
No. 24.	27, Elmside ...	√√ (55337)
No. 25.	24, Kings Road ...	√ (3286)

GROUP "F"—SECTORS 57 to 72.

Wardens Posts:

No. 26.	8, Clifton Hill	√ (4930)
No. 27.		√
No. 28.	141, Sweetbrier Lane ...	√ (54381)
No. 29.	24, Hanover Road ...	√ (55338)
No. 30.	60, Ladysmith Road ...	√ (3289)
No. 32.	1, Regents Park ...	X (4204)

GROUP "G"—SECTORS 76 to 83.

Wardens Posts:

No. 33.	13, Pennsylvania Road ...	X (4591)
No. 34.	Richmond Hotel ...	√ (55604)
No. 35.	Exe Street Institute ...	√√ (3291)
No. 36.	95, Bonhay Road ...	√ (55336)

GROUP "H"—SECTORS 84 to 90.

Wardens Posts:

No. 37.	48 Old Tiverton Road 13 Sylvan Road	√ (54138)
No. 38.	"Eling," Cowley Road ...	√ (54301)
No. 39.	Egerton School, Pennsylvania (Siren Post)	√ (3853)
No. 40.	"Osea," Higher Hoopern ...	X (54062)

GROUP "J"—SECTORS 91 to 108.

Wardens Posts:

No. 41.	11, Gervase Avenue ...	√ (3260)
No. 42.	138, Cowick Street ...	√√ (54086)
No. 44.	2, Cordery Road ...	X (3105)

3

Decontamination Services :

	Telephone Nos. : Office.	Control Room.
Executive Officer, City Engineer & Surveyor	(5032)	(55513)
Depots : Exe Island ...	(4883)	
Cleansing Dept., Exe Island ...	(3163)	
Vehicle D/c., New Cattle Market	(54879)	
Protective Clothing D/c., Baths and Wash-houses, King Street	(54519)	

Mortuary Van Parties :

Executive Officer, City Engineer & Surveyor	(5032)	(55513)
Depot : Exe Island ...	(4883)	

Water Repair Parties :

Executive Officer, City Engineer & Surveyor	(5032)	(55513)
Depots : Danes Castle ...	(3160)	
Pynes Waterworks ...	(2515)	

Furniture, Salvage Removal and Storage :

Executive Officer, City Engineer & Surveyor	(5032)	(55513)

Strutting, Shoring and Demolition of Buildings :

Executive Officer, City Engineer & Surveyor	(5032)	(55513)

Co-ordination of Gas, Electricity and other Services involving Repairs to Roads :

Co-ordinating Officer, City Engineer and Surveyor ...	(5032)	(55513)

Canal Undertaking, Cemeteries, Burials and Parks :

Executive Officer, City Engineer & Surveyor	(5032)	(55513)

ELECTRICITY.

Executive Officer, City Electrical Engineer	(4171)	(55514)
Depots : No. 1. Electricity House, Fore Street	(4171)	(55514)
No. 2. Power Station, City Basin	(3288)	(55514)

GAS.

Executive Officer : Engineer and General Manager ...	(5151)	(55516)
Depots : No. 1. Gas Company's Offices, 11/13, Southernhay East	(5151)	(55516)
No. 2. Gas Works, City Basin...	(5152)	(55516)

6

Hospital Services :

	Telephone No.	
Royal Devon & Exeter Hospital ...	(2261)	(54897)
City Hospital, Heavitree Road ...	(2671)	(55054)
Princess Elizabeth Orthopaedic Hospital	(54217)	(55896)

Mortuary :

Old Rack Street Schools ...	(2572)	(54323)

CLEANSING STATIONS FOR UNWOUNDED GAS CASUALTIES.

For Male Civil Defence Volunteers only :

No. 1. Police Station Annexe, Denmark House
No. 2. Cleansing Station, Tan Lane
No. 3. ,, ,, Exe Island
No. 4. ,, ,, Hamlin Lane
No. 5. Auxiliary Fire Station, New North Road
No. 6. ,, ,, ,, Polsloe Road
No. 7. ,, ,, ,, Magdalen Road
No. 8. ,, ,, ,, Coombe Street
No. 9. ,, ,, ,, Alphington Street
No. 10. ,, ,, ,, The Elms, Wonford

Women Civil Defence Volunteers will continue to go to the nearest First Aid Post.

For Unwounded Civilians :

No. 1. John Stocker Senior Boys' School, Dunsford Road
No. 2. Episcopal Senior Boys' and Girls' School, Dinham Road
No. 3. King's Alley Baths
No. 4. St. James' Institute, Toronto Road
No. 5. New Swimming Baths, Denmark Road

RESCUE, REPAIR, DEMOLITION AND DECONTAMINATION SERVICES.

Rescue Parties :

	Telephone Nos. : Office.	Control Room.
Executive Officer, City Engineer & Surveyor	(5032)	(55513)
Depots, Tan Lane ...	(55152)	
Hamlin Lane ...	(54853)	

Road and Sewer Repairs and Sandbag Parties :

Executive Officer : City Engineer & Surveyor	(5032)	(55513)
Depots : Tan Lane ...	(55152)	
Highways Depot, Tan Lane	(2578)	

5

EMERGENCY FEEDING CENTRES.

Telephone Nos. :
Administrative. (55435) Operational. (55435)

Executive Officer : Secretary for Education, 39, Southernhay West ... ...

Centres :

No. 1. Civic Hall, Queen Street ... (2074)

In the event of emergency, further premises will be opened as required. Information as to Centres opened at one or more of the undermentioned Schools will be communicated to Police and Wardens through A.R.P. Control Centre.

No. 1. St. Thomas Senior Girls' School (54336)
No. 2. John Stocker Junior Boys' School (55555)
No. 3. Exe Island School (55375)
No. 4. Holloway Street J.G. and I. School (55381)
No. 5. St. James Senior Girls' School (3985)
No. 6. Bradley Rowe Girls' School (3614)
No. 7. Ladysmith Girls' School (55554)

INFORMATION CENTRE.

Executive Officer : Deputy City Treasurer, 3, Southernhay West ... ... (55425)

Main Centre :
St. Sidwell's Junior Boys School, York Road (55593)

Alternative Centre :
Hele's School (4383)

POLICE A.R.P. ARRANGEMENTS.

Police Control :
Court House. Telephone Nos. (55517), (55518), (55519)

Alternative Police Control :
Old Devon County Headquarters Telephone Nos. (55414-5-6-7)

POLICE PARADE POINTS.

Tel. No.
No. 1. Denmark House, Waterbeer Street (2224)
No. 2. Red House, Whipton ... (5290)
No. 3. Basement, Odeon Cinema (55585)
No. 4. 21, Heavitree Road (3154)
No. 5. "Glenhayes," Prince of Wales Road (4911)
No. 6. "Crom-a-boo," Fore Street, Heavitree (4916)
No. 7. Basement, Bude Hotel (54291)

8

FIRE SERVICES.

Executive Officer :
Telephone Nos. :
Administrative and Operational.
Chief Officer of the Fire Brigade (55484) (55485) (55486)
Headquarters Fire Station, Howell Road (2222) (2223)
Trunks 12

Alternative Control : The Elms, Wonford (4503)
(To be used only when unable to establish contact with Headquarters).

Auxiliary Fire Stations :
No. 1. Maudes Garage, New North Road
No. 2. Autocars Service Co., Polsloe Road
No. 3. Motor Mecca, Magdalen Road
No. 4. Gayton's Garage, Coombe Street
No. 5. Pike's Garage Alphington Street
No. 6. The Elms, Wonford

REST CENTRES.

Executive Officer :
Telephone Nos. :
Administrative. (54908) Operational. (54908)
Deputy Public Assistance Officer, 46, Southernhay West ... ...

Centres :

ST. THOMAS AREA.
No. 1. Emmanuel Church Hall, Okehampton Road
No. 2. St. Thomas Methodist Institute, Cowick Street
No. 3. G.W.R. Assembly Hall, Cowick Street
No. 4. St. Andrew Cowic Hall, Willeys Avenue
No. 5. St. Thomas Salvation Army Hall, Church Road
No. 6. Exwick Parish Institute.

CENTRAL AREA.
No. 7. St. David's Institute, Haldon Road
No. 8. St. Sidwell's Methodist, Sidwell Street
No. 9. St. Matthew's Hall, The Triangle
No. 10. St. James Institute (entrance Bath Road)
No. 11. St. Mary Arches, off North Street
No. 12. Mint Methodist Schoolroom, The Mint
No. 13. Children's Hall, The Friars, Salvation Army Temple

EASTERN AREA.
No. 14. Heavitree Congregational, Fore Street, Heavitree
No. 15. St. Mark's, Manston Road
No. 16. Pinhoe Road Baptist Church Hall, Pinhoe Road
No. 17. City Mission, Burnthouse Lane (adjoining Bradley Rowe Schools)
No. 18. St. Loyes Church Hall, Burnthouse Lane
No. 19. Salvation Army Hall, Burnthouse Lane

N.B.—No specific order of opening can be given, but halls opened under this scheme will be communicated to Police and Wardens through A.R.P. Control Centre.

7

		Telephone No.
No. 8.	Hope Road Chapel, Wonford ...	(3235)
No. 9.	Eagle House, Clock Tower ...	(55627)
No. 10.	52, Buddle Lane ...	5587
No. 11.	Exwick Vicarage, Exwick ...	54325
No. 12.	Police Box, Exe Bridge	(2224 x 8b)
No. 13.	Basement, Windsor Hotel, Bonhay Road	(38811)
No. 14.	8, Queen's Road ...	(4438)
No. 15.	Salvation Army Temple, The Friars	(3208)
No. 16.	Mount Radford School, St. Leonards Road	(2425)
No. 17.	Police Sub-station, Topsham Road	(2224 x 6b)

OBSERVATION POSTS.

No. 1.	Constitutional Hill ...	(2224)
No. 2.	Ludwell Lane ...	(2224)
No. 3.	Fire Brigade Headquarters, Danes Castle	(2224)

PUBLIC SIREN STATIONS.

No. 1. Court House, Waterbeer Street
No. 2. Mount Pleasant Chapel, Pinhoe Road
No. 3. Old Whipton Infants' School, Whipton
No. 4. St. Sidwell's Methodist Church, Sidwell Street
No. 5. 2, Stafford Terrace
No. 6. Countess Wear Hotel, Countess Wear
No. 7. Crawford Hotel, Alphington Road
No. 8. Exwick Vicarage, Exwick
No. 9. Buddle Lane Community Centre
No. 10. Motor Mecca, Magdalen Road
No. 11. Exeter Gas Co., The Basin
No. 12. Fire Brigade Headquarters, Danes Castle
No. 13. Egerton School, Pennsylvania
No. 14. Shakespeare Road Community Centre
No. 15. City Mental Hospital, Digbys
No. 16. Exeter Electricity Generating Station, The Basin
No. 17. Decontamination Centre, Exe Island
No. 18. Willey & Co., Haven Road

In case of breakdown of electricity supply, or other failure of fixed sirens, four battery-operated sirens have been fixed on vehicles. The drivers of the vehicles can be contacted through Police Headquarters (2224).

9

OFFICIAL NOTICE BOARDS.

Official notices for the information and guidance of the public will be posted only on the Official Notice Boards at the following points.

Notices which purport to be official and which are posted elsewhere should be treated with suspicion and reported to the police.

No. 1. Guildhall, High Street
No. 2. Town Clerk's Office, 10, Southernhay West
No. 3. Police Station, Court House
No. 4. Police sub-station, Topsham Road
No. 5. Police detached station, Countess Weir
No. 6. Official Information Bureau, Queen Street
No. 7. City Library (News Room)
No. 8. First Aid Post, Merrivale Road
No. 9. Air-Raid Wardens' Post, The Gallows
No. 10. Air-Raid Wardens' Post, Exwick
No. 11. St. David's Church, St. David's Hill
No. 12. St. Thomas Church, Cowick Street
No. 13. Emmanuel Church, Okehampton Road
No. 14. St. Sidwell's Church, Sidwell Street
No. 15. St. Mark's Church, Pinhoe Road
No. 16. St. Leonard's Church, Topsham Road
No. 17. St. Lawrence Church, High Street
No. 18. Whipton Church, Whipton
No. 19. St. Matthew's Church, Triangle
No. 20. Roman Catholic Church, South Street
No. 21. Countess Wear Church
No. 22. St. Anne's Chapel, Sidwell Street
No. 23. Heavitree Congregational Church
No. 24. Southernhay Wesleyan Church
No. 25. Infants' School, Wonford
No. 26. Salvation Army Hall, Burnt House Lane
No. 27. St. Olave's Church, Fore Street
No. 28. Apostolic Church, Alphington Street
No. 29. Air-Raid Wardens' Post, 13, Pennsylvania Road
No. 30. Public Health Dept., 5, Southernhay West

10

Issued by the Ministry of Home Security.

WHAT TO DO ABOUT GAS

OTHER COUNTRIES LOST THEIR FREEDOM in this war because they allowed the enemy to create confusion and panic among their civilian population so that the movement of defending armies was impeded.

We are not going to allow that to happen here. It won't happen if we are all on our guard, prepared to meet anything the enemy may do.

He may use gas. THE DANGER IS NOT SERIOUS if you do the right thing, both NOW and when the time comes. If you do, this weapon will have failed and you will have helped to beat it.

Here are the things to know and do. Read them carefully and remember them well in case the day comes. Keep this leaflet and look at it again.

HOW NOT TO GET GASSED.

NOW

1. In your gas mask you have the best possible protection against gases that affect your lungs or your eyes. It is a sure defence if you use it properly and in time. Make sure your own and your children's gas masks fit and are in working order: your warden or A.R.P. post can tell you. Practise putting them on and get used to wearing them with confidence. Your life may depend on whether you can put your mask on quickly. Remember to take off your spectacles before putting on your gas mask.

2. CARRY YOUR GAS MASK ALWAYS, and have it handy at night.

3. To prevent the face-piece misting over, smear a little soap lightly on the inside once a week.

4. If your chemist has " No. 2 Anti-gas ointment " (price 6d.) in stock, buy a jar. Read the instructions on the jar and carry it always. This ointment is for use as a protection against the effects of liquid blister gas.

IF THE GAS RATTLES SOUND.

1. PUT ON YOUR GAS MASK AT ONCE, wherever you are, even in bed.

2. TAKE COVER. Get into any nearby building as soon as you hear the rattle. Go upstairs if the building is a tall one. Close all windows in your house.

Don't come out or take your gas mask off till you hear the handbells ringing the " Gas clear ".

NEVER LOOK UPWARDS—you may get a drop of liquid gas in your eyes.

COVER YOUR SKIN UP so long as you are out of doors—hands in pockets, collar turned up. Or if you have an umbrella, put it up.

IF YOU DO GET GASSED.

GAS OR VAPOUR. If you breathe any gas or vapour—

1. PUT ON YOUR GAS MASK AT ONCE.

2. KEEP YOUR MASK ON, even though you may still feel some discomfort.

3. If the irritation is serious and does not stop after a time, apply to the nearest A.R.P. warden or member of a First Aid Party.

LIQUID BLISTER GAS. If you are splashed with liquid gas from a bomb, and you can see the dark splash on your skin or clothing you must act as follows :—

SKIN.

(*a*) Dab, NOT wipe, as much of the liquid off your skin as you can with your handkerchief; then rub " No. 2 Anti-gas ointment " well into the place. Don't forget your handkerchief has become very dangerous—destroy it.

(*b*) If you haven't the ointment by you, go to the nearest chemist's shop, where you will find bleach cream and be told how to use it.

(*c*) Ointment or cream should be put on within FIVE MINUTES of your being splashed. If this is impossible, wash at once with soap and water, preferably warm—this may save you a bad burn.

CLOTHING.

(*a*) Take off any splashed outer garment AT ONCE, before the liquid soaks right through to the skin—seconds count.

(*b*) If you are within five minutes of your home or any private house or other place where you know you can get a wash, go there and wash yourself. Before going in, take off your shoes and *any* clothing which you think the liquid has splashed—your health matters more than your feelings.

(*c*) If you can't get to such a place within five minutes ask the wardens or police what to do. They will know where the public cleansing centres are.

KEEP YOUR FOOD SAFE FROM GAS

1. Poison gases will not always affect even exposed foods to such an extent that they become dangerous for human consumption, but in any case very simple precautions will protect your food entirely.

2. Food in cans or airtight bottles is perfectly safe, and flour, rice, tea, butter, etc., should be kept in tins or jars with well-fitting lids. Refrigerators are very good protection. Perishable foods would be safe in them, or in a gas-proof room. Store all your tins and jars in cupboards or in places where they cannot be splashed by liquid gas.

3. If there is any risk that your food or water may have been contaminated, on no account attempt to deal with them yourself. Notify the police or an air raid warden. Your local authority will give expert advice and treatment.

WE CAN BEAT GAS ATTACKS
—if we know what to do, and do it.

(55189) 14,100M 4 41 Hw.

55070-B

POST SECTOR MAP

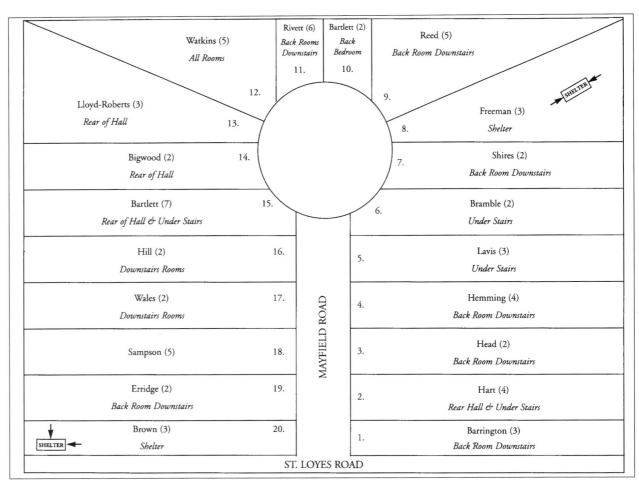

A sector map for Mayfield Road showing the rooms used when raids were in progress. This was used to assist wardens in locating people in need of help.

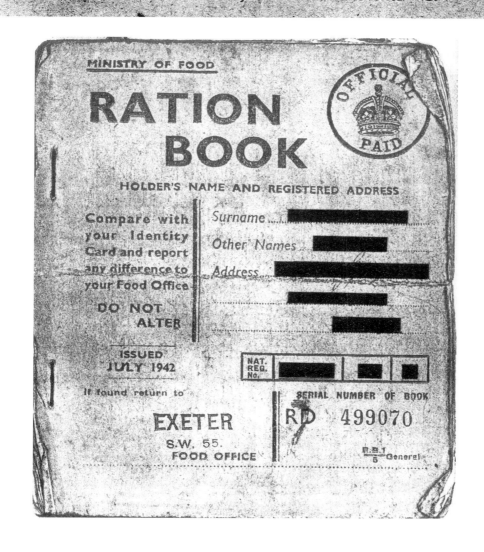

THE CURTIS CHART
Total Air Raid Warnings

Year	Jan	Feb	Mar	April	May	June	July	Aug	Sept	Oct	Nov	Dec	Total
1940	-	-	-	-	-	-	-	10	7	1	5	20	43
1941	5	8	27	39	40	19	7	1	4	10	6	-	166
1942	5	3	11	24	13	11	12	24	18	14	4	6	145
1943	12	-	-	-	-	-	-	-	-	-	-	-	12

From 7 August, 1940 to 27 January, 1943 366 Air Raid Warnings. Total 448 hours and 20 minutes equal to 18 days, 16 hours and 20 minutes.

Air Raid Warning - Exeter

No.	Year	Date	Raid	Time	am/pm	Time	am/pm	Hrs	Mins
1	1940	7 Aug	1	11.25	P	1.25	A	2	
2		13		4.20	P	4.43	P		23
3		15		5.53	P	6.25	P		32
4		16		11.50	A	11.59	A		9 (Bombs
5		16		1.35	P	1.50	P		15 dropped)
6		21		9.10	A	9.15	A		5
7		25		12.30	A	2.50	A	2	20
8		25		6.03	P	6.15	P		12
9		25		9.25	P	12.08	A	2	43
10		29		9.21	P	12.27	A	3	6
11		3 Sept		9.10	P	11.33	P	2	23 (Bomb
12		5		10.30	P	10.55	P		25 dropped)
13		14		3.20	P	3.55	P		35
14		16		9.10	P	9.50	P		40
15		25		4.30	P	5.00	P		30
16		30		11.45	A	12.08	P		23
17		30		4.30	P	4.51	P		21
18		7 Oct		8.25	P	8.55	P		30
19		4 Nov		1.20	P	1.33	P		13
20		26		6.30	P	7.53	P	1	23
21		29		2.05	A	3.07	P	1	2
22		29		3.35	P	4.05	P		30
23		29		9.45	P	11.00	P	1	15
24		1 Dec		6.55	P	7.55	P	1	
25		2		7.55	P	12.07	A	4	12
26		5		9.15	A	9.40	A		25
27		5		2.23	P	3.30	P	1	7
28		7		2.40	P	2.52	P		12
29		7		7.25	P	7.47	P		22
30		8		4.25	P	5.00	P		35
31		11		6.45	P	7.40	P		55
32		12		2.40	P	2.55	P		15
33		12		10.00	P	11.19	P	1	19
34		13		1.06	P	1.27	P		21
35		15		7.34	P	9.16	P	1	42
36		15		10.05	P	11.03	P		58
37		20		6.03	P	6.50	P		47
38		20		7.57	P	9.20	P	1	23
39		20		11.50	P	5.05	A	5	15
40		21		8.27	P	9.05	P		38
41		22		12.40	A	7.05	A	6	25
42		22		6.49	P	1.05	A	6	16

No.	Year	Date	Raid	Time	am/pm	Time	am/pm	Hrs	Mins
43		23		6.58	P	10.46	P	3	48 (hours of
44	1941	2 Jan		8.30	P	12.41	A	4	11 warning
45		4		7.06	P	1.35	A	6	29 end 1940
46		10		6.45	P	7.25	P	1	40 59 hrs 49
47		17		10.35	P	11.20	P		45 mins)
48		18		12.15	A	3.20	A	3	15
49		3 Feb		8.00	P	10.10	P	2	10
50		4		8.50	P	9.25	P		35
51		8		7.35	P	9.00	P	1	25
52		12		4.40	P	5.13	P		33
53		19		8.15	P	11.15	P	3	
54		20		7.35	P	12.35	A	5	
55		21		9.05	P	11.20	P	2	15
56		26		7.59	P	10.05	P	2	6
57		1 Mar		7.57	P	8.42	P		45
58		2		8.21	P	8.56	P		35
59		2		9.47	P	10.28	P		41
60		3		6.39	A	7.02	A		23
61		4		8.20	P	10.05	P	1	45
62		6		6.35	P	7.30	P		55
63		7		1.26	P	1.48	P		22
64		11		8.26	P	12.04	A	3	38
65		12		1.13	P	2.35	P	1	22
66		12		8.17	P	3.02	A	6	45
67		13		7.57	P	11.05	P	3	8
68		14		12.15	A	3.00	A	2	45
69		14		8.33	P	4.25	A	7	52
70		16		9.11	P	1.20	A	4	9
71		17		1.38	A	2.52	A	1	14
72		17		3.20	A	3.35	A		12
73		19		3.11	A	4.03	A		52
74		20		9.22	P	12.45	A	3	23
75		21		8.57	P	12.35	A	3	38
76		22		12.25	P	12.35	P		10
77		24		2.45	P	3.40	P		55
78		24		5.10	P	5.39	P		29
79		29		10.46	A	11.00	A		14
80		29		8.42	P	12.50	A	4	8
81		31		2.30	P	3.02	P		32
82		31		5.32	P	5.48	P		16
83		31		8.40	P	9.46	P	1	6
84		1 Apr		4.47	P	5.05	P		18
85		2		7.10	A	7.46	A		36
86		2		8.35	P	10.50	P	2	15
87		3		4.50	P	5.11	P		21
88		3		8.29	P	1.10	A	4	41 (bombs
89		4		9.02	P	1.45	A	4	43 dropped
90		5		8.03	P	9.05	P	1	2 near
91		6		5.50	P	6.17	P		27 airport)
92		6		9.59	P	10.12	P		13
93		6		11.15	P	11.30	P		15
94		7		12.30	A	3.10	A		40
95		7		4.45	P	5.43	P		58
96		7		8.37	P	4.30	A	7	53 (longest
97		8		9.08	P	9.38	P		30 warning)
98		9		1.50	A	2.30	A		40

No.	Year	Date	Raid	Time	am/pm	Time	am/pm	Hrs	Mins
99		9		9.24	P	1.35	A	4	11
100		10		1.07	P	1.45	P		32
101		10		10.20	P	2.30	A	4	10
102		11		9.29	P	5.00	A	7	31
103		12		2.02	P	2.22	P		20
104		12		8.52	P	11.20	P	2	28
105		13		10.15	P	11.30	P	1	15
106		13		11.35	P	11.45	P		10
107		14		1.55	A	2.20	A		25
108		14		5.05	A	5.25	A		20
109		14		10.50	P	12.00	P	1	10
110		15		1.55	A	2.50	A		55
111		15		4.00	A	4.15	A		15
112		15		9.55	P	5.25	A	7	30
113		16		10.15	P	10.30	P		15
114		17		3.00	A	5.50	A	2	50
115		21		10.25	P	3.15	A	4	50
116		22		9.45	P	3.10	A	5	27
117		23		9.55	P	1.55	A	4	
118		26		1.55	A	2.25	A		30
119		27		10.45	P	11.20	P		35
120		28		9.45	P	1.40	A	3	55
121		29		4.40	A	5.45	A	1	5
122		29		9.52	P	1.35	A	3	43
123		1 May		12.25	P	1.23	P		58
124		1		9.37	P	11.40	P	2	3
125		2		12.05	A	2.30	A	2	25
126		2		9.22	P	10.55	P	1	33
127		3		9.42	P	3.10	A	5	28
128		4		1.29	P	1.59	P		30
129		4		11.20	P	4.40	A	5	20
130		5		11.20	P	5.10	A	5	50
131		6		8.40	P	9.10	P		30
132		6		11.55	P	4.50	A	5	35
133		7		1.05	P	1.10	P		5
134		7		11.15	P	4.50	A	5	35
135		8		2.50	P	3.22	P		32
136		8		11.40	P	5.00	A	5	20
137		9		11.00	P	1.50	A	2	50
138		11		8.20	P	9.50	P	1	30
139		11		11.30	P	5.00	A	5	30
140		12		5.05	A	5.55	A		50
141		13		3.40	A	4.00	A		20
142		14		5.50	P	6.06	P		16
143		15		11.55	P	1.55	A	2	
144		16		3.05	A	4.45	A	1	40
145		17		12.05	A	5.00	A	4	55
146		18		1.50	A	2.20	A		30
147		18		4.00	A	5.00	A	1	
148		19		5.30	A	5.50	A		20
149		20		1.40	A	3.30	A	1	50
150		20		4.00	A	4.50	A		50
151		20		11.55	P	1.20	A	1	25
152		25		12.10	A	12.20	A		10
153		25		3.10	P	3.30	P		20
154		25		5.45	P	6.16	P		31

No.	Year	Date	Raid	Time	am/pm	Time	am/pm	Hrs	Mins
155		28		1.15	A	3.35	A	2	20
156		28		4.10	P	4.20	P		10
157		29		12.00	P	1.25	A	1	25
158		29		2.10	A	4.50	A	2	40
159		29		9.20	A	9.40	A		20
160		30		7.25	P	8.30	P	1	5
161		31		12.15	A	4.35	A	4	20
162		31		10.25	A	11.00	A		25
163		1 June		12.00	A	4.10	A	4	10
164		2		12.10	A	4.10	A	4	
165		3		12.20	A	4.00	A	3	40
166		5		12.00	A	12.50	A		50
167		7		10.55	A	11.05	A		10
168		9		12.20	P	12.30	P		10
169		9		2.25	P	3.05	P		40
170		9		8.25	P	8.40	P		15
171		10		1.15	A	1.30	A		15
172		11		5.15	P	5.27	P		12
173		11		6.55	P	7.33	P		38
174		11		8.50	P	9.30	P		40
175		15		1.50	A	2.20	A		30
176		16		12.50	A	1.45	A		55
177		17		1.30	A	2.55	A		25
178		18		5.00	P	5.40	P		40
179		21		12.05	A	12.40	A		35
180		21		11.20	A	11.50	A		30
181		28		1.50	A	3.25	A	1	35
182		1 July		12.55	A	3.05	A	2	10
183		2		12.55	A	2.05	A	1	10
184		5		1.05	P	1.40	P		35
185		5		2.40	A	4.40	A	2	
186		8		12.40	A	2.05	A	1	25
187		9		12.40	A	4.35	A	3	55
188		12		6.10	P	7.30	P	1	20
189		26 Aug		10.35	P	12.45	A	2	10
190		6 Sept		9.18	P	10.30	P	1	12
191		16		4.10	P	4.30	P		20
192		18		9.15	P	11.30	P	2	15
193		23		8.35	P	10.30	P	1	55
194		6 Oct		8.23	P	9.40	P	1	17
195		7		8.17	P	9.42	P	1	25
196		9		2.18	P	2.26	P		8
197		21		1.30	P	1.38	P		8
198		24		7.40	P	8.15	P		35
199		25		8.00	P	8.50	P		50
200		25		9.26	P	10.15	P		49
201		26		8.45	P	10.40	P	1	55
202		28		8.30	P	10.25	P	1	55
203		30		8.00	P	11.00	P	3	
204		1 Nov		8.45	P	11.35	P	2	50
205		11		4.40	P	4.55	P		15
206		23		7.35	P	9.31	P	1	56
207		25		7.05	P	8.40	P	1	35
208		26		6.55	P	7.06	P		11
209		28		6.45	P	9.25	P	2	40
210	1942	8 Jan		12.28	P	12.40	P		12

No.	Year	Date	Raid	Time	am/pm	Time	am/pm	Hrs	Mins	
211		8		1.25	P	1.45	P		20	
212		11		12.10	A	12.20	A		10	
213		11		8.33	P	8.55	P		22	
214		26		5.11	P	5.28	P		17	
215		12 Feb		8.00	A	8.40	A		40	
216		12		1.35	P	2.00	P		25	
217		16		6.40	P	6.55	P		15	
218		5 Mar		7.50	P	8.00	P		10	
219		7		9.33	A	10.07	A		34	
220		12		11.57	A	12.19	A		22	
221		18		12.12	P	12.32	P		20	
222		19		9.13	P	9.28	P		15	
223		23		1.30	P	1.47	P		17	
224		23		7.52	P	8.30	P		38	
225		24		9.30	P	10.30	P	1		
226		29		9.10	P	9.20	P		10	
227		31		1.47	P	2.04	P		17	
228		31		2.15	P	3.02	P		47	
229		2 Apr		9.35	P	11.15	P	1	40	
230		3		8.10	P	8.19	P		9	
231		5		9.00	A	9.10	A		10	
232		6		11.33	A	11.55	A		22	
233		9		12.45	P	1.20	P		35	
234		13		8.40	A	9.17	A		37	
235		16		8.15	P	8.45	P		30	
236		17		1.30	P	2.20	P		50	
237		17		3.40	P	4.00	P		20	
238		18		8.15	P	8.40	P		25	
239		23		10.45	P	12.30	A	1	45	
240		24		9.15	A	9.30	A		30	(Okehamp-
241		25		12.15	A	1.55	A	1	40	ton Rd.
242		25		3.00	A	3.10	A		10	Bombs All
243		25		11.55	A	12.15	P		20	over
244		25		10.35	P	1.25	A	2	50	Exeter 47)
245		26		4.35	A	6.15	A	1	40	(Portland
246		26		11.40	P	12.00	P		20	Street)
247		27		12.40	A	2.45	A	2	5	
248		27		2.50	A	3.05	A		15	
249		27		12.33	P	12.58	P		25	
250		27		9.35	P	10.00	P		25	
251		29		12.00	A	12.25	A		25	
252		29		2.20	P	2.40	P		20	
253		3 May		2.45	P	4.10	P	1	25	
254		4		1.40	A	3.10	A	1	30	(Bombs all
255		4		2.10	P	2.40	P		30	over Exeter
256		4		7.35	P	8.00	P		25	B. High
257		4		11.00	P	11.30	P		3	St. etc)
258		5		10.25	A	10.55	A		30	
259		7		6.00	P	6.15	P		15	
260		10		8.10	P	8.25	P		15	
261		14		7.00	P	7.15	P		15	
262		21		8.40	P	9.10	P		30	
263		23		4.50	P	5.20	P		30	
264		24		9.32	P	10.03	P		31	
265		31		1.25	P	1.45	P		20	
266		3 June		12.15	P	12.25	P		10	

No.	Year	Date	Raid	Time	am/pm	Time	am/pm	Hrs	Mins
267		7		6.50	P	7.10	P		20
268		9		9.00	A	9.10	A		10
269		10		10.50	P	11.15	P		25
270		21		8.55	A	9.13	A		18
271		23		7.40	P	8.00	P		20
272		27		5.05	P	5.20	P		15
273		28		1.05	A	3.10	A	2	5
274		29		1.40	A	3.10	A	1	30
275		29		1.40	P	2.07	P		27
276		30		8.25	A	8.30	A		5
277		2 July		1.50	A	3.40	A	1	50
278		6		5.00	P	5.20	P		20
279		6		9.10	P	9.25	P		18
280		11		6.00	P	6.08	P		8
281		13		7.20	A	7.30	A		10
282		22		6.15	A	6.25	A		10
283		22		9.40	P	9.50	P		10
284		27		6.20	A	6.42	A		22
285		28		9.08	P	9.20	P		12
286		30		8.00	A	8.14	A		14
287		31		12.45	A	2.03	A	1	18
288		31		7.15	P	7.45	P		30
289		3 Aug		1.11	P	1.26	P		15
290		3		10.55	P	11.18	P		23
291		4		2.45	P	2.55	P		10
292		5		1.55	A	3.25	A	1	30
293		5		9.20	P	9.40	P		20
294		6		8.35	P	8.45	P		10
295		8		3.45	P	3.55	P		10
296		9		5.40	A	5.50	P		10
297		9		9.15	A	9.33	A		18
298		11		7.40	A	7.50	A		10
299		12		6.37	P	6.59	P		22
300		13		12.30	P	12.43	P		13
301		13		5.38	P	6.03	P		25
302		16		8.20	P	8.31	P		11 (also on this
303		16		9.13	P	9.32	P		19 day, test of
304		17		3.20	P	3.43	P		23 sirens
305		17		5.55	P	6.10	P		15 10am)
306		17		11.20	P	11.40	P		20
307		18		12.01	A	12.40	A		39
308		20		4.50	P	5.00	P		10
309		25		1.17	P	1.37	P		20
310		28		9.18	A	9.34	A		16
311		28		9.45	A	9.57	A		12
312		30		12.44	P	1.03	P		19
313		1 Sept		12.40	P	1.00	P		20
314		2		3.57	P	4.10	P		13
315		4		6.30	A	6.40	A		10
316		4		6.53	P	7.10	P		18
317		5		9.07	P	10.01	P		54
318		10		1.07	P	1.15	P		8
319		10		8.45	P	9.05	P		20
320		12		8.50	A	9.00	A		10
321		12		1.58	P	2.30	P		32
322		13		8.24	P	8.46	P		22

No.	Year	Date	Raid	Time	am/pm	Time	am/pm	Hrs	Mins
323		16		8.05	A	8.10	A		5
324		16		9.20	A	9.40	A		20
325		18		11.33	A	11.51	A		18
326		19		6.45	A	7.11	A		26
327		25		7.14	A	7.22	A		8
328		27		3.22	P	3.48	P		26
329		28		7.26	A	7.47	A		21
330		29		8.16	A	8.54	A		38
331		11 Oct		2.20	P	2.33	P		13
332		14		7.27	A	7.47	A		20
333		15		5.45	P	6.02	P		17
334		16		11.15	A	11.32	A		17
335		21		10.25	A	10.40	A		15
336		23		4.15	P	4.45	P		30
337		24		10.52	P	11.18	P		26
338		24		11.30	P	11.50	P		20
339		25		11.41	A	11.51	A		10
340		26		9.45	A	10.15	A		30
341		26		12.51	P	1.11	P		20
342		28		9.45	A	10.20	A		35
343		29		1.40	P	2.05	P		25
344		31		5.05	P	5.27	P		22
345		3 Nov		12.50	P	1.07	P		17
346		13		4.03	P	4.07	P		4
347		25		2.55	P	3.10	P		15
348		30		12.50	P	1.20	P		30
349		6 Dec		6.00	P	6.25	P		25
350		16		1.52	P	1.52	P		15
351		16		6.00	P	6.05	P		5
352		18		2.25	P	2.35	P		10
353		20		5.43	P	5.54	P		11
354		30		10.05	A	10.40	A		35
355	1943	8 Jan		1.10	P	1.30	P		20 (18 days 11
356		9		2.53	P	3.40	P		47 hrs 23
357		10		2.30	P	3.00	P		30 mins)
358		14		3.50	P	4.00	P		10
359		17		8.20	P	8.30	P		10
360		21		1.25	P	1.40	P		15
361		22		8.35		9.20			45
362		26		11.00	A	11.20	A		20
363		26		2.00	P	2.30	P		30
364		26		2.35	P	2.50	P		15
365		26		4.00	P	4.30	P		30
366		27		12.30		12.45			15

EXETER AIR RAIDS
LISTINGS FROM CHIEF CONSTABLES NOTEBOOK

No. (Air Raids)	Date	Time of Alert	Time (Bombs)	No.	Area of Incidents	Casualities Fatal	Ser.	Slt.	Remarks
1	7.8.40	23.19	23.26	5 H.E.	Saville Rd., Buller Rd. Charnley Ave.	-	1	-	Damage to residential property.
2	16.8.40	None	03.25	2 H.E.	Field nr Bovemoor Lane & Field at Mile Lane	-	-	-	Slight damage to buildings.
3	6.9.40	22.36	22.36	1 UXB	Normandy Rd.	-	-	-	Slight damage
4	16.9.40	None	21.00	2 H.E.	Field at Exwick	-	-	-	Slight damage
5	17.9.40	None	22.06	6 H.E.	Blackboy Road Polsloe Road Magdalen Road	4	1	2	Serious damage 3 U.X.B.
6	19.9.40	None	None	-	After investigation found to be out of city.				
7	28.10.40	None	21.26	2 Mines	Cranbrook Road & field nearby	4	-	23	Extensive damage.
8	16.1.41	None	22.48	4 H.E.	Magdalen Bridge				Slight damage.
9	4.3.41	None	None	-	Exmouth Junction				Machine gunning.
10	5.5.41	23.16	00.20	3 H.E.	Western Road				Damage to railway.
11	6.5.41	23.13	02.30	9 H.E.	Warwick Road, Hill Barton Road, etc				Damage to several houses.
12	17.6.41	01.35	01.20	5 H.E.	Burnthouse Lane				Damage to houses.
13	23.4.42	22.43	23.31	6 H.E.	Okehampton Road, etc	5	2	15	Several houses demolished.
14	24.4.42	00.06	004-0110	H.E. & I.B.	Paris Street, King Street, etc	73	20	53	Severe damage to all types of property.
15	25.4.42	04.25	05.50	H.E. & I.B.	Portland Street				Several houses demolished.
16	4.5.42	01.36	01.36 - 02.50	-	Exeter's Blitz. 160 H.E. 10, 000 incendiaries 6 paramines.	161	70	406	
17	30.12.42	10.05	10.05	6. H.E.	Holloway Street Isca Rd, Polsloe Rd	18	18	79	Hit and run raid.
					TOTAL	268	115	594	

SUMMARY OF AIR RAIDS IN APRIL AND MAY, 1942

Date	Time	Number	Type (Bombs)	Fatal (Casualties)	Others	Area of Damage
23.4.42	23.31	Six	250kg H.E.	5	17	Okehampton Street
25.4.42	00.06	65	H.E. approx. 30 tons	73	73	Pennsylvania, Paris St, King St, Wonford etc
26.4.42	05.45	One 702	H.E. Incendiary Bombs	3	16	Portland Street
4.5.42	01.36 to 02.50	160	H.E. approx. 75 tons			Widespread.
		10,000	Incendiary Bombs	161	70 Ser. 406 Slt.	
		Six	Paramines			

PRE-WAR MAP

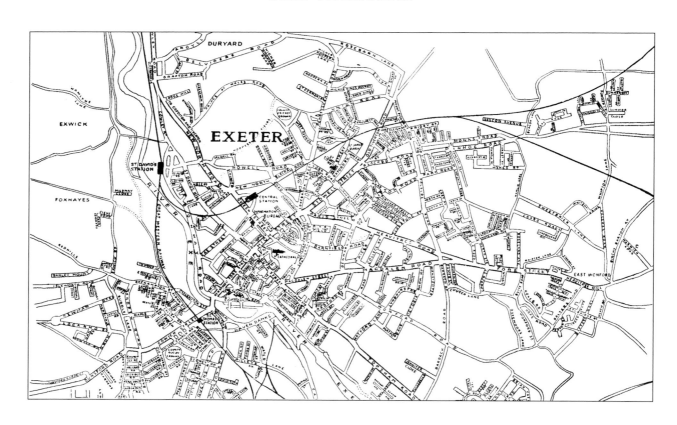

THE VENNING MAPS – BOMBED AREAS 1945

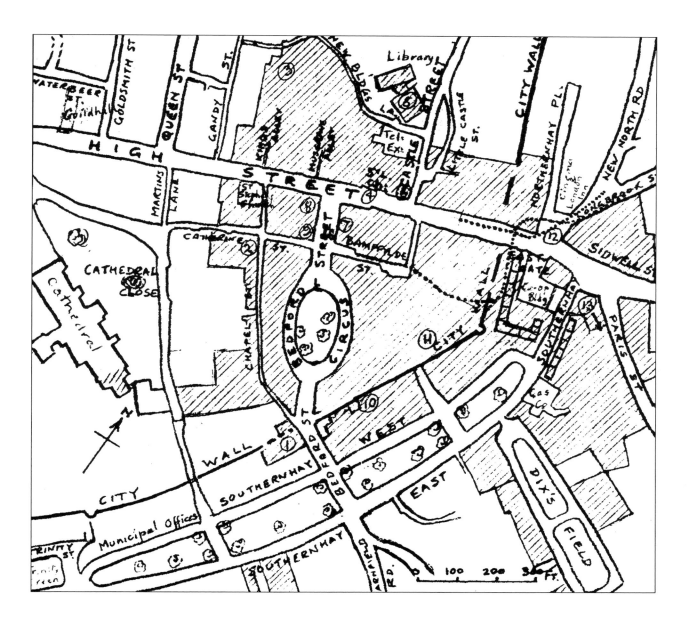

High Street Area
Blitzed Areas & Old Road Layout, 1945.

City Wall	⌐⌐
"Blitzed Area"	▨
Underground Passages	•••••
L. &. G. *Underground Conveniences	

1. Site of Drill Hall
2. Site of St Catherine's Almshouses
3. Site of Former Swimming Bath

4. Site of St Lawrence Church
5. Site of City Library
6. Standing Westminster Bank (remains)
7. Standing Barclays Bank (remains)
8. Site of Lloyds Bank
9. Site of Dellers Cafe
10. Site of Former Elec. Sub Stn
11. Site of Bluecoat School
12. London Inn Square
13. Bude Hotel (remains)
Temporary Shops later (1947)   ▭▭

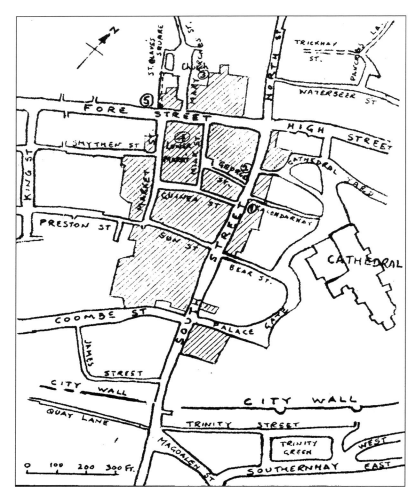

Fore St/South St Area
Blitzed Areas & Old Road
Layout, 1945

City Wall   ⌓
"Blitzed" Area   ▨

1. Site of Hall of Vicars
   Choral
2. Site of St Georges Church
3. Mary Arches Church
4. Temporary Shops later
   (1948)
5. St Olave's Church

Sidwell St Area
Blitzed Areas & Old Road Layout,
1945

"Blitzed" Areas   ▨

1. Warren Lane
2. Church Lane
3. Leighton Terrace
4. Cheeke Street
5. Stover Place
6. King William Street
7. Belgrave Road
8. Summerland Crescent
9. Russell Street
10. Verney Place

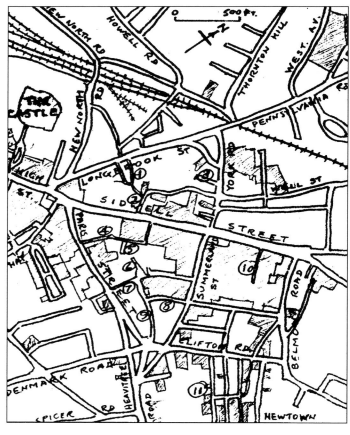

CHIEF CONSTABLES NOTEBOOK

CIVIL DEFENCE WARDENS' SERVICE

The organisation of the Wardens' Service is arranged so that the City is divided into *10 Groups* which in turn are sub-divided into 130 Sectors.

Each *group* has a Head Warden who is responsible for his group and is assisted by a Deputy Head Warden, together with a paid Staff Warden. Groups A/B and H have 2 Deputy Head Wardens owing to the size of the Groups. Each *Sector* has in charge a Senior Warden who is assisted by a Second Warden.

Strength. 1943. The authorised strength is 1,310 and the actual strength is made up as follows:-

Designations	Whole-time paid	Part-time unpaid
Chief Warden	—	1
Head Warden	—	10
Deputy Head Wardens	—	12
Senior Warden	—	130
Second Warden	—	130
Wardens - Male	47	631
. . . - Female	—	308
	47	1,222

TOTAL: 1,269

Wardens' Posts. There are 44 Wardens' Posts fully equipped.

Equipment. Each Warden has been issued with the following equipment:

Battledress	Steel Helmet
Greatcoat	Respirator [C.D.]
Boots or Shoes	Eyeshields
Hat or Beret	Whistle and Torch

Up to August, 1943, the following respirators were on issue from the Wardens' Department:

Baby's Protective Helmet- 1,794
Small Childs respirator - 2,443
Small Civilian respirator- 2,336
Civilian respirator - 60,000 [approx]
Civilian Duty respirator - 1,356
Special types - 347

The Repair Depot, Pancras Lane, effect on an average 600 repairs to respirators every month.

Key points.
The following list was supplied by the Town Clerk in accordance with instructions set out in Circ: S.W.102/1942.
1. Exeter Corporation Power Station. The Basin.
2. Exeter T.S., C.E.B., Water Lane.
3. United Gas Industries [Willey & Co., Haven Road]
4. Delaney Gallay Ltd., Exwick.
5. Exeter Gaslight & Coke Co., The Basin.
6. Air Service Training Ltd., General Garage, Blackboy Road.
7. Veale's Warehouse, Pye & Counties - Magnesium storage. Transport, Haven Road.
8. Air Service Training Ltd., Metropolitan Transport Garage, Polsloe Bridge.
9. Air Service Training Ltd., Cox Bros. Garage, Sidwell Street.
10. Air Service Training Ltd., Pike's Garage, Alphington Street.
11. Folland Aircraft Ltd., [Garton & King], Tan Lane.
12. B.B.C. St. Leonards Place.

Special Constabulary

In 1931 the Special Constabulary was reorganised and had a strength of 101. Warrant cards and armlets were issued and the majority of the Special Constables were sworn in. In 1938 it was found necessary to take the reorganisation further and consequently the strength was built up, all members were sworn in, a file was made for each man together with a record card. Lectures were commenced on police law and duties, A.R.P., First Aid etc. Arrangements were put in hand in December, 1939, for uniform to be supplied and it was possible to issue full uniform to a number of the Special Constables. By June 1940, all members of the Special Constabulary were supplied with full uniform, which consists of the following: Overcoat, Raincoat, Tunic, Trousers, Cap, Gloves, Leggings, Cape, Respirator, Steel Helmet, Rubber Boots, Whistle and Truncheon.

Strength 1943
The authorised strength is 250 and the actual strength is maintained up to the limit, and is made up as follows:
1 Commandant. Appointed October 1938
7 Divisional Officers.
13 Special Sergeants. Appointed May 1939
229 Special Constables.

The establishment is arranged as follows:

Headquarters
1 Staff Divisional Commander.

Mobile Division.
This Division was formed in April, 1939, with the following strength:
1 Divisional Commander   7 motor cars
2 Special Sergeants   and also 4 S.C's
5 Special Constables   with cars who
                         act as reserves
There is a reserve of 15 cars owned by S.C's which are available for use in emergencies.

Patrol Section
4 Divisional Commanders
11 Special Sergeants
121 Special Constables
(The 4 who act as reserve for the Mobile Div: also do patrol)

Observer Section
This section commenced duties on the 18th January, 1941.
1 Divisional Commander
99 Special Constables
2 Posts manned from 4 p.m. to 8 a.m. daily. Times relaxed in summer.

Duties
Each man should do 48 hours a month - 8 hours a week patrol duty [this is reckoned as 10 hours a week]. The other 8 hours is made up by answering the sirens and other duties.

Medals
87 Long Service medals have been awarded and 18 Bars thereto.

Classes of Instruction

Summer	1937	Anti-gas training.
Nov.	1938	Police law, first aid
	to	and Foot Drill.
March	1939	
Jan.	1939	Anti-gas training for new members.
March	1939	Beat patrol with a regular P.C.
April	1939	Special Driving course and instruction for Mobile Division
May	1939	Special Course on Police law etc. for Special Sergeants.
May	1939	Specials commenced beat patrol.
May to July	1939	Refresher course in anti-gas and once a week foot drill followed by practical

demonstrations in dealing with accidents together with traffic drill.

CLASSES OF INSTRUCTION

Regularly up to 1939 instruction classes were held for the members of the force together with periodical Refresher courses. During the war period the following classes have been held:

1. December 1939 - Two regulars and thirty-two Police War Constables. Three weeks course. 4 hours a day.

2. April 1940 - Seven Regulars and seventeen Police War Constables [New entrants]. Four weeks course. 4 hours a day.

3. November 1940 - Twenty Police War Constables [New entrants]. Four weeks course. 4 hours a day.

4. October 1941 - Twenty-two Police War Constables [New entrants]. Five weeks course. 4 hours a day.

5. March-April 1942 - Refresher Course of two weeks - 8 hours a day. All members of the War Reserve.

6. July-August 1942 - Eleven Police War Constables [New entrants]. Five weeks course. 4 hours a day.

During these courses, at the end of each week, an examination is held. In addition to instruction in Police law and procedure, the above classes were given instruction in the use of firearms [rifle, Sten and Bren guns], first aid, foot drill, traffic drill, physical training and unarmed combat.

To ensure that all members of the force and Special Constabulary are keeping abreast of the multifarious inser-

tions in Daily Orders, sets of questions are issued to sergeants each week who question the men on the subjects and if they cannot answer correctly the sergeants advise them. For Special Constabulary training see 'S'.

May to July 1949	Course in Police duties and first aid for new entrants.
Sept.1939	Course of 10 lectures in Police law and first aid for new entrants.
January 1940	Refresher course for all members in first aid.
February 1940	Course on Police duties for new entrants.

Since 1940 Courses have been held as required for new entrants and refresher courses have been arranged for all members of the Special Constabulary which included, in addition to those subjects mentioned above, lectures on H.E. and Incendiary bombs, physical training, unarmed combat and the use of firearms [Rifle, Sten and Bren guns]. In June, 1943, a course of safety first lectures were given to all members, outlining the way they could best help on their beat to prevent road accidents.

On the outbreak of war 32 members of the Special Constabulary were enrolled into the Police War Reserve and since then other members have been enrolled making a total of 66 enrolments from the Special Constabulary. At present there are 42 members of the Special Constabulary in the War Reserve.

August 1944	Patrol section duties reduced to three each fortnight.
September 1944	Observer Section. Manning of Posts suspended as from 0800 hours 29th September.
November 1944	Patrol section duties reduced to one each week.
January 1945	Fifteen members of C.D. Service trained and sworn in

as Special Constables to fill vacancies.

February 1945 Divisional Commanders now known as Special Inspectors.

Awards to date - Long Service medals. Patrol Section 94. Observer Section 26.

Strength - Aug 1943	*Authorised*	*Actual*
Regular force	98+3	52 5/45
First Police Reserve	3	3
Police War Reserve	76	75
Women's Auxiliary Police Corps	16	16
Special Constabulary	250	250
Police Auxiliary Messenger Service	100	94
May 1946	110+2	80+ 1

policewomen
+9 civilian women +8
For further details see C.C.K's Dept.

CHURCHES, CHAPELS AND OTHER PLACES OF WORSHIP DESTROYED AND DAMAGED

Destroyed
1. Bedford Church, Bedford Circus.
2. St. James Church, St. James Road.
3. St. Lawrence Church, High Street.
4. St. Sidwell's Church, Sidwell Street.
5. Christ Scientist Church, Dix's Field.
6. Gospel Hall, Fore Street.
7. Spiritual Church, Milk Street.
8. Locomotive Church Institute, Sidwell St.

Severely Damaged
1. Cathedral Church of St. Peter.
2. Emmanuel Church, Okehampton Road.
3. St. Mary Arches Church, Mary Arches St.
4. St. Matthews Church, Clifton Road.
5. Congregational Church, Heavitree.
6. Congregational Church, Southernhay.
7. St. Sidwell's Methodist Church, Sidwell Street.
8. Church of the Blessed Sacrament, Heavitree.
9. Elim Tabernacle, Paris Street.
10. Christ Church, Grosvenor Place.
11. St. Stephen's Church, High Street.

In addition to the above twelve other churches etc., were slightly damaged.

MANPOWER STATE

Monday 4 May 42
250 Rescue Work
100 Royal Engineers
100 Police duties
20 Royal Corps Signals. Post Office.
20 Cooks, Whipton
20 Water Carts **Total 514**

Tuesday 5 May 42
100 R.Es.
250 Debris clearing
100 Police
100 Rescue
6 Stoking
20 Water carts **Total 576**

Wednesday 6 May 42
20 Cooking
100 R.Es
250 Debris
100 Police [Traffic Control]
24 Salvage [Flour]
50 Rescue
14 Stoking
100 Grave Digging
30 Rescue [City Hospital]
20 Water Carts
6 Lorries **Total 714**

Thursday 7 May 42
300 Debris
100 Grave Digging
50 Rescue
18 Stoking
20 Cooking
20 Water Carts

4 D.Rs and Signallers
100 Police assistance
25 Salvage [Grain]   **Total 637**

Friday 8 May 42
        260 Debris clearance
350   40 Salvage
        50 Rescue
100 Police assistance [Traffic Control]
50 Grave filling
18 Stoking
21 Cooking
30 Food Salvage
4 D.Rs and Signallers
22 Lorries
20 Water Carts   **Total 615**

Saturday 9 May 42
300   250 Debris Clearance
        50 Rescue
100 Police assistance [Traffic Control]
18 Stoking
21 Cooking
4 D.Rs and Signallers
20 Furniture Salvage 5
0 Salvage [Grain]
18 Lorries
20 Water Carts   **Total 551**

Sunday 10 May 42
250   200 Debris clearance
        50 Rescue
50 Police assistance [Traffic Control]
18 Stoking
21 Cooking
20 Furniture salvage
4 D.Rs and Signallers
50 Salvage [Grain]
18 Lorries
20 Water Carts   **Total 451**

Monday 11 May 42
200 Rescue and Debris
50 Police assistance [Traffic Control]
18 Stoking
21 Cooking
20 Furniture salvage

50 Grain salvage
4 D.Rs and Signallers
16 Lorries
20 Water Carts   **Total 399**

Tuesday 12 May 42
222 Debris and rescue
50 Police assistance [Traffic Control]
50 Grain salvage
18 Stoking
21 Cooking
20 Furniture salvage
4 D.Rs and Signallers
16 Lorries
20 Water Carts   **Total 421**

Wednesday 13 May 42
230 Rescue and debris
50 Police duties
50 Grain salvage
21 Cooking
12 Stoking
4 D.Rs and Signallers
8 Transporting food
12 Salvage work for Aircraft Production
9 Lorries
20 Water Carts   **Total 416**

Total manpower supply by Military up to date [13.5.42] 5,234

        **J. Hepburn GRA for
        Major Chichester
        Military Commander.**

AWARDS FOR CONDUCT DURING AIR RAIDS
Police
P.W.R. Hutchings   GEORGE MEDAL
P.S. Fraser   Commended by H.M.
                    The King
P.A.M. Reynolds   -ditto-
13 members of the   Commended by the
Regulars   Watch Committee
3 members of the   -ditto-
War Reserve
4 members of the   -ditto-
Special Constabulary

P.A.M. Matthews -ditto-
Other Awards
C.J. Newman Esq., O.B.E.
A.R.P. Controller
Mrs. E.A.M. Knee, GEORGE MEDAL
Nurse at City Hospital
Mr. E. Howard, GEORGE MEDAL
A.R.P. Warden
Mrs. M. Britt, B.E.M.
Nurse at City Hospital
Miss A.D. Walker, B.E.M.
Nurse at City Hospital
Mr. J.P. Cundy, B.E.M.
Exeter Co-operative Society
Mr. L. Turner, B.E.M.
Casualty Service
Mr. C. Leonard, B.E.M.
Rescue Party

Mr. E. Eveleigh, B.E.M.
Aircraft Fitter
Mr. F. Hannington, B.E.M.
G.P.O. Sorting Clerk
Mr. S. Pike, B.E.M.
G.P.O. Night Supervisor
Mr. H. Tagg, B.E.M.
Southern Railway
Mr. C. Wells, B.E.M.
G.P.O. Postman
Mr. F. Sansom, M.B.E [Civil Div.]
Exeter Gas Co.
3 Firemen Commended by H.M.
the King
1 Storekeeper -ditto-
7 members of Staff -ditto-
Chief Constable O.B.E.

THE RAIDS
AIR RAID – 7TH AUGUST 1940

EXETER CITY POLICE REPORTS

AIR RAID DAMAGE: CHARNLEY AVENUE AND VICINITY

7.55am Thursday 8th August, 1940

At about 11.25pm Wednesday 7th August 1940, a high explosive bomb was dropped in Charnley Avenue, Larby Homes Estate, Redhills. The bomb made contact with the pavement outside a semi-detached house called "Moretonia". A crater about five feet deep was made and a 4" water main immediately under the point of impact was split open. Shrapnel and other debris were thrown over an extensive area seriously damaging adjoining property within a radius of about 50 yards.

Senior Warden Stabbett, with other wardens, was on the scene within a minute or so, he being in Prescott Avenue [a road adjoining] at the time of the explosion. A message was put through to Report Centre and within a short time the Water Repair Party were on the scene. The water was turned off at a nearby junction and repairs put immediately in hand. Owing to the near proximity of a gas main the Gas Repair Party were also in attendance, but their services were not required. P.C. Tyrell, with two War Reserve constables, was soon at the incident and took control. There were no personal injuries sustained and no obstruction of traffic.

Damage:

Moretonia, Charnley Avenue
Warwick, Charnley Ave. - general damage
Glenbar, 3 Charnley Ave.
Glenella, 1 Charnley Ave.
2, 4, 6, Green Lane - general damage
9, 11, 17, 19, 21, 23, 27, Prescott Rd - general damage

County Library - general damage
Stokes Nurseries - general damage

In every case the occupiers were on the premises and were aware of the damage.

With the exception of two households, everyone on whom I called stated they heard the sirens. The caretaker at County Library informed me that he could hear one of the sirens sounding the all clear when the others were sounding the warning. I was on duty at Exe Bridge when the warning was sounded, and I too, distinctly heard one of the sirens sounding a steady note.

There was some confusion at Exe Bridge because the public shelter next door to the Seven Stars was not unlocked. In response to our instructions to take cover, some persons shouted back strong criticisms about the shelter being locked. They were directed to Gervase Avenue.

In contact with the public during the raid and immediately after I did not see any signs of panic.

Signed *S.W. Moore Police-sergeant No. 4*

DAMAGE TO PROPERTY IN SAVILE ROW DURING AN AIR RAID

8.15pm Thursday 8th August, 1940

On Wednesday August 7th, 1940, at about 11.35pm a H.E. bomb was dropped from an aircraft onto the footpath at the junction of Savile Road and Merrivale Road and extensive damage was caused, all the house property in Savile Road was damaged in varying degrees, some with windows smashed, others with doors blown off and ceilings blown down, extensive damage was also caused to furniture in these premises, in all there are 19 houses in Savile Road all of which are the property of the Exeter City Council, the following houses in Merrivale Road, also the property of the Exeter City Council, were damaged, damage to these mainly consisting of smashed windows:

54, 58, 62, 64, 66, 68, 70, 72, 74, 76, 78, 100, 102, 103, 107, 111, 113, 115, 119, 121, 123, Merrivale Road - general damage.

Frank COCKRAN, aged 45 years, a Railway Employee, residing at 121 Merrivale Road, was either standing at or passing by the landing window at the top of the stairs at his house when he was struck by either a piece of flying glass or a piece of bomb casing [a piece of which was found near where he was at the time] and sustained injuries to his hand and in the groin, he walked to the First Aid Post in Savile Road where he was treated and later removed in an A.R.P. Ambulance to the Royal Devon and Exeter Hospital, where he was detained, an enquiry at his home the morning after elicited that his condition was serious. There appeared to be no injuries to any other person in the district.

The First Aid Post at Savile Road was also extensively damaged, both pairs of double doors were blown out, a number of panes of glass in the front of the building were smashed and ceilings in the hall fell, the work of the Post was not affected by this. The following premises in Buddle Lane were damaged by the force of the explosion, and the only damage to these properties were broken window panes:
52, 54, 55, 56, 58, 59, 60, 62, Buddle Lane

The footpath at the junction of Savile Road and Merrivale Road was damaged and a small crater caused by the bomb, this was topped off by the Road Repair Party and made safe, one P.C. was left on the scene all night. Several Ambulances and First Aid Parties were soon on the scene as also was the Road Repair Party. The Police attending the inci-

dent were, one Sergeant, 4 P.C.s, 4 P.W.R.s, 14 Special Constables.
Signed *Sidney Geo. Collins Sergeant, No. 9*

DAMAGE CAUSED BY AIR RAID
1pm Thursday 8th August, 1940
On Wednesday 7th August 1940, at about 11.30pm an H.E. bomb dropped in the garden at the rear of Messrs. French & Co., No. 169 Cowick Street, Exeter, the bomb demolished several garden walls and did extensive damage to a number of buildings in the vicinity as follows:

Exeter Munition Co. Buller Road, Exeter, all windows at the rear of the premises broken, roof at rear damaged, rear door blown off, acetylene generator holed, heating furnace damaged. Windows in the front of the premises were also broken and the roof of the oil store was damaged, the owner of this property is Messrs. Leighton Steer.

Dellers Baker
31, 36, 38, 40?, Cowick Street
83 Buller Road
Turks Head Inn - general damage
Morton Inn Court
Morton Inn
169 Cowick Street
Union Place
163 Cowick Street

There were no personal injuries and all the damage to the properties is being dealt with by the respective owners, officials of the City Authority have been to the scene. There was no crater caused by the bomb, it apparently struck a wall in falling and demolished it.
Signed *Sidney Geo. Collins Sergeant No. 9*

DAMAGE TO PROPERTY FOLLOWING ENEMY ACTION: HIGH EXPLOSIVE BOMB
10.15am Thursday 8th August, 1940
At 6am Thursday 8th August, 1940 I

commenced enquiries respecting an H.E. bomb which was dropped from enemy aircraft at 23.25 hours on Wednesday 7th instant, at the rear of 3 Shooting Marsh Stile, Alphington Street. The bomb fell on soft ground in the garden at the rear of the house mentioned and about 12 feet from the building. It caused a crater which measured approximately 14 feet in diameter and 3' 6" deep. Considerable damage was occasioned to property but there were no serious personal injuries. For the purpose of elucidation I beg to submit the detail under address headings:

2 Shooting Marsh Stile - Occupants of the house were John Lee, aged 65 years, his wife Susanna Jane, aged 60 years, and a lodger William Came, aged 66 years. Mr and Mrs Lee went to bed shortly after 10pm and did not hear anything until the explosion occurred and then glass from the window fell on the bed, which was in a bedroom on the first floor. Mrs Lee sustained a very slight cut on the right side of the nose. Mr Came who was occupying a bedroom on the top floor heard the warning siren but remained in bed. He heard two explosions and then there was a flash which illuminated his bedroom. His bed was then covered with falling plaster and rubbish. When the dust had cleared he got up and went downstairs.

Damage: Room No. 1 on top floor, windows smashed and ceiling damaged. Room No. 2 on same floor, window smashed. Living room on the ground floor, window measuring 6'x6' smashed, ceiling cracked. Scullery: window smashed, ceiling and wall damaged. A lean-to shed in the yard was completely demolished. House owned by Mrs Sherry, 4 Prospect Place, Topsham Road, Exeter.

The occupants of this house were temporarily homeless and I referred them to Mr Huish, at the Public Assistance Office.

3 Shooting Marsh Stile - Occupants of this house were James Daniel Darby aged 73 years, his wife Kate, aged 75 years and their son Frederick aged 44 years. These persons occupied the upper part of the house. The ground floor rooms were occupied by Cyril Bird aged 41 years and his wife Lillian aged 43 years. Mr Darby was sleeping in a bedroom on the top floor which faced on to Shooting Marsh Stile, and his son was occupying a bedroom on the same floor. Both remained in bed until the debris commenced to fall on the beds. Mrs Darby was in bed in a room on the first floor and immediately she heard the siren she got up and went into a living room on the same floor. Mr and Mrs Bird were undressing preparatory to going to bed, in a bedroom on the ground floor, when the siren sounded. Mr Bird went outside and as he did so he heard the bomb falling and immediately fell flat on the ground. After the explosion he picked himself up and on trying to re-enter the house found that the front door had been partly blown from its hinges and he had to force the door down to enter. The whole of the household were taken in by neighbours.

Damage: This house contained eleven rooms and there was extensive damage throughout the building, the rooms facing the rear being more extensively damaged. A large wash house, glass lean-to verandah, and lavatory at the rear were completely demolished. The occupants of this house are likely to require assistance as homeless persons, and in view of this I advised them accordingly. There is a large attic in these premises and during my investigations I saw that it contained a large quantity of paper and rubbish.

4 Shooting Marsh Stile - The occupier of this house is Mrs Lucy Ellen Roper, aged 63 years, but her house was practically undamaged, there being only very slight removal of plaster. Both these houses are owned by Mrs Sherry, mentioned above in respect of No. 2 Shooting Marsh Stile.

1 Rattenburys Place, Shooting Marsh Stile
This house is occupied by William George Havill, aged 71 years, his wife Florence, 51 years, and their son George William, aged 15 years. The boy was sleeping in a room on the top floor which faces the rear, close to where the bomb dropped, and glass and debris was thrown onto his bed. There was damage to walls, ceilings and windows, but the house was habitable. This house is also owned by Mrs Sherry.

2 Rattenburys Place, Shooting Marsh Stile
The occupants of this house were, William John Carpenter, aged 50 years, his mother Mary, aged 78 years, and a lodger George Watson, aged 45 years. Watson was sleeping in a room at the top of the house when the bomb exploded and he miraculously escaped injury. Two windows were blown out and the ceiling fell in on the bed in which he was, but he received no injury.

This house was very extensively damaged and is not habitable. The occupants left and have gone to stay with friends. This house is also owned by Mrs Sherry.

3 Rattenburys Place, Shooting Marsh Stile
Leonard Phillip Kelly, aged 44 years, his wife Margaret Annie, aged 47 years, and his mother-in-law Emma Tuckfield, aged 80 years who is a cripple and blind, occupy this house. This house was badly damaged and it may be that it will not be habitable. I have informed the occupants as to their course should they be rendered homeless. This house is also owned by Mrs Sherry.

4 Rattenburys Place, Shooting Marsh Stile
The occupiers of this house are Mrs Fanny Stone, aged 80 years, and her daughter

Bessie Agnes Stone, aged 47 years. Mrs Stone had a lucky escape in that a large quantity of glass and debris was thrown onto the bed in which she was sleeping but she was unhurt. The house was damaged but not so extensive as to make it uninhabitable. This house is also owned by Mrs Sherry. An outside wash-house and lavatories used by the residents of Rattenburys Place were badly damaged, the roof and windows being smashed.

'The Forge' Shooting Marsh Stile - This workshop is owned by Mrs Sherry and tenanted by Victor Edward Beer, of "Eddy's", Kennford. The roof was damaged, windows smashed, and wooden sides of the building broken.

Stephens & Stephens, Shooting Marsh Stile - The above mentioned are the owners of a builder's yard. Very slight damage was occasioned to glass in the offices there.

Royal Oak Inn, Alphington Street - These premises are owned by Messrs. Norman & Pring Ltd., and occupied by Mrs Hilda Ellen Walkey, aged 33 years. A large plate glass window valued at about £30 was smashed, as was a window measuring approximately 3'6"x2'.

29 Alphington Street - This is a shop occupied by Miss Florence Mingo, 38 years, who is part owner of the premises together with her sister Mrs Bolt. A large front window of the premises was completely smashed, the window measuring approximately 6'x7'6". Slight damage was also occasioned to a wall at the rear. The premises are insured against damage with The Wesleyan & General Insurance Co. Ltd.

27 Alphington Street - This is a shop occupied by Henry Mingo, aged 55 years, and owned by Mr Oswell of 26, Alphington Street. A small window in the front of the premises measuring approximately 3'x3' was smashed. Not insured.

26 Alphington Street - This is a shop owned and occupied by William Hedley Oswell, aged 68 years, and the damage occasioned was to windows. A large shop window measuring 7'6"x5' was smashed and a similar window was badly cracked. Several other panes of glass were either smashed or cracked. Not insured.

P. Pike & Co., Alphington Street - The premises belonging to the above firm are those situated at the junction of Alphington Street and Shooting Marsh Stile. One portion of the premises is occupied by the A.F.S. and the other by the firm in question. A window measuring approximately 8'x8' was smashed in the motor section and a similar window was smashed in the A.F.S. section. The whole of the windows of the A.F.S. premises had been sandbagged but at the point where the window was smashed, the sandbags had been removed some few days ago with the object of replacement, those that were removed being faulty.

'Wylie House', Alphington Street - The occupier of this house is Mrs Sonia Hetty May Remington, aged 45 years, and the owner is Mrs Sherry. A window on the ground floor was smashed, the window measured approximately 3'x3'6".

Wheelwrights Workshop, Shooting Marsh Stile - These premises are owned and tenanted by Leonard Owen Fry, aged 35 years who resides at 27, Okehampton Street, Exeter. The damage caused to the premises consisted of corrugated side broken, window frame blown out, wooden partition damaged, and slight damage to materials. Not insured.

Damage to property following enemy action: High explosive bomb - The property that required immediate shoring up or demolition, was attended to by the City Architect's Department. When I left Messrs. Stephens & Stephens acting for the City Council, were making arrangements for further shoring up and removal of debris.   Signed *H. Arnold Sergeant*

REPORT OF INCENDIARY BOMB POCOMBE HILL

9.45am Thursday 8th August, 1940
On Wednesday night during the Air Raid on the city a report was received at my Parade Point, saying that an incendiary bomb was seen to fall at the "Crows Nest", Pocombe Hill, I immediately sent two Specials, they went there and saw the person who complained, she pointed out the position of the bomb to them which she stated fell in a field adjoining her house, search of the field was made but no trace of any incendiary bomb was traced, this was later reported to me at the Parade Point, Buddle Lane and Head Quarters were informed.

At about 7.15am this morning I went to the "Crows Nest", Pocombe Hill and saw the occupier, she pointed out to me the position of the alleged incendiary bomb, I searched the field but could trace nothing which might suggest an incendiary bomb. Just before the bombs were dropped last night I was in Buddle Lane and saw a bright light coming from the direction of Pocombe Bridge, this light suggested to me that it was a parachute flare dropped by the aircraft. There is nothing to suggest either an incendiary bomb or an unexploded bomb.
Signed *Sidney Geo. Collins Sergeant, No. 9*

DAMAGE BY HIGH EXPLOSIVE BOMB DROPPED IN WARDREW ROAD

7.25am Thursday 8th August, 1940
At about 11.30pm on Wednesday, 7th August, 1940, a high explosive bomb was

dropped by enemy aircraft in the back garden of 88 Wardrew Road, a dwelling house, owned and occupied by Reginald Bertram Fulford, causing a crater about three feet deep and measuring about 10 feet in diameter. Extensive exterior damage was done to the rear of Fulford's House. Similar damage was done to the following houses in the same district:

82, 84, 86, 90, 92, 94, 96 Wardrew Road
46, 48, 50, 52, 54 Maple Road
77, 85, 87, 89, 91 Wardrew Road

There were no fatalities at this incident. Only one person was injured namely, John Arthur Lavers, aged 68 years, of 86 Wardrew Road, who sustained a slight cut on his head due, it is believed, to a piece of plaster falling from the ceiling at his house. First aid was rendered by a member of the First Aid Party at the scene.

Police, Air Raid Wardens, and a First Aid Party were on duty at the incident. The military later placed a guard on duty. A constable was detailed to stand by pending further instructions. In the course of my enquiries I learned that all the occupiers of the above-named premises, with the exception of one, heard the warning siren and were able to make preparations for their safety, this no doubt prevented a heavy casualty list.

Signed *C. FRASER P.S.56*

AIR RAID – 6TH SEPTEMBER 1940

5.30AM, UNEXPLODED BOMB IN DWELLING HOUSE NO. 48 NORMANDY ROAD

Saturday 7th September, 1940

On Friday September 6th 1940 at about 11.30pm an H.E. bomb was dropped from an enemy plane. The bomb was heard by a number of people, who described it as giving a swishing noise as it descended. It collided with the front of No. 48 Normandy Road, causing that part of the building to collapse into the roadway, and damaging the interior of the premises. The occupiers, a Mrs F.M. Ford and her daughter Miss V.M. Ford who were asleep on the premises, were unhurt and immediately vacated the premises. This is confirmed by a member of the Home Guard, Mr Phillip Aggett, of 26 East John Street, who was on duty at the Drill Hall, Normandy Road, who heard the bomb crash into the house, but heard no explosion. Aggett saw the occupants vacate the house, but it is not known yet where they took shelter.

Wardens on duty in this Sector No. 68 under the Senior Warden, Mr Warren, were soon at the scene of the incident and they were followed by a number of police officers which included Sergeants Carr, and Brown and six constables. The nature of the incident was soon ascertained and Headquarters were immediately informed. Owing to the imminent danger of an explosion, the inhabitants of the following streets were evacuated.

Normandy Road, Stuart Road, Antony Road and Hanover Road. Temporary accommodation was provided by friends in the Heavitree district, those who were unable to be accommodated in this manner were temporarily accommodated in various public halls under the supervision of the Town Clerk's staff. They were conveyed to these places of shelter in Corporation buses.

Services arriving on the scene following the report of the incident were. First Aid Party No. 1, A.F.S. Squads Nos. 1 and 6, and Rescue Party No. 1. Their services were not required and they returned to their respective depots. The evacuation of this area which numbered approximately

300 people was carried out smoothly with the full and willing co-operation of the persons concerned, without any disorder. Major Lock the Head Warden was in attendance and supervised the Wardens and Superintendent A.E. Rowsell was present and in charge of police arrangements.

All road approaches to the incident were closed and guarded by police officers. The Military have not attended up to the time of reporting and a further report on the progress of the incident will be submitted as soon as possible.
Signed *Trevor Brown Police Sergeant No. 6*

CITY AND COUNTY OF THE CITY OF EXETER POLICE AUXILIARY SERVICES INFORMATION NO. 242. MONDAY 9TH SEPTEMBER, 1940

Air Raid Damge Incident - Unexploded Bomb
At 2330 hours on Friday 6th instant, following an air raid warning period in respect of which the "Raiders Passed" signal was received at 2253 hours a high explosive bomb was dropped from an enemy aircraft, penetrated the roof of 48 Normandy Road and became deeply embedded in the pavement of the house, unexploded. The incident was dealt with as a Delayed Action bomb and all dwelling-houses within a radius of 150 yards evacuated, those not finding accommodation with friends or neighbours being temporarily provided for in the Food and Shelter Stations at St. Sidwell's Methodist Church Hall, St. James' Institute, Heavitree Congregational Church Hall, and St. Mary Arches Parish Hall. The incident was inspected by an officer of No. 100 Bomb Disposal Section, R.E. who advised that the evacuated area could be reduced in radius, the following dwelling-houses continuing to be evacuated:

Stuart Road, Nos. 25 to 53 [odd numbers only, inclusive]

Normandy Road Nos. 16 to 52 [even numbers inclusive] and Nos. 17 to 47 [odd numbers inclusive]

Hanover Road, Nos. 17 to 25 [inclusive].
An Incident Post was set up at Wardens' Post No. 30 and later transferred and is now located at Normandy Road Drill Hall. All persons occupying houses other than those above were advised that they could return to their homes. Pending further instructions from the Officer-in-Charge of the Bomb Disposal Section, persons are to be directed not to loiter in the locality, to keep as far as possible in the part of the house which is farthest from the bomb, and to keep windows facing in the direction of the bomb open. Although it is possible that the bomb in question is a "dud" it must be regarded as a delayed action bomb until disposed of. Notice will be given to all concerned as soon as it has been dealt with by the Bomb Disposal Section, Royal Engineers, and the incident is closed.

CITY AND COUNTY OF THE CITY OF EXETER POLICE AUXILIARY SERVICES INFORMATION NO. 245 THURSDAY 12TH SEPTEMBER, 1940

Air Raid Damage Incident - Unexploded Bomb
Adverting to Information No. 242, the U.X.B. Incident in Normandy Road was transferred to Heavitree Brook at 1800 hours on Tuesday, 10th instant, the Officer-in-Charge of the 99th Bomb Disposal Section, R.E., having excavated the bomb [a 250 kilo delayed-action H.E.] and decided to move it to a safer place for destruction. The bomb was found to have a clock which had ceased ticking, but the mechanism of which might resume at any time, hence the need for moving the bomb the shortest possible distance. The bomb was exploded at 15.45 on 11th instant, resulting in slight damage to ceilings and windows in various parts of Heavitree.

Arrangements for the repair of damaged property are being dealt with by the A.R.P. Controller. The incident is now closed.

Incident No. 1: 48 Normandy Road
H.E. Bomb Delayed Action
10.45am - Lieut. Goffin, 99 Bomb disposal section, Plymouth. [Arrival]
10.45am - Chief Constable informed of above arrival.
11.00am - Arrival of Chief Constable, Superintendent and Commandant.
11.15am - Chief Constable to Mr. Clithero.
11.55am - Chief Constable to Town Clerk.
11.58am - Arrival of Surveyor's men.
12.10pm - Chief Constable to Cullompton.
12.15pm - Danger area reduced by Lieut. Goffin and Chief Constable.
12.50pm - Foreman Jefferys reported building shored up.
2.40pm - Lieut. Goffin to Bristol.
3.00pm - Lieut. Goffin to Chief Constable. Bomb is delayed action but clock has ceased ticking. Will pull it into position to see if clock resumes ticking.
3.20pm - To SO Cancel letters re evacuated persons returning to homes.
4.40pm - Lieut. Goffin to Chief Constable. Delayed action bomb has been removed from house. Will put it on lorry and wants road cleared in order to take bomb to place of safety.
5.05pm - Progress report.
6.00pm - -do- Incident transferred.
6.05pm - To S.O. Unexploded bomb removed from district. It is now safe for everyone to return to see if everything is alright at home.
7.00pm - To S.O. Police guard posted at approaches to field where delayed action bomb is situated.
7.15am - Council Foreman asks for permission to work on 'dump' with 10 men. Instructed to keep 200 yards away from position of bomb.

We will inform him of time of detonation.
11.50am - Chief Constable enquiring for position. Informed that Lieut. Goffin had not been on scene today; believed to be in County area.
2.25pm - Lieut. Goffin 2 NCOs and 5 men arrived. Further examination made. Hole dug and bomb replaced in it.
2.40pm - Lieut. Goffin: "We can do nothing further, so will explode bomb at 3.45 p.m. today."
3.50pm - Bomb exploded: No injury. General damage as follows:-
Nos. 35,36,17,21,5,7,67, *Sweetbrier Lane,* 71 *Hamlin Lane.*

CITY AND COUNTY OF THE CITY OF EXETER AIR RAID WARDENS

Tel. No. 4930
Please reply to - B.B.Whitaker
8, Clifton Hill,
EXETER.
9th September 1940
Dear Sir,
UNEXPLODED BOMB. 48 Normandy Road 23.30 Hours. 6th September 1940.
Statement by WARDEN F.J. Rockey, 51 Anthony Road. Sector 68.
While in my Garden, I heard the Bomb drop and immediately dashed out to ascertain its whereabouts. It was very dark and I stumbled over the debris in the road and then observed that a house had been hit. I immediately went into the house and observed a small blue flame and heard loud hissing. There was no sign of the occupants, and I therefore tried to get into the back part of the house but the communicating door was jammed. Fearing that the occupants were trapped I left the house and contacted Warden J.W. Brooks who had arrived on the scene a few seconds after me. I hurriedly explained the position and left him to deal with matters while I communicated with Control Centre.

Hearing no explosion and having observed the light and noises I concluded that the Bomb was one of the large type incendiary which had not yet fully come into operation.

I went to the Kiosk in Hamlin's Lane but after twice making attempt to communicate decided that the telephone was out of action, especially that on pressing button 'B' twice my money was not returned. I then went to the Police Box in Hamlin Lane. Sergeant Carr was there and he could not get through to the Police Station and recommended me to try Thorne's Garage on Heavitree Hill from whence I eventually got my message through.

Before leaving Sgt. Carr I asked him to send Police to the scene. I did not write out my M1 but was assisted in sending it by the Control Room Operator.

I then returned and contacted Sgt. Brown.

Yours faithfully,
Head Warden "F" To Chief Warden, A.R.P. HQ., Exeter.

AIR RAID – 11TH SEPTEMBER 1940

REPORTS OF DAMAGE CAUSED BY BOMB AT SWEETBRIER LANE 11TH SEPTEMBER 1940.

Reported by Occupiers to Sergeant Healey, Incident Officer

Sweetbrier Lane - Nos. 35, 17, 67, 5, 21, 7, 37, 59, 39, 52, 134, 65, 33, 29, 25, 27, 23, 15.

Whiteway Drive - No. 16. *Hamlin Lane* - Hamlin Farm, 71, 109. *Stuart Road* - No. 53.

Reports of Unexploded Bombs etc.

1 Saxon Road - Suspected delayed action bomb
2 Avondale Rd - Long-drawn wailing noise
3 North St. Heavitree - Suspected delayed action bomb
4 Mile Lane - as above
7 St. Leonards Road - Unexploded bomb
8 Countess Wear - Time bomb dropped
9 Polsloe Bridge - Unexploded bomb
Polsloe Bridge - Suspected delayed action bomb, Polsloe Bridge - as above.
10 Fore St., Heavitree - Unexploded bomb
11 Thompson Road - Delayed action bomb
12 Duryard Estate - as above
13 South Lawn Terrace - Suspected heavy bomb. Distinct whistling noise
14 Sandford Street - Delayed action bomb
15 School House, Heavitree - -do- -do-
16 Whipton Reformatory - Suspected bomb on fields nearby
17 Briar Crescent -do- delayed action bomb
18 Russell St - Bullets struck roof of house
19 Sweetbrier Lane - Unexploded bomb
20 St. Leonards Road - as above
21 Hope Rd - Suspected unexploded bomb
22 Coronation Road - -do- -do-
25 Topsham Road - -do- -do-
26 63 Pinhoe Road - -do- -do-
27 Polsloe Bridge - -do- -do-
45 Pinhoe Road - Large hole in garden
28 Denmark Road - Whistling noise

AIR RAID – 17TH SEPTEMBER 1940

WARDENS' REPORTS

Statement of Miss Minnie Anna Dwelly, 31 St Johns Road, Exeter. Now Residing at 12 Princes Square, Exeter.
"On Tuesday 17th September, 1940, at about 10.10pm I was sitting in my house 31 St. Johns Road, I was in the front room on the first floor when I heard a swishing noise and part of the rear and the side of the house collapsed. The next thing I remember was switching off the electric fire, picking up my handbag and walking across the room and standing by the table. The next thing I remember was when Mr Bryant came into the room, I do not know how he got there, he then took me, he half carried me I think to the side that had collapsed and then lowered me down to a Mr Lake and Mr White who were standing on the pile of bricks and I was taken into Mr Bryant's house. I really do not remember very much about it all."

This statement has been read over to me and is true. Signed *M.A. Dwelly.*

Statement of Percival George White, Butcher, Residing at 17 Park Road, Exeter.
"At about 10.10pm on Tuesday 17th September 1940, I was in my house when I heard a crash, I came from my house and ran into the road and saw that a house No. 31 St. Johns Road had been partly demolished, when I got there Mr Bryant was climbing over a pile of bricks apparently to get into the first floor of the house, I could not see the woman at that time but later Mr Bryant lowered her down to where I was standing, with Mr Evans and Mr Lake, the woman was able to walk and there was no difficulty in getting her out."

This statement has been read over to me and is true. Signed *P. G. White*
Court House, Exeter.
11.15am Tuesday 1st October 1940.

Statement of Thomas Evans, Residing at 41 St Johns Road, Exeter. Air Raid Warden.
"On Tuesday 17th September 1940, at about 10.10pm I was in my house when I heard bombs drop, I heard a crash, I ran out of my house and found that 31 St. Johns Road had been partly demolished.

I saw a woman, Miss Dwelly, standing in the front room of the house on the first floor, with me at that time was Mr White of 17 Park Road, Exeter, and Mr Lake, Parkfield Road, Exeter. Mr Bryant was at that time climbing over a pile of bricks going towards the rear room on the first floor, myself and Mr White also climbed over the pile of bricks and attempted to get into the room where Miss Dwelly was standing, I caught hold of a piece of furniture and found it was giving away so I gave up the attempt to get into that room. By this time Mr Bryant had got into the rear room and entered the front room where Miss Dwelly was, he led her into the rear room and lowered her down on to the pile of bricks to where I and a Fireman was standing, where the woman was lowered, the pile of bricks were about 5 feet lower than the first floor of the house. Miss Dwelly was taken over the bricks into Mr Bryants' home where she received attention. No difficulty was experienced in getting Miss Dwelly from the house, she was uninjured and able to walk which she did from the front room into the back room and then with assistance over the bricks."

This statement has been read over to me and is true. Signed *T. Evans.*
8 Clifton Hill, Exeter.
8.45pm Friday 27th Sept. 1940.

Statement of Head Warden Whitaker, "F" Group, Residing at Clifton Hill.
"On Tuesday 17th September 1940, at 10.6pm bombs were dropped from aircraft

in this City, at the time I was in my house, I went to the basement immediately and contacted Wardens Pawley, Sanders, Nowell and Hopkins, who were at the Post, we waited about 2 seconds to make sure that everything was all clear and then we all ran up Clifton Hill towards Polsloe Road, meeting Warden Godsland who reported the position and damage of the incident in St. Johns Road, I shouted to him to put in an M.1. and dashed straight to the house, 31 St. Johns Road.

On arrival at the house I observed a woman standing on the edge of the first floor, the side of the house had been demolished, there was a man with the woman but I do not know who it was, the electric light was on in the room, below the room standing on the pile of debris were two men, one I have since found out was Warden Evans, who lives close by, Wardens Pawley, Sanders and I went up the pile of debris to assist in lowering the woman and she was assisted over the debris into Mr Bryant's garden, on the way across the debris I asked the woman if there were any others in the house, she stated there were two people below, two of the Wardens returned to the damaged house while I left to go into the street by way of Bryant's garden gate and on observing that the two trapped were being assisted by two Wardens from the ground floor I assembled the other Wardens now on the spot and instructed them as to their duties in connection with the incident.

At the time the Wardens from my Post assisted the woman from the house I did not know who the man was on the first floor and at the time the woman was assisted from the house I did not see Mr Bryant. A little later Mr Bryant was extremely excited and was walking up and down in front of his house complaining of the delay in sending an Ambulance to remove people from the house to a place of safety, he was later joined by a Mr Dyer of

Park Road, who was also agitated in this respect and I informed both of them that they must leave the scene of the incident and not interfere as we were perfectly capable of dealing with the situation!"

This statement has been read over to me and is true. Signed *B. W. Whitaker*. Statement taken and signature witnessed by me *S. G. Collins P.S. 9.*

Statement of Leonard Sanders, Staff Warden, "F" Group, Residing at 11 Clifton Road.
"On Tuesday 17th September, 1940 at 10.6pm I was walking down Clifton Hill, towards Belmont Road, when I heard bombs being dropped from an aircraft. I ran back to the Wardens Post and, with Mr Whitaker, I ran towards Polsloe Road, when someone said to us there is a house demolished in St. Johns Road. We immediately went there and saw that the side of a house, No. 31 St. Johns Road had been demolished. I saw Mr Bryant, he was standing on the pile of bricks at the side of the house, I spoke to him saying, "Hello Bert", the woman at the time was standing on the first floor and the pile of bricks was almost up to where the woman was standing.

Mr Bryant, Mr Whitaker and myself were standing on the bricks and someone who was standing in the room with the woman lowered her down to us and Mr Bryant caught hold of one of her arms and Mr Whitaker the other. I took the woman's arm from Mr Whitaker and with Bryant, assisted the woman down over the bricks into Mr Bryant's garden and then into his house, the whole time the woman was being assisted from the house Mr Bryant was standing on the bricks with Mr Whitaker and myself, the woman was later taken away in the A.R.P. Ambulance.

Mr Bryant could not have assisted the two other people from the house because he was with me in his own house whilst they were being got out."

This statement has been read over to me and is true. Signed *L. Sanders*.

AIR RAID DAMAGE IN THE BLACKBOY ROAD DISTRICT

1pm Wednesday 18th September, 1940.

On Tuesday September 17th 1940, at about 10.10pm six bombs were dropped from enemy aircraft on property in Blackboy Road, Alexander Terrace and Polsloe Road, all the bombs were of the H.E. type and caused serious damage to property and persons.

One bomb dropped on house and shop property where a fire was caused, these premises were 25, 26, 27 and 28 Blackboy Road, the whole of these properties were extensively damaged and two people residing in them sustained injuries, they were Mrs Alice F. Alexander, aged 72 years, slight injuries, Mr J.W. Clarke, aged 61 years, slight injuries and Mrs J.W. Clarke, whose injuries were serious, she is 45 years of age, all these people resided at 26 Blackboy Road. Three were removed in A.R.P. Ambulances to First Aid Posts and after examination Mrs J.W. Clarke was removed to the Royal Devon & Exeter Hospital. The fire caused by the bomb was quickly dealt with and extinguished by the A.F.S. from the Station in Polsloe Road.

Another H.E. bomb fell and demolished the rear of the house of No. 3, Alexandra Terrace, Blackboy Road, this house is used as a private Nursing Home and at the time there were two invalids in bed there, no one sustained any injury and the invalids were removed by First Aid Parties to the First Aid Station and later to the City Hospital.

An H.E. bomb fell and completely demolished the house, No. 72 Blackboy Road, this house is in the occupation of Mr William Squire, who was away at the time, but in the house were his Wife, Mrs Florence Squire aged 44 years and their four sons, George Alfred Squire aged 17 years and 9 months; John Arnall Squire aged 11 years and 6 months; James William Squire aged 9 years and 11 months, and Sidney Robert Squire aged 3 years and 5 months, all of these five persons were trapped under the debris and were rescued with great difficulty by several parties of Rescue Workers, George Alfred Squire was the first to be rescued, he was under debris in the front garden of the house and it was found that he was dead, Mrs Squire was the next to be rescued and except for shock and several slight injuries she was unharmed, the other three were later rescued and it was found that they were all dead at the time of being rescued. Mrs Squire was removed by the First Aid Party to No. 1 First Aid Post and the bodies of the four children were removed in the Mortuary van to the Public Mortuary.

Three more H.E. Bombs fell in the grounds of the Devon & Exeter Girls Training School, Polsloe Road, two of these had exploded and fell in the garden and one was unexploded which fell on the tennis courts, a brick wall was demolished on these premises and the blast from the exploded bombs also demolished several garden walls at the rear of houses in Blackboy Road.

No. 29, Blackboy Road which is licensed premises in the occupation of Richard Arthur Doncaster and known as the Ropemakers Arms was also slightly damaged by a bomb but there were no injuries.

On examination the whole of the above incidents except the two bombs which were known to have exploded, were treated as unexploded and a large number of houses in the district were evacuated and the occupants were sent and accommodated as a temporary measure in the Elmside Conservative Club and St. Sidwells Methodist Church Institute, Sidwell Street.

All the houses in the following streets were evaucated of all their residents, several of whom were bedridden and had to be removed by A.R.P. Ambulances:

Blackboy Road - from its junction with Polsloe Road to and including Kendalls Buildings, and each side of the road.

Polsloe Road - from just the Heavitree side of Clifton Hill to its junction of Blackboy Road, both sides of the road.

Alexandra Terr. - the whole of Alexandra Terrace.

Prospect Blds. - the whole of Prospect Buildings.

Elmside Close - the whole of Elmside Close.

Hampton Place - the whole of Hampton Place.

Elmside - from Blackboy Road to May Street, also all Toronto Road.
All the people left in the district in houses adjoining those evacuated were instructed to use only that side of the house which was most distant to where the bombs had fallen.

An Incident Post was established at No. 54b Blackboy Road, a house that was evacuated but was some distance from the nearest bomb and in which a telephone was installed.

Arrangements were later made for all the persons who had been evacuated and had been unable to go with friends, to be removed in Corporation omnibuses to Food & Shelter Stations which the City has provided for such cases.

There were a number of various A.R.P. Parties on the scene, and were as follows:

Wardens, there were approximately 30 of these, Rescue Parties, First Aid Parties, Gas Party, Electricity and a number of Police, Police War Reserves and Special Constables.

A very high tribute must be paid to the manner in which the parties on the scene worked, their co-operation and the very valuable assistance rendered by them.

Traffic, both vehicular and pedestrian, was diverted via Mt. Pleasant Road, Mansfield Road, Old Tiverton Road to Sidwell Street and Policemen were stationed at a number of points to deal with this matter, Blackboy Road for its whole length was closed, also Polsloe Road from Clifton Hill and Elmside to May Street. Police were on duty all night for this purpose until relieved at 6am. Two A.F.S. men were left on duty at the Fire Incident all night.
Signed *Sidney Geo. Collins Sergeant No. 9*

AIR RAID INCIDENTS AT POLSLOE ROAD, ST JOHNS ROAD AND PARK ROAD.

8.15pm Thursday 19th September, 1940.
On Tuesday 17th September 1940, at about 10.10pm an H.E. bomb was dropped from enemy aircraft and fell in Polsloe Road immediately outside Messrs. Autocars Service Garage at a point about 3 feet from the footpath, this bomb failed to explode but penetrated the roadway to a depth as yet unknown, the approximate diameter of this is about 20 inches and as far as can be ascertained no mains were damaged.

At the same time another H.E. bomb fell and struck a house, No. 33 Park Road, Polsloe Park, this penetrated the roof, the front bedroom floors and ceilings and buried itself in the earth under the floor to a depth as yet unknown, this bomb also failed to explode. I have as yet been unable to locate the occupier or the owner and I do not know the real extent of the damage but Bomb Disposal Squads of the Royal Engineers are now at work on all three unexploded bomb incidents.

A third bomb in this vicinity fell and partly demolished two houses, Nos. 31 and 30 St. Johns Road, this bomb exploded. No. 31 St. Johns Road is owned and occupied by Miss Dwelly who occupies the top flat, other occupants were Mr Cockram and his mother, Mrs Gay. The side of this house is completely demolished and there is considerable internal damage and also to the rear of the house and garden walls. The house adjoining this, No. 30 owned by Mr J.H. Simpson who is also the occupier, sustained considerable damage to the rear, part of the wall of the rear bedroom being blown out, back garden walls down and there is extensive damage to all rooms of this house, also the roof.

No. 29 St. Johns Road, owned by Mr Radford of Messrs. Jarman & Radford, Bedford Circus, Exeter and occupied by Mr D.T. Clement and his wife, sustained damage to a fireplace in the rear room, roof at the rear badly damaged and rear walls cracked, slight damage was also caused to 28 St. Johns Road owned by Mr Hoare of 37 Old Tiverton Road and occupied by Mr Ball and his wife, the roof at the rear of the premises was damaged, there were also several panes of glass broken at the rear of the house. This bomb also caused damage to the rear garden walls of No. 7 Park Road owned and occupied by Mr Bert Bryant and the rear garden walls of Nos. 1, 3 and 5 Park Road, the damage to No. 1 was very slight. I have as yet been unable to locate the owners or occupiers of these houses.

The whole of the roads in the district within 100 yards of the unexploded bombs were evacuated and the residents were sent to St. Sidwells Methodist's Church Hall until other arrangements could be made for them.

Another bomb has been located in the rear garden of 68 Blackboy Road this demolished three garden walls but caused no other damage. I have not been able to find the whole extent of the damage in this case.

In all incidents further enquiries are being made with the view of submitting a full report.

There were no serious injuries in any of these incidents but I think some of the residents sustained slight injuries, several aged persons who were bedridden were removed in A.R.P. Ambulances to First Aid Posts and later to the City Hospital.
Signed *Sidney Geo. Collins Sergeant No. 9*
Air Raid Damage, Blackboy Road, 17 September 1940.

Property Involved:
Blackboy Road - Nos. 25 - 29, 67 - 74.
Alexandra Terrace - Nos. 2, 3, 4, 5, 6, 7.
Polsloe Road - Girls Training School.
Park Road, Polsloe Park - No. 1, 3, 5, 7, 33.
St. Johns Road - No. 28, 29, 30, 31.

CRATER IN BACK GARDEN OF 68 BLACKBOY ROAD.

Monday 4th November 1940.
With reference to the attached telephone message, I went to 68 Blackboy Road, where I saw Mrs Hughes, wife of the occupier of the house, she took me into the rear garden of the house and showed me a crater measuring about 6 feet wide and 8 feet deep. She stated that this crater had opened up on Saturday last 2nd instant, it was then about one foot wide and very deep, since the surrounding earth had fallen in, causing the crater to become its present size.

On the night of 17th September 1940, when bombs were dropped in this City one of the bombs fell in this spot in the garden of 68 Blackboy Road, it was treated as an unexploded bomb and was examined by the bomb disposal squad of the R.E. they stated that the bomb had exploded. What has happened now is that this bomb exploded under ground causing a cavity rather deep down and with the recent heavy rains it has caused the earth to sink leaving a crater.

Mr. Hughes himself is apparently not very much concerned respecting this and his wife informed me that he was making arrangements to have the crater filled in.
Signed *Sidney Geo. Collins Sergeant No. 9*

AIR RAID – 28TH NOVEMBER 1940

AIR RAID DAMAGE INCIDENT AT FORE ST, HEAVITREE, CASUALTIES, SLIGHT INJURIES.

11.50pm Thursday 28th November 1940.

At approximately 9.25pm on Thursday, 28th November 1940, I went to Fore Street, Heavitree, where air raid damage has occurred from enemy action. The below mentioned business premises received damage, the amount of which, as yet known, is as follows:

Devonshire Meat Co., 11 Fore Street
Eastmans Ltd., Butchers, 18, Fore Street
11, Fore Street, Heavitree, Ironmongers
26, Fore Street, Heavitree, Butchers
All general damage.

I also went to the Horse and Groom Hotel, Fore Street, Heavitree and rendered first aid to several persons who had been involved in air raid damage at Cranford Road, Heavitree.
Signed *Trevor Brown Sergeant No. 36*

AIR RAID DAMAGE AT ST LOYES.

2.50am Saturday 30th November 1940.

On Thursday 28th November 1940 at about 9.30pm information was received at Head Quarters that damage had been caused to property in Cranbrook Road, St. Loyes, Exeter, by enemy action. I was sent there with some constables. I immediately went there in the Police van and on arriving found that a number of houses had been demolished, others badly damaged and that some people were trapped under the debris of Nos. 15 and 16 Cranbrook Road. I was informed by the Wardens that the necessary reports had been sent through for assistance and that it was on the way. I established an Incident Post at No. 1 Cranbrook Road and communicated with Head Quarters when additional Police assistance was sent.

I at once started the evacuation of the whole of Cranbrook Road and Woodstock Road, and parts of St. Loyes Road, Durling Road, Broom Close, and with the assistance of a number of Wardens, was able to partly release some of the persons trapped in the debris, by that time all the parties concerned arrived and continued the work.

Inspector Reeve arrived and took charge of the Incident. At 3.40am I was in Cranbrook Road when I thought I heard someone groaning, the sound came from under the wreckage of No. 15. This sound continued for some time and in view of this I communicated with Head Quarters and spoke to the Town Clerk. I explained the position to him and a Rescue party was sent, whilst they were arriving P.Cs Addicott and Powell dug amongst the debris and found a dog trapped. The Rescue Party arrived and dug in the debris for some time but were unable to find anyone trapped.

I remained at the Incident with 5 PCs all night and at 6 a.m. was relieved by Sergeant Norden.
Signed *Sidney Geo. Collins Sergeant No. 9*

AIR RAID INCIDENTS - ST LOYES ESTATE AND DISTRICT.

8.00am Friday 29th November 1940.

At about 9.30pm on Thursday, 28th November 1940, two large bombs believed to be Land Mines were dropped by means of parachute attachments, from an enemy aeroplane in a residential district lying to the South East of this City. One landed between Cranbrook Road, and Woodstock Road, good class districts, and the other landed in an open hilly field about 250 yards from houses of the Council type.

The former exploded with terrific force, and very considerable damage was caused to houses within a wide area which, for the most part, were badly damaged. Further afield, houses were damaged to a lesser extent, but for a circle of 1/4 mile, the damage was severe. The second one also caused a large amount of blast, but the damage was not so considerable as it was dropped in open space.

A small fire was caused in the Cranbrook Road incident, believed in a garage at the rear of one of the houses. This was quickly put out by the A.F.S. who attended. The effect of these explosions were felt over a very wide area, reaching in two freak results at least 1 mile away, in opposite directions.

All services were in attendance, and worked well. The amount of damage is so great, that further reports will be necessary to cover the whole of the extent.

An incident post was established near the spot of the former explosion, at No. 1 Cranbrook Road, in the house of Mr F. Stanlake and also this house was badly damaged, the post was able to be carried on throughout the night.

Unfortunately the incident resulted in four dead and 26 injured.

In all cases, the injuries were fortunately slight, some injured were detained in the R.D.&E. Hospital and some were able to make their way to friends' houses.

The force of the two explosions left craters to the depth of about 15' and to a diameter of about 40' showing that the missiles were of very heavy calibre.

A large number of persons were rendered homeless and these were removed in 'buses and cars to St. Sidwell's Methodist Chapel premises and St. David's Institute.

A large number of ambulances were in attendance and used, and wardens generally were present in good numbers, and rendered valuable services.

A large number of regular and auxiliary police were in attendance, together with the Chief Constable, Superintendent, Inspector Reeve and Sergeants.

It is not able to the moment, to estimate the amount or enumerate the size of the damage, but P.C's Cody and Holman are busy compiling a complete list of the damage for record purposes.

A large Council building estate adjoins both incidents, and they were damaged to a lesser degree than the private estate at St. Loyes. Further reports will be submitted as particulars are obtained.

Signed *Alexander E. Reeve Inspector*

Damage to Properties:

Woodstock Road - Nos. 1 - 20.

Cranbrook Road - Nos. 1 - 21.

Avondale Road - Nos. 1 - 21.

Mayfield Road - Nos. 1 - 20.

Glenmore Road - Nos. 2 - 6, 11 - 20.

St. Loyes Road - Nos. 1 -19, 21, 23, 25, 27.

Attwyll Avenue - Nos. 1, 3, 5, 7, 11, 13, 15, 17, 19, 21, 23, 25, 27, 29, 31, 33, 35, 37, 39, 41, 43, 94, 92, 90, 88, 86, 84, 82, 80, 78, 76, 74, 72, 70, 68, 66, 64, 62, 60, 58, 56, 54, 52, 42, 40, 38, 36, 34, 32, 30, 28, 26, 24, 22, 20, 16, 14, 12, 2.

Sidwell Street - No. 71

Wellington Road - No. 54

East Wonford Hill - Nos. 1, 3, 5, 7, 9, 11, 13, 15, 17, 19, 21, 23, 25, 27, 29, 31, 33, 35, 37, 39, 41, 43, 45, 47, 49, 51, 53, 55, 57, 59, 72, 74, 67, 69, 71, 73, 75, 77, 79, 81, 83, 85, 87.

Lethbridge Road - Nos. 1 - 29, 38, 36, 34, 32.

Heath Road - Nos. 2, 4, 6, 8, 10, 12, 14, 16, 18, 20, 22, 24, 26, 28, 30, 32, 34, 36, 38, 40, 42, 44.

Quarry Lane - Nos. 1, 2, 3.

Hoker Road - Nos. 15, 17, 27, 35, 49, 55, 57, "Sandhurst", 66, 64, 60, 58, 56, 54, 50, 48, 46, 44, 42, 38, 36, 34, 32, 30.

Stafford Terrace - Nos. 2, 4, 5, 6, 7.

Rifford Road - Nos. 15 - 54, 93 -179 (odd nos. only), 64 - 94 (even nos only) 120, 118, 112, 110, 108, 104, 102, 100, 98.

Cross Park Terrace - Nos. 7, 11, 13, 15, 17, 21, 23, 25, 27, 29, 31, 33, 35, 37, 39.

Heavitree Park - Nos. 2, 3, 4, 5, "Mowbray House", "The Cabin".

Hurst Avenue - Nos. 1 - 28, 33, 35, 32, 34, 36, 38, 40, 42, 44, 46, 48, 50, 52, 54.

Durling Road - Nos. 1 - 29.

Peryam Crescent - Nos. 1 - 4, 6 - 13, 16, 18, 20 - 27, 30, 32, 36, 38, 40, 44, 46, 48, 50, 52, 54, 56, 58, 60, 62, 15, 17, 29, 31, 33, 35.

Woodwater Lane - Nos.1 - 25.

Hope Road - Nos. 1, 2, 3, 4, 5, 6, 7, 8, Shop, "St. Loyes Stores", "Fort Villa".

Hope Place - Nos. 1, 2, 3, 4, 5, 6.

Sivell Place - Nos. 5, 6, 8, 12, 13.

Cholwell Cottages - Nos. 1, 2, 3, 4, 5, 6, 7, 8.

Ludwell Lane - Nos. 2, 4, 6, 8, 10, 12, Council A.R.P. Depot.

Rutherford Street - Nos. 1, 3, 5, 7, 9, 2, 6, 8, 12, 14, 16, 18, 20, Field off Ludwell Lane [scene of explosion Rifle Range - Exeter School - completely destroyed].

Broom Close - Nos. 1 - 11, "Stores".

Salters Road - Nos. 23, 25, 27, 29, 31, 33, 35, 37, 39, 41, 43, 79, 81, 83, 85, 87, 89, 91, 93, 95, 97, 99, 101, 103, 105, "Wyndout House", "Wyndout Cottage".

St Loyes Almshouses - Nos. 1, 2, 3, 4.

Wilford Road - Nos. 1 - 28, 30, 32, 34, 36, 38, 40, 42, 44.

Fore Street, Heavitree - Nos. 18, 62, 62A, Hunsdon Lodge, 26, Thorn's Garage.

Regent Square - Nos. 4, 18, 22, 46, 62.

Victor Street - 52 houses slightly damaged.

Stanwey - 23 houses slightly damaged.

St Loyes Terr. - 21 houses slightly damaged.

Salters Hill - 4 houses slightly damaged.

Cummings Buildings - 15 houses slightly damaged.

Coronation Road - 18 houses slightly damaged.

Wonford Village - Gardener's Arms and Post Office - slight damage.

Wonford Street - Wonford Inn, School, Baptist Chapel, 46 houses slight damage.

Sweets Cottages - 2 houses, 1 shop slightly damaged.

Morgans Building - Country House Inn and 17 cottages slightly damaged.

Cyprus Terr. - 3 cottages slightly damaged.

Bovemoors Lane - 2 bungalows and 2 houses slightly damaged.

Wonford Road - Wonford House - extensive damage to windows.

AIR RAID – 5TH MAY 1940

EXETER CITY POLICE REPORTS

Monday 5 May 1941

I beg to report that at approximately 12.20am today, three H.E. bombs were dropped in this City from enemy aircraft. The first two fell in allotments known as Flowerpot Field which adjoins the River Exe. They did negligible damage and caused craters from 35-45ft deep, and about 45ft in diameter. It is, however, worth noting that this field was formerly a refuse tip and the ground is therefore recently made up. This would lend itself to large and deep craters.

The third bomb fell on the main Great Western Railway line about 600 yards south of St. David's Station and damaged both tracks. It appears to have fallen between the up and down tracks, and has dislodged sleepers and two lengths of rails. One was thrown into Emmanuel Road and the other into Lynwood Avenue. This bomb caused a crater in the embankment 34x43ft, and 20ft deep. Railway traffic on this section was immediately suspended, and repairs are in hand.

No person was injured in the incident, but the bomb which fell on the railway caused damage to 14 of the 17 houses in Lynwood Avenue and some in Emmanuel Buildings were damaged also. The damage is confined mainly to roofs and windows, but not one of the houses was rendered uninhabitable. The premises known as the Exe Valley Joinery Works were also damaged, chiefly roof and windows. Damage was also done to ceilings in Lynwood Ave. and Emmanuel Buildings.

An Incident Post was quickly established at 25 Okehampton Road, where, by the kind permission of Mr P. Yandell Rose, the telephone was placed at the disposal of the police [No. 5392]. Police Constables were posted at the junction of Emmanuel Road with Okehampton Road and at the end of the path field leading into the allotments. Barriers and danger lamps were later placed, one at the end of Emmanuel Road and the other in St. Andrew's Road, leading into Exwick Fields. Search was made over a wide area by police and wardens for any unexploded bombs, but this search proved negative. Very able assistance was given to the police by the wardens in this section, and I should like to place on record our appreciation of their whole-hearted support and assistance.

My opinion is that the bombs were of fairly large calibre, and they were dropped from a low altitude. All three fell within about 80 yards. I was in Bonhay Road by the weir and saw the plane pass over and the bombs hit the ground, but I have no clear recollection of the one exploding on the railway. Soil and pieces of stone fell on my side of the weir, but the explosions did not impress me as being very loud. I understand that passenger traffic on the railway is being conveyed by buses between St. David's and St. Thomas stations in both directions. This arrangement will increase vehicular traffic in both directions for a short time. Telegraph and signal communications between the two stations is disrupted until repairs have been effected.

A precis of this report has been passed to the A.R.P. Controller for the City and further and more comprehensive information may be obtained during daylight hours, when the full extent of damage may be assessed.

Signed *F.J. Healey Sergeant, 7.*

AIR RAID INCIDENT, WESTERN ROAD, LYNWOOD AVENUE & DISTRICT

Wednesday 7th May 1941.

With reference to the Air Raid Incident in the Western Road, Lynwood Avenue, Emmanuel Buildings and district on the 5th instant, a survey of the district shows that the following property is damaged, for the most part only slightly.

Western Road - Film Transport [Great Britain] Ltd., Western Road, slight damage to asbestos roofing.
Exe Valley Joinery Works, Western Road, extensive damage to asbestos roofing, light damage to glass.
Emmanuel Buildings, in these buildings there are a number of flats all contained under one roof. I have been unable to interview occupiers in all cases, but there were a number of holes in the roof on each side of the buildings and several ceilings down

or damaged, and slight damage to glass. Emmanuel Road, Emmanuel Church Hall, damage to two ceilings.

Lynwood Avenue - There are 17 houses in this Avenue of the semi-detached type, all sustained some damage.
No. 1, 2, 3, 4, 5, 6, 7, 8, 9, 10, 11, 12, 13, 14, 15, 16, 17 Lynwood Avenue all were generally damaged.

Exe Street - Exe Street, Council Yard, slight damage to roof.

Bonhay Road - Slight damage.

AIR RAID – 6TH MAY 1941

POLICE REPORT

At approximately 2.30am on Tuesday 6th May 1941, I was at headquarters when a series of explosions were heard in the Heavitree district. At 2.38am I was instructed by the A/Chief Constable to go the Gallows immediately with six men. I immediately left with the van taking PC's 82, 18, 27 and 85. Arriving at East Wonford Hill we were informed that bombs had dropped at the rear of Warwick Road where we proceeded.

In Warwick Road we met several Wardens and PCs 75, 27, and PWR 131 who came on the scene. We commenced searching for bomb craters in the fields which are situated between Warwick Road and Ringswell Ave. About 50yds from Warwick Road was the first crater and 25yds further along in a straight line towards Ringswell Ave was another crater. Continuing our search a bomb crater was found in the field at the top of Ringswell Ave which had apparently fractured a water main as water was running away rapidly. Further along towards Hill Barton Road five craters were found immediately at the rear of "Hawcroft"

and "Trelake" detached dwelling houses. In making a final survey at daybreak I found the ninth crater at the top of Ringswell Ave about 50yds to the left.

Making a rapid survey with the assistance of Wardens it was ascertained that no personal injuries had been sustained and the damage to property was not serious.

ARD report was made to the Report Centre at 3.25am and an additional ARD Report put through at 6am covering the presence of the ninth crater.

Sgt Healey had also attended the incident and had been investigating from Hill Barton Road and had set up the incident post at "Westbourne" Lower Hill Barton Road, where we made contact. A search of the surrounding district, the By-pass road and neighbouring railway line and bridge did not reveal any further damage or possibility of delayed action bombs. PCs were stationed at Warwick Road, Ringswell Ave and Lower Hill Barton Road. The Reserve men who were sent to the incident were not required and were returned to HQ.

A survey of the damage was made, but extremely poor visibility and the absence of many people who had decided to spend the rest of the night elsewhere prevented a comprehensive list being made, but the following is some indication of the nature of the damage.

Damage:
Warwick Road
From No. 1 to 31 inclusive; rear windows and verandahs smashed and door blown in. Nos 9, 1 1, 12 and 15 being damaged rather more than the others. The roofs of these houses also suffered damage.

Birchy Barton Hill
"Innisfree"
"Westfield"
"Belvedere"
Houses rear windows smashed.

Hill Barton Road
"Hawcroft"
"Trelake"
"Westbourne"
Houses rear windows broken, roofs damaged and ceilings down.

Sgt Collins who relieved me of IO duties at 6am is preparing a detailed list of damage.

Major Locke, Head Warden contacted me at the Incident Room and arranged for two Wardens to remain on duty at the incident.

During the morning of the 6th instant I made a survey of the properties on the Lower Hill Barton Road and Ringswell Ave and Warwick Road district to find that the damage is as follows, all damage caused was comparatively light and mostly confined to broken glass, slates and tiles damaged as well as ceilings cracked and down, in a few cases there was slight damage to furniture and interior walls.

Warwick Road
There are 35 buildings in Warwick Road, mixed type, bungalows and semi-detached houses, the whole of these properties sustained some damage, either glass broken or roofs damaged.

Warwick Avenue
The 4 properties in this avenue all sustained some slight damage, all confined to glass being broken.

Ringswell Avenue
The 9 houses in this avenue also sustained some slight damage, such as glass broken, roofs damaged, ceilings and doors damaged.

Birchy Barton Hill -
"Belvedere"
"Innisfree"
"Westfield"
"Donbar"
"The Ness"
"The Chalet".

Honiton Road
Gallows Filling Station
"Heimet"

Lower Hill Barton Road
"Hawcroft"
"Trelake"
"Westbourne"
14, Lower Hill Barton Road,
"Laburnam House"
"Avril"
11, Lower Hill Barton Road
9, Lower Hill Barton Road
"Montigo"
"Wilaine"
"Willesley"
"Wellington"
"Three Corners"

Pinhoe Road
"Honeylands"
The Incident was closed at 12.45 pm, two PWR's were left at the scene as repairs were still being carried out to the properties.

AIR RAID – 17TH JUNE 1941

POLICE REPORT

I beg to report that at 1.20am Tuesday 17th June 1941, five bombs were dropped from enemy aircraft in Exeter. All five fell within a distance of about 300 yds, the location being at the rear of residential property beside the main Exeter - Exmouth road, and between Burnthouse Lane and Topsham Barracks on that side. Fairly large craters were caused and damage to roofs, windows, outhouses, walls etc., was fairly wide-spread. City Council property in Burnthouse Lane area appears to have suffered over a wide area, but this damage is not serious and in no case was a house rendered uninhabitable. PWR 122 Goodridge was near the Dolphin Inn when the bombs fell, and apart from a cut finger (he is unable to say how this was caused), this officer is uninjured. According to him the bombs fell in this order:

No.1. In the centre of the roadway in Burnthouse Lane outside the Sub-Station.
No.2. In waste ground at the rear of Rosemount, Topsham Road.
No.3. In a small field at the rear of Prospect Dairy, Topsham Road.
No.4. In a garden at the rear of the Red House.
No.5. In a garden at the rear of No. 1 Prospect Place, Topsham Road.

The incident caused the following casualities and these were treated at the First Aid Post on the Estate. No. 1 being later removed to hospital.
No.1. Maurice TUCKER, 10 years, 21, Spencer Ave. Serious internal injury.
No.2. Isabella TUCKER, his mother, 47 years, same address. Rt hip & shock.
No.3. Denner MURCH, 11 months, 3 Milton Road. Slight injury.
No.4. Mrs Martha HODGE, 48 years, Fairfield Cottage, Topsham Road. Shock.

Arrival of the police was prompt under the Acting Chief Constable, and the Incident Post was established at the Sub-station. Other services who attended promptly were: Water, Gas, Electricity. Road repair & Wardens. No. 1 incident fractured a 4in water main in the centre of the roadway, but this was quickly controlled. This control, however, cut the water off the whole of the Shakespeare Road side supply. Neither gas nor electricity supplies were affected. Shortly after the incident a message was received from Dr Boyd giving instructions that all water in the vicinity was to be boiled for at least 5 minutes before use, and this message was quickly passed to all police and wardens on duty for circulation, and I have reason to believe that the circulation was good. No services were affected by the other four bombs.

At 3.15am all police, wardens, messengers etc., with the exception of PC 24 PWR 122 and 162, were dismissed. Before leaving the incident at 6am (I was relieved by Sergt Collins), I made contact with Inspr. Speare, Corporation Transport, and subject to certain modifications if found necessary, the following traffic diversion will operate. All double-decker buses will turn at Topsham Road end of Burnthouse Lane and circular shuttle service will be operated by single-deckers around the estate, passengers changing outside the Post Office. All other traffic to and from the estate to go via Barrack Lane, Wonford Road and enter the estate from the Wonford end.

Details of the incidents and a brief survey of damage, and details of casualties were passed to the ARP Controller at 5.40am but a more detailed survey is being made by my relief with a view to arriving at a more correct estimate of the damage caused.
F.J. Healey, Sergt, 7.

With reference to the Air Raid incident in

the Burnthouse Lane district at 1.20am this morning, the 17th instant, I have made a survey of the district and find that 85 premises in all sustained some damage, the largest portion of which was very slight, being mainly holes in roofs caused by falling stones and masonry.

The crater at the junction of Burnthouse Lane and Briar Crescent, caused a dislocation of traffic and all traffic including Corporation buses had to be diverted, the Corporation buses coming to and from the City had to be turned at the junction of Burnthouse Lane and Topsham Road, another single-deck bus ran from Briar Crescent to Chestnut Ave, other trafffic was directed via Barrack Road, Wonford Road into Burnthouse Lane, 5 men were used for this purpose.

The following is a list of the damaged property:

Shakespeare Road, Nos. 6, 29, 35.
Tennyson Ave, Nos. 2, 3, 7, 23.
Chaucer Ave, Nos. 10, 2, 6, 1, 3, 5, 11, 9.
Milton Road, Nos. 18 to 21, 16, 14 ,1 to 7, 9, 13, 15.
Burnthouse Lane, Nos. 36, 38, 40, 45, 24, 25, 26, 28, 23, 19, 20, 22, 16, 18, 15, 17, 14, 13, 11, 7, 5, Dolphin Inn, Exeter Co-op Soc.
Briar Crescent, Nos. 2, 4, Electricity Sub-power Station.
Hawthorn Road, Nos. 2, 4, 6, 8.
Spencer Ave, No. 21.
Earl Richards Road, Nos. 89, 90, 91, 92.
Fernpark Close, Nos. 1, 3, 4, 5, 7.
Topsham Road, Police Sub-Station, "Mile End", "Fairfield Cottage", "Prospect Dairy", "Withenfield", "The Red House".
Prospect Place, Nos. 1, 2, 3, 4. Topsham Barracks.

The repair parties were soon at work on the damaged buildings and on the crater in the roadway in Burnthouse Lane, the surface of the whole width of the road is badly damaged but by 12.45pm single line traffic was working, the City Transport Depot

were informed of this.

At the request of Dr. Boyd, the Police car loud speaker was used for the purpose of warning persons residing in the locality to boil all water before use and leaflets to this effect were distributed. At 12.30pm, I was relieved by Sgt. Brown.   *Sgt. No. 9.*

11.50am Tuesday 17th June 1941.
Telephone message received by the Acting Chief Constable, from Dr. Boyd, Deputy MOH.

The City Surveyor informs me that the water supply is possibly affected by the air raid incident, and people in the Burnthouse Lane Estate and in Topsham Road from the crater to the Country House Inn should be advised to boil all water for 5 minutes before use. I shall be glad if you can arrange for loud speaker announcements and for the posting in Burnthouse Lane of notices.

Announcement immediately made by Police car as follows: "Police Message. The MOH directs that owing to damaged water mains all water must be boiled for 5 minutes before use". Handbills posted in district by Wardens. 4.30pm Mr Howells, Public Health Dept. "We are now informed that the area in which the water supply is possibly affected should be extended to Rydon Lane and Topsham Road on southeast side from Country House Inn to Roundabout."

Announced by loud-speaker (police and bills distributed).

AIR RAID PRECAUTIONS - GROUP "L" HEAD WARDEN'S DIARY OF EVENTS DURING INVESTIGATION OF INCIDENTS AT BURNTHOUSE LANE

At 01.13 hours I was seated in my Dining Room and heard a low flying plane pass overhead, followed almost immediately by the whistle of a bomb, and a protracted thud, suggesting that two HEs had exploded almost together. Phoned Post 15 but could get no definite information.

Topsham Barracks reported bomb near their buildings.

I got into my car, picked up Staff Warden Bath and proceeded to Burnthouse Lane, at Topsham Road end steering of the car became very difficult, investigation revealed considerable debris and a large crater in Burnthouse Lane.

I instructed Bath to warn Topsham Road traffic and then examined crater. Saw road was completely blocked and water main damaged. Constable emerging from Sub Station stated a report had been sent in. Two Wardens arrived and relieved Bath in Topsham Road to investigate with me the wreckage at rear of Mr Pitkin's house. Senior Wardens Sampson and Hogden arrived and I instructed them to look for other craters on the opposite side of Topsham Road and in the open space around St Loye's Church.

Chief Constable and other Wardens arrive. On Chief's instructions 2 Wardens were sent to St Loye's Training Centre and one to all the houses in Mr Pitkin's block to enquire if all was well. Senior Warden Murch reported that he had taken his child to First Aid Post for treatment.

Located stop cock for representative of Water Department to turn off water.

Examined gardens at rear of Red House and observed large crater near St Loye's Church. Bath reported a crater behind Rosemont. Advised Report Centre that 2 bombs had been located.

Phoned Warden Pitts on duty at Countess Wear to return home.

On arrival at Substation I was informed that location of four bombs had been reported.

Warden Hodge reported that his wife was suffering from shock and that she had been moved to a neighbour's house where she was comfortable. Wardens assisted in keeping crowd back from edge of crater.

About 03.00 hours Chief Constable dismissed Wardens and intimated that Police would remain in charge.

About 03.30 hours I reported general situation to Sgt Baker and suggested crater at rear of Mr Whitton's premises and the one by St Loye's Church was one and the same. Also reported what I knew of the casualties (2).   17/6/41

Court House, Exeter.
SECRET

Dear Sir,
    Reporting of Enemy Air Activity
            DS. 127/RA

As requested in your memo of the 28th May 1941, I forward, for your information, details respecting a bombing attack on this City.

(a) *Location; date, time and strength* - Burnthouse Lane and rear of private property abutting on Topsham Road between Burnthouse Lane and Topsham Barracks; Tuesday, 17th June, 1941: 01.20 hours: 5 HEs estimated 500 Ibs.

(b) *Damage to civilian property directly affecting war effort* - Nil.

(c) *Damage to civilian property not directly affecting war effort* - Damage to private dwelling houses, not serious.

(d) *Damage to communications. Traffic diversions approx. time of repair when assessable* - Unclassified road, Burnthouse Lane, blocked. Traffic diversion - Barrack Rd and Wonford Rd. About 5pm 17th June 1941.

(e) *Military help required* - None.

(f) *Short impression of raid, eg., civilian casualties, morale, evacuees, enemy a/c down* - Alert not in progress. Bombs dropped by single enemy aircraft. Four persons injured, one serious. Morale good, No evacuation.

Yours faithfully,
Chief Constable.
Date 17th June 1941.

AIR RAID – 23RD APRIL 1942

POLICE REPORT

The raid on Exeter on the night of the 23rd April 1942, consisted of seven H.E. bombs, including a stick of four on Okehampton Street and Okehampton Road (K/118 and K/119), and resulted in four fatal casualties and about 18 injured with varying degrees of severity. Very considerable damage was done to property and to service mains. The blast effect was very noticeable.

In addition to this stick of bombs, two fell on Marsh Barton without causing damage or injury, and a further one at Redhills with the same effect.

Incendiary bombs, apparently directed at the City, fell on the outskirts without causing any fires within the City boundary.

The raid on the City on the night of the 24th April 1942 was the first of its kind we have experienced and was noteworthy for its severity. Incendiary bombs fell in considerable numbers in the higher part of the City and some fires resulted. Another feature was that the bombs were unusually plentiful, in some places about six yards apart. The City was lit up by a considerable number of flares, and the enemy adopted his usual dive-bombing tactics. Most of the bombs used were of very heavy calibre and the damage was spread throughout the City.

The known fatalities are 41, but it is anticipated that this number will rise to about 50. In addition the persons injured in varying degrees are in the region of 70. A number of unexploded bombs remain to be dealt with, and are proving themselves to be the usual nuisances.

The Police and Civil Defence Services have been re-inforced by calls on neighbouring authorities, and as far as can be, reliefs are being arranged to ensure a suitable period of rest being given.

The experience of this night indicates that the enemy has not forgotten his earlier tactics, and all Civil Defence personnel must have in mind that his treatment of towns on previous occasions has often extended over three or more nights.

The Chief Constable and the Chief Warden look with the greatest confidence to all ranks of the CD Wardens to maintain the keenness and devotion to duty which they have shown to date. All must remember that only by taking as much rest as the occasion allows and by taking care of their personal comfort and wellbeing, will they be in the physical condition to withstand the demands on their service which these conditions make.

POLICE REPORT

At 22.40 hours on Thursday 23rd April 1942, A.R.M. "Purple" was received and three minutes later the A.R.M. "Red". The sirens were accordingly put into operation.

At 23.31 hours the falling of bombs was reported by the Police Observer Section from Observation Post No. 2 (Ludwell Lane) and their bearing proved to be accurate.

It was found that four bombs had fallen in Okehampton Street and Road in the following positions:

(1) In the roadway of Okehampton Street Opposite No. 8.
(2) Okehampton Street opposite the premises of Messrs. Kerswell and Sons.
(3) In the roadway of Okehampton Road opposite No. 19.
(4) In roadway of Okehampton Road opposite No. 30.

The craters formed indicated that bombs of the 250 Kg. type had been used. Roads were impassible and Police arrangements for traffic diversion were immediately put into action. Damage was occasioned to water, gas, electric and sewer mains and a number of persons were trapped beneath the wreckage.

A.R.M. "White" was received at 00.30 hours. It was subsequently found that the following persons were killed:

(1) Hedley William LENDON, aged 46 years, master painter and decorator of 13, King William Terrace, Exeter.
(2) Kenneth William LENDON, aged 17 years, unemployed - son of the above named. Address as above.
(3) William Henry PADDON, aged 45 years, hide and skin merchant, of 35, Okehampton Road, Exeter.
(4) Henrietta BAXTER, aged 42 years, married woman, of 6 Okehampton Street, Exeter.
(5) Cissie WRIGHT, aged approx. 45 years, general dealer, of 17, Okehampton Road, Exeter.

In addition two persons were seriously injured and fifteen received slight injuries. A summary of damage to property revealed that a total of eight houses and business premises were demolished, thirty-six were extensively damaged and two hundred and forty-one were slightly damaged. The summary of damage in respect of the various streets is as follows:

APPENDIX 1

Hill Barton Road	Longbrook Street
Union Road	Belgrave Road
Well Street	Beaufort Road
Oxford Road	Cox's Garage
Woodbine Place	Paris Street
Claridges	West Avenue
Hoopern Lane	Barton Road
Kings Avenue	Devonshire Place
Duckworth Road	Victoria Street
Waterloo Place	Hope Hall
Springfield Road	

Swiss Cottage
Bonhay Road
St. Germans House
Pennsylvania Hill
Pennsylvania Road
Victoria Inn, Union Road
Marlpool Cottage, Union Rd
Kelstones, Staplegrove, Union Road
A Doctor's Garage, St Germans
St. Catherines Priory
Edgerton Park Road
King William Terrace
Queen's Crescent
Powderham Crescent
Hillsborough Avenue
Pennsylvania Close
Pennsylvania Crescent
Edgerton Park Laundry
City Steam Laundry
Nr. Gardeners Arms, Wonford
Brook Green Terrace
Bradley Rowe House
Northcotts Garage
Port House Laundry
Parkins Foundry
Ham & Passmore

APPENDIX 2

Cathedral Close	Wonford St.
Glass House Lane	Carlisle Road
Hill Barton Road	Regent's Park
Isleworth Road	King Street
New North Road	Regent's Street
Bonhay Road	Barton Road
Exwick Cemetery	Howell Road

Paris Street
Prospect Park
Streatham Rise and Cowley Road district
Alphington Street and Shooting Marsh Stile Area
Hoker Road and Attwyll Avenue District
Matford Avenue and Wonford Road
Topsham Road District
Okehampton Road
Culverland Road
Old Vicarage Road

AIR RAID – 25TH APRIL 1942

POLICE REPORT.

On the night of the 24th-25th April 1942, Exeter suffered damage as a result of an enemy air raid. The "Alert" was sounded at 00.06 hours on Saturday the 25th April and shortly afterwards the City was seen to be encircled with flares of the four candle type suspended by parachutes. This provided tremendous illumination and there was complete visibility of the City.

Enemy planes then dive-bombed within the circle and H.E. bombs of heavy calibre were dropped causing casualties and doing considerable damage. Large numbers of 1 Kg incendiary bombs were released and fell mainly on residential property in the Pennsylvania district, but others fell in various parts of the City as shown in Appendix 1. Serious fires were caused but they were effectively dealt with by the National Fire Service. The number of H.E. bombs dropped has been estimated to be 65 with a total weight of approximately 30 tons, and the number of hostile aircraft taking part were thought to be about 25.

Damage caused by H.E.s was widespread and incidents were reported in the districts as shown in Appendix 2, the order being in sequence of priority in respect of the damage extensiveness.

Numerous reports were received of suspected UXBs and these were investigated by trained Police Reconnaissance Officers. It was found that only five were actual UXBs and these were removed by the Bomb Disposal Unit without any damage or injury being occasioned. The location of these bombs was:

(1) Wonford Road at the side entrance to "Newstead".
(2) In the garden at the rear of "Newstead", Wonford Road.
(3) In the garden of 27 Culverland Road.

(4) In the works of Messrs. Townsend's, Gandy Street.
(5) In the roadway of West Street near Fore Street.

The large number of reports received, and the correspondingly small number of actual UXB's found, amply illustrates the value of having Police personnel properly trained in Bomb reconnaissance work. It will be easily understood that early reconnaissance prevented considerable inconvenience to the public by unnecessarily closing roads and evacuating them from their homes, and further, that it saved the wastage of valuable man-power. Traffic was temporarily disorganised and to cope with this situation military assistance was obtained, the contingent which arrived consisting of 1 sergeant, 2 corporals, and 22 lance corporals.

AIR RAID AND DAMAGE BY ENEMY ACTION ON THE NIGHT 24TH-25TH APRIL 1942

In order to deal with the situation as a whole it was necessary to have Police reinforcements, and this was arranged by putting into effect the Local Mutual Aid Scheme. As a result of this, 1 Inspector, 3 Sergeants and 30 Constables of the Devon Constabulary were drafted into the City. These men were housed at "Downes", Crediton.

A large number of persons were rendered homeless and they were accommodated at Rest Centres in the City. Emergency feeding centres were arranged and mobile canteens were used.

Morale generally was good, but it was found that quite a considerable number of civilians were leaving the City at night to stay in the Country. Loud speakers were used to make announcements deprecating the policy of civil evacuation and it was found that there was an appreciable decrease as a result.

Police loud speaker cars were used to good purpose in making announcements of public interest.

A summary of the position is as follows:

Casualties:
Fatal 73
Seriously injured 20
Slightly injured 53
Damage to property (approximate)
Premises demolished 76
Premises for demolition 102
Premises repairable incl:
Slightly damaged 795

It was genuinely considered that all services worked well and in complete harmony. A special mention was received from Police Sergeant Brown, who was engaged on the Paris Street incident, to the effect that soldiers were assisting in the rescue of trapped persons and he especially commended the work of Sergeant Clarke and Bombardier Reason of the Royal Artillery. The "Raiders Past" was sounded at 01.53 hours. This signal was followed at 02.53 hours by a second "Alert" and at 03.10 hours by the "Raiders Past". During this period no bombs were dropped and there were no incidents reported.   *H. Arnold, Insp. 12th May 1942.*

Statement of Police Constable No 21,
Horace Reginald DEAN:
"On Friday, 24th April 1942, I came on duty at 10pm, and was working Beat 5 (Fore Street). At 12.06am on Saturday 25th April 1942, the air raid alert was sounded in the City. At that time I was talking to about eight men who were sheltering at the entrance to Messrs. Wheaton's premises in Fore Street. They were fire watchers. I remained talking to them for some minutes

until enemy aircraft began to drop flares over the City and I then advised the fire watchers to split up. I began to walk down King Street and I there saw a group of about five fire watchers standing outside Messrs. Brock's premises. I began to walk towards them and as I did so I heard a bomb whistling down. I immediately ran around the corner into Smythen Street and lay down on the ground. As I did so I heard the bomb explode close by and a small quantity of debris fall around me.

I heard a woman screaming and I got up and ran back around the corner into King Street. I saw that the bomb had exploded on the footpath in King Street about ten yards from where I had seen the men standing. I saw five men lying on the footpath and on the roadway in King Street. A woman was also lying in the roadway. About five houses on each side of the road had been demolished. I examined the men and saw immediately that three of them were dead, as also was the woman. The two other men were groaning and both had paving stones lying on them. I took the paving stones off one of the men, Thompson, and saw that his back and leg were very badly injured. I then ran to Messrs. Wheaton's premises in Fore Street and found a group of fire watchers still lying on the ground in the passageway taking cover. I asked them to help me as there were several people dead, and one of them named Blake accompanied me immediately back to the scene of the damage.

I left him with the two injured men and told him to look after them while I telephoned for assistance. I ran to the Police telephone pillar at the end of King Street, and while I was telephoning to the Police Control, Police Sergeant Collins came up Fore Street to me. I told the Sergeant what had happened and he carried on telephoning particulars to Headquarters, and I ran back to King Street. I rendered first aid to one of the injured men and shortly afterwards Police Constables Bishop, Smith and Reed arrived. Sergeant Collins was also on the scene and I endeavoured to procure a conveyance to take the injured men to hospital. A bystander fetched a large furniture van from the Smythen Street Car Park.

Blake and I placed the injured man Thompson, whose back was injured on two planks and placed him inside the van and a boy living in Kings' Dwellings also jumped in the van. He was suffering from a broken arm. Then a woman, Mrs Mortimore, who was injured, and also placed in the van. Blake got into the van with me and someone drove the van to hospital.

When we arrived at the hospital Blake and I assisted in taking the injured persons into the casualty ward.

I then returned to King Street and found that the dead bodies had been removed. I remained on duty at the scene of the incident and was present when the Rescue Party recovered the bodies of Mrs Frost and Mr Blunt. I supervised their removal to the mortuary.

At about 5.30am I found a man with a head injury still sleeping in a bomb damaged house in King Street. He was in bed on the first floor, although the end of the house had been blown away. I assisted in getting him down over the debris and he was taken on a stretcher to Evans Gadd to await removal to the hospital.

All the officers present assisted in rendering first aid to the injured, and assisted in their removal to the hospital."

Exeter City Police.
2.20am 8th May 1942
Subject: Damage by enemy action on Saturday, 25 April 1942 (Incident at King Street)

To the Chief Constable
"I beg to report that on Saturday, 25th April, 1942, at 12.06am the 'alert' was sounded in the City, and soon afterwards bombs began to fall. I was making my way to my Parade Point, at Headquarters, I was coming along Fore Street, opposite the entrance to King Street, when I heard bombs falling close to where I was, and after they had exploded I saw that they had fallen in King Street. I went there immediately with PC 21 Dean, who was also in Fore Street, to render what assistance I could. Laying on the footpath and in the roadway outside Messrs. Brocks premises in King Street were five men and one woman all of whom had been killed by the explosion.

A number of houses, garages and other property had been demolished and PC Dean went to the Police Box at the junction of King Street and Fore Street to send through his Express Report. Then, with the assistance of two Wardens, I searched the district for injured persons, and after locating several and setting the Wardens to work rendering what First Aid they could, I saw Inspector Kelly in Smythen Street. I established an Incident Post at Messrs Evans and Gadd's premises, Smythen Street, notified HQ, and fully reported the incident to the ARP Control Centre. PCs 59 Bishop and 69, Smith, who had been sent from HQ, then arrived, I placed PC Bishop in charge of the Incident Post and returned to King Street with PC Smith to deal with the incident from there.

Bombs could still be heard falling, but I was able to obtain the assistance of a civilian and a soldier (unknown), and with the PCs Dean, Smith and the two Wardens made a further search, and found a man and his wife and three children in a partly demolished house. The man and his wife were slightly injured. These I sent to the First Aid Post in charge of a Warden; they were not badly injured and could walk. Nothing else could be done at the time, and I went to the Incident Post and sent a further report to the Control Centre. Whilst I was doing this assistance was being rendered to the badly injured persons by the persons helping me. I again returned to King Street, and decided it would not be wise to keep the badly injured persons in the street longer, so I attempted to obtain a suitable vehicle to move them to hospital in, and after a while succeeded in obtaining a large furniture van. I obtained a stretcher from Messrs. Evans & Gadd, and placed a badly injured man on this. I placed all the injured persons that I could on the floor of the van, and told the driver to take them to the hospital, a civilian going with him to assist and show him the way. I do not know the driver of the van. I then made a further examination of the persons thought to be dead and found one man who had sustained head injuries to be still alive.

In Messrs, Brocks premises, which had been badly damaged, were some motor vans and as by this time several soldiers had arrived on the scene I asked them if they could drive, and on being told that they could I told them to take the vehicles from the garage. In one van I placed the man who was at first thought to be dead and another person who I had by this time received information had been injured in a house in Stepcote Hill, and sent them to hospital with a Warden.

This removed all the injured persons that at that time could be found, and until the Rescue Parties arrived nothing else could be done, and I could not find out whether anyone else was trapped under the demolished buildings.

The persons who had been killed were covered over, and I then left PC Bishop in charge of the Incident Post, and PCs Dean and Smith in King Street, and reported myself to Police Control to see if I could be of assistance at any other incident. I was sent to examine several incidents that had been reported to the Police as UXBs".

Signed *Sidney Geo. Collins, Sergeant No. 9.*

WEB/SB   The City Treasurer,
17th June 1942   Southernhay West.
Air Raids - 25th April and 4th May 1942

With reference to your memo of the 11th instant the following is a list of streets which have been closed, as a result of enemy action, to residents or occupiers of business premises, for periods of 7 days or more, together with the approximate dates such streets were closed and re-opened.

From 27.4.42 to 10.5.42: *Westgate Slip* (Nos 57, 58, 59, 60), *Fore Street* (Nos 130, 131).
From 25.4.42 to 3.5.42: *Wonford Road* by 'Newstead', *Victoria Park Road* by *Wonford Rd*, *Matford Avenue* by "Newstead".
From 26.4.42 to 3.5.42: *Prospect Park* by *Culverland Rd*, *Culverland Rd* by *Prospect Park*, *Springfield Rd* by *Culverland Rd.*
From 25.4.42 to 18.5.42: *Paris Street*
From 4.5.42 to 10.5.42: *New North Road* by *Northernhay*, *Longbrook Terrace* by *New North Road*
From 4.5.42 to 10.5.42: *Pennsylvania* by *Hillscourt Bridge*, *Thornton Hill* by *Blackall Road*, *Blackall Road* by *Pennsylvania*
From 4.5.42 (still closed): *Castle Street, New Buildings, Bampfylde Street, Catherine Street, Post Office Lane, Chapel Street, Bedford Street* and *Circus, High Street* between *Gandy St* and *London Inn Square.*
From 4.5.42 to 12.5.42: *York Road* between *Oxford Road* and *Longbrook Street, Leighton Tce* and *Church Lane, Queen's Crescent.*
From 4.5.42 to 11.5.42: *Well Street* by *Cambridge Terrace, Cambridge Terrace, Oxford Road* by *Cambridge Terrace.*
From 4.5.42 (still closed): *Fore Street* between *Market Street* and *High Street, Milk Street, Market Street* between *Preston St* and *Smythen Street, Guinea Street, George Street, Bear Street, Sun Street, South Street* between *Palace Gate* and *High Street.*

Paris Street, Exeter. 10th June 1942.

Statement of Edmond Joseph SPETTIGUE, age 38, new residing at 45 Howell Road, Exeter, who saith:

"Prior to Saturday, 25th April 1942 I resided at 20 Paris Street, Exeter, where I carried on business as a cycle fitter and mechanic.

I am an Air Raid Warden, and I was on duty at No 2 Post (St Sidwells Methodist Church) when the Alert sounded at 00.07 hours on Saturday, 25th April 1942, and I then took up my duties patrolling Sidwell Street and Paris Street.

At about 12.35am I was near the top of Paris Street when I heard the sound of a bomb exploding at the bottom of Paris Street near Eaton Place. I came down Paris Street to contact my Second Warden (Mr Hackworthy) and I asked Mr Ball if he had seen Mr Hackworthy, and he told me that he had gone to the bottom of Paris Street where a bomb had fallen.

I then assisted some person into the shelter under Collings, and as I was coming out I was buried by debris caused by bombs which I later found had dropped at the entrance to Brunswick Place and at the rear of 82 Paris Street.

I am sure that the bomb at the bottom of Paris Street dropped three to five minutes before those which fell in (1) Morgan Square (2) entrance to Brunswick Place, (3) the rear of 82 Paris Street and (4) in Cumberland Terrace".

Court House, Exeter, 9am 7th May 1942.
Statement of Marine Walter John VAUGHAN:
"I am the husband of Eva Mary Ann Vaughan, who resided at 48 Paris Street, Exeter, until Saturday, 25th April, 1942. Our two children, Michael, aged 6, and David aged 5, also resided at this address. My wife and children resided at 48 Paris Street, for the past seven years, and I lived there with them until the 15th March 1941, when I joined HM Forces, and for about the last two years my sister-in-law, Mrs Mary White, also lived there, and I know she was killed in the air raid on the night of the 24th/25th April.

I last saw my wife and children on the 13th and 14th April, 1942, when I came home on 24 hours leave, and the last letter which I received from her was on Saturday, 25th April. The postmark showed that this had been posted at 4pm on the 24th April at Exeter, and the address shown at the top of the letter was 48 Paris Street. My house was completely destroyed by a direct hit in the raid, and since that time I have not seen my wife and children, or received any information which would suggest that they are alive."

Further statement of Marine Walter John Vaughan, who saith:

"I have been to the mortuary at Rack Street on two occasions, and to the mortuary at Whipton once, but I was unable to identify anything which may have been my wife and children or any of their clothing."

11.30am 29th May 1942.
Statement of Mrs Virginia Louise MARSDEN:

"Until 4th May last I resided at 43 Paris Street, Exeter, and I knew Mrs Eva Vaughan who lived with her two sons David and Terence at 48 Paris Street. I used to help in my sister-in-law's shop at 42 Paris Street and Mrs Vaughan and the children often came there, with the result that I knew them very well and saw them every day. I also knew Mrs Mary White who used to live with her.

I know that Mrs Vaughan normally slept at home with her two sons, and I last saw her at about 6pm on Friday 24th April last. I was then standing at the door of my sister-in-law's shop and Mrs Vaughan passed me on her way down Paris Street towards her house. I remember that she spoke to me but I cannot recall just what she said. Since her house was destroyed on the morning of the 25th April last I have not seen Mrs Vaughan or her children, and I have not received any information which would suggest that they are still alive."

Corporation Transport Depot, Exeter.
10.30am 13th May 1942.
Statement of Tom HUTCHINGS, age 54, a fitters mate employed at the Corporation Transport Department:

"For about 30 years my father, and my mother have resided at 49 Paris Street, Exeter. My sister, who was 51 years of age and unmarried had also lived with them all her life. My other widowed sister, and her son, aged 18, have also resided there for about six years.

At about 12.40am on Saturday 25th April, 1942, during an air raid, their house was hit by a high explosive bomb and was completely demolished. The bodies of my father, Thomas Hutchings, my sister Florence Theresa Hutchings, and my nephew. Leonard Charles Hellier, were recovered and identified, but no trace has since been found of my mother Mrs Elizabeth Hutchings, or my sister, Alice Mary Hellier, and I have received no information which would suggest that they are still alive. I last saw my mother at about 1.30pm on Friday 24th April, and I believe that I saw Mrs Hellier at the same time, and I certainly saw her on the Thursday. I know that they slept at 49 Paris Street every night and when I last saw them they were in their normal good health.

When the 'alert' sounded it was the practice of the family to take shelter under the stairs and on examining the crater where the house used to stand I formed the opinion that the bomb must have fallen right in the kitchen, which was only a few yards from where they took shelter."

59 Paris Street, Exeter.
7.30pm 28th May 1942.
Statement of Miss Victoria May GOVIER:

"I am the niece of Mr & Mrs Hutchings, who resided at 49 Paris Street, and I am the cousin of Mrs Alice Mary Hellier, who resided with them with her son, Leonard George Hellier. Miss Florence Hutchings, who also lived there, was another cousin of mine.

I know that since the air raid in the early morning of Saturday 25th April, last, the bodies of my uncle, Thomas Hutchings, Miss Florence Hutchings and Leonard Hellier were recovered and identified, but since that date I have not seen or heard anything of Mrs Elizabeth Hutchings or Mrs Alice Mary Hellier.

I last saw Mrs Hellier at about 12.30pm on Friday 24th April, when I called at her house. She was then in her normal state of health. I cannot remember exactly when I last saw Mrs Hutchings, but I used to see her practically every day.

I know that the family always slept at 49 Paris Street and they always remained indoors when the 'alert' sounded and usually sheltered beneath the staircase. I also know that it was the custom of the family to remain together during an 'alert' as Mrs Hutchings has sometimes been in to see my mother and I, but when the siren has sounded she has returned to her own home and if she did not go quickly one of the others would come and fetch her."

3, Myrtle Cottages, Stoke Canon.
3.45pm 17th May 1942.
Statement of Frederick John HUTCHINGS, age 48, a mill hand, employed at Silverton Paper Mills:

"I am the son of Mrs Elizabeth Hutchings and the brother of Mrs Alice Mary Hellier, both of whom resided at 49 Paris Street, Exeter, and who are missing, presumed killed, after the air raid during the morning of Saturday 25th April, 1942.

After the raid took place I went to the public mortuary on several occasions and I was able to identify the bodies of my father, Thomas Hutchings, my sister, Florence Hutchings, and my nephew Leonard Charles Hellier. I was unable, however, to identify any body which might have been Mrs Elizabeth Hutchings or Mrs Hellier, and I saw no clothing which I could identify as belonging to them.

Since the date of the raid I have not seen Mrs Elizabeth Hutchings or Mrs Hellier and I have received no information which would suggest that they are still alive."

Criminal Investigation Dept.
12.30pm 11.6.42
Statement of Ernest Fraser, Police Sergt No 56.

"At about 12.50am on Saturday 25th April 1942, I went to the bottom of Paris Street, opposite the Transport Depot where I saw that a number of houses had been demolished by a high explosive bomb due to enemy action. Among the houses which were demolished were Nos. 47, 48 and 49, Paris Street, the bomb having fallen among these houses.

Rescue Parties were summoned and a number of injured persons and bodies were recovered from these and the adjoining houses."

Watch Committee, 17th June 1942.
Air Raids on the City.

I have to submit the following brief statement on the work of the police during and after the raids on this City which occurred between 24th April and 4th May last, and of the casualties which resulted and the damage sustained.

I am glad to be in a position to report that police casualties in all these raids were comparatively slight, but it is with deep regret that I have to record that Special Constable Harold Rowland Luxton was killed whilst performing his duties in Sidwell Street. Police sergeant Frederick Harris sustained a slight fracture of the spine and will be off duty for several months but he has been released from hospital and is able to reside at his home; a plaster jacket has been applied and this he will have to wear for some time. Police constable Roy Weeks also sustained severe bruising of the spine and back but has been able to return to light duties and should soon be fully recovered. The following members also received slight injuries: Sergeant Andrew Murray; Constable Walter Addicott; War Constable Ronald Lee; War Constable Leslie Hancocks.

The results of the attack on 25th April were beyond my own resources and I was obliged to obtain two units each of ten men and a sergeant from the Chief Constable of Devon under the Mutual Support Scheme. These were billeted at my Reinforcement Depot at Downes, and remained for three days. The raid on 4th May necessitated my calling in reinforcements from Somerset, Devon and Plymouth, numbering 100 men in all, who were billeted at 'Downes' and arrangements for their feeding were made there and at the Police Canteen.

Six members of the Force had their homes totally demolished, 4 sustained serious damage to their houses, and a further number sustained slight damage.

The effects of the raids resulted in very considerably extended duties and loss of rest days being required of the Force, but I should like to place on record my appreciation of the manner in which all ranks carried out their duties in very difficult and dangerous circumstances. The assistance rendered by the Special Constabulary, Woman's Auxiliary Police Corps, and the Police Auxiliary Messenger Service was of the highest order.

A special word is due from me to the Commandant, Officers and men of the Special Constabulary who were called upon to perform dangerous and exacting duties during the raids, and who, after the raids, worked for long hours with courage and high efficiency.

AIR RAID – 26TH APRIL 1942

POLICE REPORT

At 04.15 hours, Sunday 26th April 1942, air raid message "Purple" was received and 9 minutes later the air raid warning "Red". The sirens were accordingly put into operation.

At 05.45 hours during the period of this "Alert" a load of 1 Kg incendiary bombs, which it was affirmed were being carried in the El type container containing 702 bombs, together with one HE bomb, were released and fell in the Newtown Area. An Express Report was received by the A.R.P. Control, and relayed to the Police Liaison Officer to the Police Controller, to the effect that houses were on fire in Heavitree Road by College Road, the Fire Brigade having been informed.

Immediately on receipt of this message Sergeant Brown and Special Sergeant Hartnell were sent to the scene and shortly afterwards were augmented by Sergeants Pittkin and Moore together with five PCs.

On arrival Sergeant Brown found that residential property at 51 and 57 Heavitree Road had been set on fire by incendiary bombs and the N.F.S. were dealing with the outbreaks. The property in question is owned by Exeter City Council and the houses respectively are used as a sick bay and nurses' hostel by the Exeter Public Health Department.

An "Incident Post" was established at 43 Heavitree Road and from there the necessary reports were transmitted by telephone to A.R.P. and Police Controls. The fires were completely extinguished at about 07.30 hours, only slight damage having been caused to roofs and floorings.

Stirrup Pumps were used with good effect on the interior of the premises by Police Officers under the direction of Sergeants Pittkin and Moore. This incident

was closed at 07.40 hours.

Reports were also received that fires of a minor nature had started in the roofs of several terrace houses in Sandford Street, East John Street, Clifton Street and Portland Street. These fires were dealt with by the NFS and by resident firewatchers and householders. The fires caused fairly extensive damage to several of the houses and numerous others received damage in lesser degrees.

The H.E. bomb fell in the roadway outside No. 80 Portland Street and damage was caused to water and gas mains. Nos. 80, 82, 84, 79, and 81, Portland Street were practically demolished and several persons were trapped beneath the wreckage in the houses Nos. 82, and 84.

The other essential services arrived and took over their respective duties. Sergeants' Norden and Searle, together with several PCs were sent to the scene and other policemen including Sergeants Pittkin and Moore were drafted from the fire incidents in Heavitree Road. A Mr. Simmons was extricated alive from No. 84 but his wife was found dead there. Two men named Wood were taken alive from No. 82 but their mother Mrs. Wood was found dead.

Subsequently it was found that the deceased persons were:

Mrs. Minnie Simmons, (Adult) 84 Portland Street.
Mrs. Ellen Wood (Adult) 82 Portland Street.
Mr. Charles D. Hackett (77) 80 Portland Street. (Died in hospital).
In addition two persons were seriously injured and 14 slightly injured.

Blast damage extended over a large area including Portland Street, Clifton Street, East John Street and Sandford Street and roofs were damaged over a much wider area from flying debris which reached premises as far away as Baring Crescent and Spicer Road.

Members of the Devon County Constabulary who were in the City under the reinforcement scheme were used later to police the area. Mobile Canteens were also in use.

H. Arnold. Inspector. 29/4/42

No. 2 Post	-	
No. 4 Post	-	
No. 5 Post	-	Total 4
Fractures or suspected fractures	-	
Other serious injuries	-	
Burns	1	
Eye Cases	-	
Slight injuries	3	
Mainly shock	-	

ANALYSIS OF AIR RAID CASUALTIES DEALT WITH AT FIRST AID POSTS, APRIL AND MAY 1942, ACCORDING TO RETURNS ON FORM MPC. 44.

Raid on 24th April 1942   persons treated.

No. 1 Post	1	
No. 2 Post	-	
No. 4 Post	-	
No. 5 Post	12	Total 13
Fractures or suspected fractures	1	
Other serious injuries	-	
Burns	-	
Eye cases	-	
Slight injuries	8	
Mainly shock	4	

Raid on 25th April 1942

No. 1 Post	7	
No. 2 Post	21	
No. 4 Post	4	
No. 5 Post	12	Total 44
Fractures or suspected fractures	2	
Other serious injuries	5	
Burns	-	
Eye cases	1	
Slight injuries	30	
Mainly shock	6	

Raid on 26th April 1942

No. 1 Post	4

ANALYSIS OF AIR RAID CASUALTIES DEALT WITH AT HOSPITALS, APRIL AND MAY 1942

Air Raid on 24th April 1942	Civilian	Service
Dead	5	-
Hospital - serious	2	-
slight	3	-
Out Patient Dept	3	-
Air Raid on 25th April 1942		
Dead	73	1
Hospital - serious	18	2
slight	24	-
Out Patient Dept	12	-
Air Raid on 26th April 1942		
Dead	4	-
Hospital - serious	1	-
slight	10	-
Out Patient Dept	-	-
Air Raid on 4th May 1942		
Dead	156	8
Hospital - serious	62	8
slight	67	10
Out Patient Dept	161	8

NOTE:- Because of the evacuation of a large number of the above out of the City on 4 May, owing to damage to one hospital and UXBs at another, it is impossible to carry analysis further at present.

AIR RAID – 3RD MAY 1942

POLICE REPORT

At the time of the air raid on this City at 1.30am Sunday 3rd May 1942, I was on duty at Paris Street Incident Post, also assisting me in the various duties were, PCs Draper, Tarr and PWRs Sprosen and Dyer.

All returned to the Post "Messrs. Chudley's shop" and collected their steel helmets and respirators, leaving behind their caps and other equipment. Within a short time of the alert being sounded incendiary bombs fell in Paris Street and Eastgate and we all set about extinguishing them and surrounding property which was affected. We were able to put out two fires and a number of bombs.

I returned to the Incident Post about 1.50am to report the huge fire burning in Sidwell Street and at the Gas Company's Office, but the phone was out of order, as PC Draper and I were leaving the Post the blast from a H.E. falling blew out Chudley's shutters and a passage door which fell on top of me slightly injuring my left little finger (3/4" of skin missing) I did not regard this slight injury of any consequence and only report it because of the instruction issued in DO 108.

Our duties seemed to draw us farther away from the Incident Post and we split up and went in different directions. PC Draper and I left the Paris Street locality when the all clear sounded and went to London Inn Square. From then onwards one job seemed to lead to another and when I returned to the Incident Post at 6am to remove our property I found the premises gutted by fire. There was no fire near the post at the time we left it, and with the Brigade fighting the fires in Eastgate I never anticipated that the fire would reach Chudley's shop.

I regret that the following equipment was lost in the fire, I have made efforts to salvage it, but there is no trace. *Police Property:* Incident Box and contents. Three ropes Salvaged Property Receipt Book. Three lamps. I P flag.
Private Property: There were about four lots of property. (Including a metal wrist watch found in Cumberland Terrace, a wallet containing 10/- note)
Sgt Moore: One helmet.
The other police offficers mentioned above lost equipment, which has I believe, been the subject of separate reports.

Up to the time of leaving the post we had made about 95 telephone calls, and payment for these should be made to Messrs. Chudleys, North Street, Exeter.

Sgt. Moore, No. 4.

AIR RAID – 4TH MAY 1942

Bill Brewer
St Thomas, Bowhay Lane, Exeter.

THE EXETER BLITZ, 4TH MAY 1942

The wailing of sirens woke us at around 1.30am and sleepily we climbed out of bed and made our way downstairs, someone put the kettle on, and we sat around, disinterested, not wanting to talk, and listening for the expected sound of enemy aircraft passing overhead.

We were getting used to this in 1942, as apart from the occasional bomb dropped on us, the Exe Valley seemed to be on the navigational flight plans of the German Air Force. Cities such as Bristol, Cardiff and Liverpool were directly attacked through this route. So on the night of 3rd/4th May, our indifference was understandable.

Eileen, a friend of mine, arrived shortly, she felt safer in my house, and would quickly join us whenever the sirens went.

The unmistakable sound of German aircraft was heard and dad went outside to look around, calling me a few moments later to join him. There in the garden the noise and concentration of aircraft was greater than we had ever heard previously. They appeared to be circling the City, and within a short while flares were criss-crossing the night sky, slowly descending to light up the buildings below.

The whistling of bombs, followed by heavy explosions, galvanised us into action and whipping up our helmets and gasmasks, all the family raced across the road to a dried up ditch opposite the house. It afforded little protection, a couple of feet deep, but with an orchard wall behind us, we felt more secure.

It was obvious that this was the start of a planned and heavy raid, bombs rained down, it seemed without a break, onto a defenceless City. There were no searchlights or anti-aircraft guns to scatter the enemy.

Apart from a few strays, the main bomb loads were falling on the City Centre, flames reaching high into the night sky.

Having worked in the City for a number of years, I knew many of the people living and working there, and some of those firewatching that night. I decided to do something and called to dad to say I was going into town to see if I could help. Despite objections, I ran down the road with Eileen following, insisting she was coming along. Passing quickly through Cowick Street we saw no visible signs of damage, until crossing over Exe Bridge, away to our right, downriver, a large gasometer was burning itself out. Running up Fore Street was a very eerie experience, with not a single other person in sight. It was almost as bright as day, so much so, that we automatically kept to the shadows cast by the sunblinds, still out across the pavement. The noise all around was deafening, although the frontages we passed appeared so far to be untouched.

Ahead of us, however, was a blazing inferno and on reaching the corner of Market Street we could go no further. Bombs and incendiaries were still raining down into the fires, but being so close, all we noticed was the final whoosh and muffled crumps as they arrived, collapsing walls and scattering myriads of sparks into the air.

There were, at this corner, perhaps five or six people, the first we had seen since leaving home, two or three being firemen directing a hose onto what I believe was the Army and Navy Stores on the corner. We tried to assist in clearing some of the stock, helping some folks move their belongings away from the area, and when extra firemen arrived, manhandled hoses and equipment up from the river. Waves of wood smoke and hot air dried our throats, and brought tears to our eyes. These having to be brushed away with the back of the hand, smearing our faces, already black and streaked with sweat.

We had intended to get to the top of South Street where my manager, Mr. Kinch, lived with his family over the premises, but this was impossible, every building on either side of the street burning fiercely. We could not see beyond, and imagined there could be no hope for anyone in that area.

At some time in the early hours, the all-clear must have sounded, although we did not hear it. We felt eventually that the position was hopeless, and all we could do then was to stand and watch.

Around seven o'clock we decided to retrace our steps. Returning down Fore Street, hose pipes covered the road, running up from the river, with here and there auxiliary pumps attached, working away on their own, with no attendants in sight.

Our clothes crumpled and smelling of smoke, eyes burning, faces streaked, hair flattened and wet with sweat from under our helmets, we arrived home.

We had accomplished little, but we were left with a sense of achievement at having "done something" in fighting back.

Within a few weeks we were both in service, having volunteered, with the Royal Air Force, and going our separate ways, but remembering for all time the night of the Exeter Blitz.   *Bill Brewer*

REPORT ON THE DAMAGE CAUSED BY FIRE AND FIRE BOMBS AT EXETER BY THE RAID ON MONDAY THE 4TH MAY 1942 AND THE WORK OF THE EXETER FIRE GUARDS

Business Premises Section
The number of persons doing duty at the premises is taken from the records at the Fire Guard Office and the number of prem-

ises calculated in each Group is based on Ordnance Survey Map as supplied by the Local Authority.

B.P. Group No. 1 comprising premises from the London Inn Square to Castle Street consisting of 18 premises with 9 Fire Guards on duty. The damage to this particular business premises group appears to have been caused by a bomb which fell on the Plaza Cinema almost entirely demolishing the building. This building was a converted theatre of the old type and a very bad fire risk; the explosion caused a sheet of flame which seemed to envelop the premises immediately. The wind, being in a north-easterly direction, fanned the flames on to the adjoining premises, spreading rapidly, the fire guards on duty found it impossible to cope with the resulting fire. The roofs of the premises involved were of such a nature that access was difficult and whilst the number of incendiary bombs which actually fell on the block was small, all the premises were destroyed from the fire originating at the Plaza Cinema.

A number of incendiary bombs fell on the properties at the junction of Castle Street and High Street and these, in turn, started a fire in the next Group. H.E.s also fell in the vicinity rendering work by the fire guard party difficult, and they vacated the premises to take shelter.

The fires having gained a fierce hold in this particular section of the High Street, the wind carried the flames on to the Westminster Bank premises.

This property was part of Business Premises Group No. 2 - the premises from Castle Street down to and including the St. Lawrence Church. The number of fire guards on duty nightly in this Group was 3 and comprised approx. 8 premises. One heavy calibre bomb had fallen on the premises of Messrs. Singers on the opposite side of the street and the blast had done considerable damage to the premises in B.P. Group No. 2, blowing out most of the windows and doors.

Mr. Thomas, a fire watcher, at the Westminster Bank, realising the danger which the nearby fire was likely to be to the Bank property, contacted the N.F.S. and requested their assistance as up to this time the N.F.S. had not appeared in the High Street, but he received a reply that they were unable to assist and he returned to the building. By this time, the flames had spread across Castle Street, through the open doors and windows of the Bank and the building was well alight. He and the other fire watchers found the task of dealing with the fires impossible and they vacated the premises having been defeated by the spreading fire and not by incendiary bombs. The fire eventually spread through this block as far as the Church which is the end of B.P. Group No. 2 and the Church was completely gutted.

In the case of the adjacent B.P. 3 - Devon & Somerset Stores, 247 High Street to Martins & Musgrave Alley, including the Exeter County Club - the number of fire guards on duty was 9 with 5 large premises in the Group. Incendiary bombs fell in very large numbers on to Messrs. Wippell Bros. & Row's premises and got such a hold that despite every effort of the fire guard, the fires got beyond their control and spread rapidly. This was aggravated by the draught caused by open doors and windows which had been blown out by the large bomb on Messrs. Singer's premises previously mentioned.

The fire guards at the Devon & Somerset Stores - the other large premises in the Group - were posted at the top of the building and dealt with all the incendiaries that fell on their premises, as they did with numbers that fell at the rear of the premises, and they also gave assistance to the fire guards at Messrs. Wippell Bros. & Row whose premises were adjoining and where the fire was getting beyond control. Mr.

Matthews, who was in charge of the fire guards at the Devon & Somerset Stores realising that the fires were getting out of hand, sent a messenger to the N.F.S. asking if he could have the use of one length of hose as he felt he could save the block if he had this additional equipment.

This request, however, was refused, and the N.F.S. did not come to his assistance. At an interview, he stated that there was a hydrant opposite the front of the building with five connections which was not used, a static water tank at the rear of the premises holding hundreds of gallons of water, which was also not used during the raid, and easy access at the rear to the Rougemont Gardens where ample supplies of static water were available. It is his opinion that one hosepipe would have been sufficient with the amount of water available to have saved the Devon and Somerset Stores as all the bombs had been extinguished and the fire, which eventually completely destroyed the building, did not spread to the premises until after the "raiders past". The fire guard fought the flames in the premises until 4.17am when they were driven out by the size of the conflagration, which subsequently gutted both these premises, and the Group mentioned. B.P. 182, the adjacent Group was involved with B.P. 181 and being several properties in behind the premises fronting the main street, having 3 fire guards on duty in each of these Groups. The premises of the Musgrave Club which were, by this time, well alight, collapsed on to Messrs. Brufords and the subsequent fire was of such a size as to be beyond the fire guards' powers, therefore, the building was completely destroyed. The fire in High Street by then had considerably developed and was spreading from building to building being fanned by the fresh wind. The N.F.S. had arrived at a point opposite Messrs. Colsons at approx. 3.30am and by playing hoses on the premises of Messrs.

Lyons prevented the fire from spreading further down High Street. A number of G.E. bombs fell in business premises at the rear of Groups 3, 4, 181 and 182, demolishing the Baths, Messrs. Mortimores and B.P. 154. A small portion of B.P. 171 comprising the Castle Hotel to Messrs. Lake, Friend & Tarbet and comprising 9 premises [having 9 fire guards] was partially destroyed. This again was a result of flames spreading to the Castle Hotel from Messrs. Mountain's Cafe in B.P. 1. Fire Guards in B.P. 1 and B.P. 4 remained in action at the edge of the fire and undoubtedly prevented the spreading of the fire at Northernhay Place, holding it in check until the arrival of the N.F.S. and saving the properties from Messrs. Stone & Co. upwards.

On the opposite side of High Street the first fires were observed at B.P. 13 and 14 comprising the Arcade - some 20 small shop premises [with 6 fire guards on duty]. The fire guards here did their best to tackle the large number of I.B.s which fell, but owing to the lack of access to the rear of the properties and the difficulty of getting on to the glass room of the Arcade, their efforts were without avail. Here again the draught caused by this Arcade increased the fire which was overpowering and they had to give up their efforts to save the premises which were completely destroyed.

B.P. 12 adjoining the premises - 48 Southernhay West and 127 East Gate - about 10 premises including the Co-operative Society. There, fire guards were able, in this modern Co-operative Society Building, to tackle the I.B.s as they fell. The fire guards were stationed on the concrete roof, and not only were they able to deal with all their I.B.s, but kept the building intact, and defeated the flames which would otherwise have spread through the windows, etc., of the property from the nearby fires.

Coming down High Street on the same side, the older properties immediately on the corner of Southernhay and High Street were destroyed, but here again, the roofs being inaccessible, nothing could be done to prevent the fire from spreading to these premises.

The Post Office was, by this time, well alight and the fire guard in B.P. 15 comprising Nos. 1/6 High Street and 2/5 Bampfylde Street - [6 fire guards on duty] - endeavoured to deal with the I.B.s which fell on and around the block, but in spite of their dealing with the bombs successfully, the flames spread down High Street and fired the premises of this block, rendering their work ineffective. It was mentioned by a fire guard official that considerable difficulty had been experienced in making fire prevention arrangements for this part of the street owing to the attitude of the local Post Office Authority. The local fire prevention office had no knowledge of the fire prevention scheme and were informed that night workers were responsible for fire prevention arrangements in case of emergency. He was of the opinion that there was no sufficiently organised scheme in operation when the raid occurred, and that there was obviously a lack of desire to co-operate with the local authority in this particular instance.

It was at this point that the H.E. bomb fell on Messrs. Singer's property and started a fire on the Group premises known as B.P. 93, with 3 fire guards on duty, Messrs. Randalls and Singers adjacent to B.P. 16 comprising Depaoli's Cafe to Kendalls Ltd., High Street, Bampfylde Street and premises at the rear of Catherine Street, with a further 6 fire guards. On these 2 Groups a number of fire guards were killed by the bomb falling on Messrs. Singers which must have been of very heavy calibre and it is obvious that the fire guards on these premises went down to the basement early in the raid and did not stay up at their posts very long, and that, coupled with a large number of I.B.s on this Group rendered the remainder of the fire guards ineffective. The fire at Messrs. Elands on the opposite side of the street gained such a hold that the flames spread across the street and set fire to the premises of Messrs. Bobby & Co. The fire guards at Messrs. Bobby & Co., were on duty on the roof and were successfully dealing with I.B.s but were continually driven off the roof by machine gun fire. Between this menace and the flames spreading across the street they were unable to cope with both diffficulties and the flames starting from Messrs. Bobby's spread to Messrs. Deller's Cafe through the portion of the building above Lloyds Bank.

The fire guards at Deller's Cafe consider that an oil bomb fell through the roof of their building, but it is very probable that the mass of flames spreading from Messrs. Bobby's, together with I.B.s started a fire in the kitchen portion where certain inflammable materials would have caused the effect mistaken for an oil bomb. The fire on this block, by this time, was out of control and carried on to the corner premises of Lloyds Bank after the "raiders past" had sounded. The fire guards on this particular section did magnificent work, doing their best to control an impossible situation.

In the adjacent premises of Messrs. Cann Bros. B.P. 18 - 32/35 High Street, where 6 fire guards were on duty, the fire spread from Messrs. Bobby's and it was undoubtedly the Arcade portion of Messrs. Bobby's premises that formed a funnel through which the increased draught fanned the flames and made the fire uncontrollable.

Messrs. Colsons adjacent to B.P. 18 caught fire from a heavy concentration of I.B.s coupled with the blast from H.E.s dropped in B.P. 169. These comprised the Church Army Home to H.E. Williams, Catherine Street, and these premises did not catch alight until the end of the raid, and were brought under control by the N.F.S. which arrived later. B.P. 153, a large Group comprising Messrs. Hughes of Exeter and the Bedford Garage, was destroyed by communicated fires from High Street and a heavy concentration of I.B.s which resulted in fires which were uncontrollable. Explosions from petrol tanks, etc., in Hughes Garage blew up burning debris, which was carried by the wind, on to Bedford Circus and set alight several properties there. This was aggravated by an H.E. dropping on the Drill Hall, which caused a fire there, and the flames spread to other properties. At the other end of Bedford Circus a heavy calibre bomb fell on properties adjoining the Devon & Exeter Savings Bank, and caused a fire. Nine men were posted for duty in this area, 7 being present at the time of the attack, and it is fairly certain that they took cover in the strong room in the basement of the Bank early in the raid as they were killed and burnt. Their presence was checked by another fire guard at 2am who advised them to come out of the basement, but their watches stopped at 2.15am and it is fairly certain that the fire started along the Circus after they were dead.

B.P. 159, comprising the Public Assistance Dept., 45, 46 and 47 Southernhay West, with 3 fire guards on duty, was completely destroyed by the fire which spread from the Arcade, and the fire guard were useless in dealing with a communicated fire of this size. B.P. 54 comprising 37/44 Southernhay West was completely destroyed by fires caused by I.B.s and as these premises were under the control of several appropriate authorities, it would appear that a co-ordinated effort to deal with the bombs and fires was lacking, and in checking the matter with the local fire guard officer, I found that they had considerable trouble in this particular block and it was referred to as having been the worst in the City.

B.P. 13, 112, 114 and 168 comprising No. 26/36 Southernhay West - 10 Premises with 12 fire guards - were all destroyed by fire caused by I.B.s which fell in such numbers as to get out of control before the fire guards available could deal with them. Portion of B.P. 155 was also destroyed for the same reason. B.P. 166 - 4/10 Southernhay East with 3 fire guards on duty. B.P. 41 - Exeter Gaslight & Coke Co., Southernhay East with 6 fire guards on duty. B.P. 79 - 1/8 Dix's Field with 3 fire guards on duty. B.P. 248 - 24/27 Dix's Field with 3 fire guards on duty. B.P. 137 - 12/23 Dix's Field with 3 fire guards on duty. These Groups were all destroyed by communicated fires and heavy concentrations of I.B.s which fell in such numbers as to make it impossible for fire guards to deal with them all. Machine gun fire compelled the fire guards to take cover and thus the fires spread and assistance or reinforcements were not available in time.

B.P. 39, comprising Messrs. Fearis, the Bude [with 3 fire guards on duty] was hit by a large number of I.B.s, several falling into the kitchens where quantities of fat and highly inflammable materials were stored. The fire which broke out very suddenly became almost immediately beyond the control of the fire guards concerned, and assistance was given to them from adjacent Groups, but subsequently, they had to give up as it was hopeless.

B.P. 65, the Savoy Cinema [with 3 fire guards on duty] - 18 fire bombs fell on the roof, four of which penetrated, and 14 lodged in the false ceiling and were fought there and controlled. All the I.B.s were dealt with by the fire guards and they have confirmed that the bomb which hit the Plaza Cinema opposite as mentioned earlier in this report, caused a tremendous sheet of flame, which enveloped the building immediately. Fire also broke out in the New London Inn which is underneath the

Savoy Cinema, but was held by the fire guards and extinguished. B.P. 48 [with 6 fire guards on duty] comprising 2, 4, 6, 8, 10, 12 and 14 Longbrook Street and 1, 2, 3, 4, 5 and 6 Sidwell Street was set alight from the Wessex Garage, which is in the adjacent Group B.P. 157. The petrol in this garage caught alight and the flames spread to the adjacent buildings and into Messrs. Standfield & White's Garage with great rapidity, and it was beyond the power of the fire guards to deal with the fires which developed. The fires thus created in Standfield & White's Garage spread to Messrs. MacFisheries and Dunsfords, which were completely destroyed. The N.F.S. checked the fires from spreading further up Sidwell Street, and kept the main portion of B.P. 43, Messrs. Freeths to Maynards, intact.

B.P. 51 [with 9 fire guards on duty] comprising 19/31a Sidwell Street, the adjacent Group to B.P. 43, had 6 I.B.s on the block which were promptly dealt with by the fire guard and extinguished. While doing so, a heavy calibre H.E. bomb fell at the rear of the premises, but they carried on and saved the group completely.

B.P. 89 [with 9 fire guards on duty] comprising premises from 34/57 Sidwell Street, old and congested with impossible roofs and very high fire risk, considered one of the worst in the City - was completely destroyed by fires caused through I.B.s. The attack, which developed on the City, starting in Sidwell Street, and the concentration of I.B.s which were put down in this area, was so great, together with machine gun attack at the same time, that the fire guards found that the buildings were on fire before they could even operate, and the property being very old, and without access to the roofs, made fire fighting in such circumstances almost impossible. Cox's Garage [A.S.T.] which is in this Group, caught fire very quickly and the wind carried the flames down Sidwell

Street with great rapidity. This would also apply to B.P. 121 comprising Summerland Street to Cheeke Street [with 9 fire guards on duty] where Messrs. Eveleigh's Garage [A.S.T.] also caught fire very quickly, and the adjacent property was a mass of flames in a very short space of time. An H.E. bomb was also dropped on the Group, as did one on B.P. 76 - 157/167 Sidwell Street [with 9 fire guards on duty] where the congested area, coupled with the suddenness of the attack, prevented the fire guards from acting as they would wish to have done. B.P. 239 [with 6 fire guards on duty], Messrs. Motor Macs, was set alight, but was got under control by Mr. Forgham, Manager of the Savoy Cinema, who borrowed a length of hose from the N.F.S. and played water on the flames until the arrival of the N.F.S. and prevented the flames from spreading to the adjacent property.

Messrs. Saunders & Bliss's workshop in B.P. [with 6 fire guards on duty] - 170/172a Sidwell Street, caught fire after the "raiders past" had sounded, and it is believed that burning debris carried by the wind fell on the building, but the flames were got under control.

Business Premises

A very large portion of the business premises in Exeter were gutted by fire and one's first reaction was that the fire guard in business premises was a failure. That was my first opinion but I have been compelled to modify it considerably as my enquiries have progressed.

Exeter, with its old properties, very congested patchwork roofs, lath and plaster walls, narrow streets etc., presented to the enemy an ideal incendiary bomb target.

My enquiries show that the business premises' fire guards were at their posts, their equipment was ready, their organisation was satisfactory, but their number was not sufficient for the major part of the task. I feel that they would probably have put up an even better show than they did, had they been able to take the stirrup pump team training at the actual premises where they worked, to a more advanced stage. I have had enquiries made by my officers from group to group at the premises involved, and I find that in many cases, the fire bomb parties were able to cope with the incendiary bombs which fell on their buildings. Some of the H.E. bombs which fell in the main streets were obviously of large calibre and the fire guards indicate that the blast from these bombs, breaking windows, throwing down doors and in some places removing walls, presented them with a problem which they had not anticipated. Instead of fighting incendiary bombs in the premises to which they had become accustomed, they found themselves in buildings which presented a very much greater fire risk than hitherto, the whole building having resolved itself into a series of draught channels which, as soon as the fire commenced, provided it with the air which made it spread very rapidly.

Messrs. Marks & Spencer in Fore Street was a modern steel framed structure. The fire guards there were ready to deal with incendiary bombs but they were presented with a heavy high explosive bomb which shattered their building and set it on fire. The fire guards at the Devon & Somerset Stores in the High Street and at Messrs. Wippell Bros. adjoining, succeeded in extinguishing a considerable number of incendiary bombs which fell on their premises, but they were then presented with a cluster of bombs which, despite all their efforts, was beyond them. A large high explosive bomb had fallen in the street near their premises and this had blown all their windows out, with the result that as soon as the fire got hold, it was able to spread with unforeseen rapidity, leaping from window to window.

The Co-operative Stores at Eastgate, which is a modern steel framed building, was in the centre of very considerable fires. The buildings round it were destroyed, but the fire guards on the new building dealt with half a dozen bombs which fell on this roof and succeeded in preventing the fires in adjoining premises involving theirs. That building was saved.

A high explosive bomb demolished the Plaza Cinema and a sheet of flame was seen to envelop the building immediately afterwards. This quickly spread to the adjoining building which, having been damaged, was soon involved. The National Fire Service had been contacted by the fire guard but were unable to render assistance, apparently being unable to get to the scene, and consequently the flames spread down to, and then across Castle Street through the open doors and windows into the Bank on the corner. The Musgrave Club appears to have received a large number of incendiary bombs, more than the fire guard could tackle, and that building rapidly becoming alight, involved Messrs. Brufords adjoining. Several high explosive bombs fell in this vicinity and demolished the Baths, Messrs. Mortimer's premises etc. Some premises in Castle Street were involved but here the fire guard kept the fire from spreading.

The fire at the Plaza Cinema threatened to involve Northernhay Place, but the fire guards seem there to have held it in check until the arrival of the National Fire Service, thus saving a considerable portion of the terrace.

The fire watchers at the Arcade had great difficulty in getting on to the roof and dealing with the very large number of bombs which fell there. The result was that the job was beyond them and the Arcade was destroyed. This fire seems to have involved Southernhay and the Post Office and, together with the falling of a high explosive bomb at Kendall's shop, ren-dered the action of the fire guard ineffective. A number of fire guards were killed by this high explosive bomb.

The fire at Elands in High Street is said to have assumed such proportions that it affected Bobby's on the other side of the High Street. The fire guards there were on the roof dealing with incendiary bombs when they were driven to cover by machine gunning, when this was over they endeavoured to regain the roof, but by this time it was on fire and they were unable to attack it. This fire seems to have involved Lloyds Bank and Deller's Cafe. The fire watchers at Deller's consider that an oil bomb fell on their building as they say that one portion of the building was suddenly involved by a fire which was too big for them to control. Incidentally, we have had reports of a number of oil bombs having fallen on business premises but there is no evidence to support the opinions of observers. The story seems to have got about owing to the fact that undoubtedly in many cases the fires spread with considerable rapidity and to use the expression of one of the fire guards "the fire was all over the place at once". This was probably due to the fact that the high explosives fell thick and the wind caused the resulting fires to spread quickly. The Bedford Garage seems to have caught on fire, through the flames from the High Street premises, and from there it spread to Bedford Circus.

A high explosive bomb dropped on the Drill Hall at the end of Bedford Circus and another at the Devon & Exeter Savings Bank, where it caused a fire. There are reports of machine gunning in the Circus and it seems that with a high explosive bomb at each end, fires spreading from High Street, incendiary bombs falling on the roof and machine gunning, the task was completely beyond the fire guard. The fire watchers at the Public Assistance Department in Southernhay say their premises were caught by the Arcade fire and they were unable to deal with it.

Messrs. Fearis, the Bude Cafe, was burnt out, although it is a modern steel framed structure. The fire guards there say that quantities of fat and highly inflammable material in the kitchens, which were next to the roof, became involved by incendiary bombs and the fire spread so rapidly that they quickly had to give up their task as they found it useless.

The Savoy Cinema, another steel framed structure, appears to have received 18 fire bombs on its roof. Four penetrated and were dealt with by the fire watchers, who say that here the H.E. which hit the nearby Plaza, sent up a big sheet of flame. The fire guards saved the Savoy Cinema.

The Manager of Messrs. Hammett's Dairies in Sidwell Street visited me to tell me that undoubtedly the fire guards saved his premises, which are considerable and situate in a high fire risk area in Sidwell Street. They dealt with 4 I.B.s which fell on their premises and then assisted on the other side of the road, undoubtedly saving a considerable conflagration in this district.

Messrs. Stone's premises in Fore Street was another building saved by fire guards, and further, there seems to be no doubt that but for their efforts the fire would have spread further down the street. The 3 fire guards at these premises tackled the fire which broke out at 2.40am and confined it to the street, working the stirrup pump until 7am when the fire brigade arrived from the fire at St. Mary Arches Church and assisted them in putting it out.

The story could be continued much further but the above will give the general picture of the fire raid on Exeter. Certain premises were saved by the efforts of the fire guard, but it is apparent that although the fire guards can be expected to deal with incendiary bombs when they fall, yet the resulting fires, if any of them get out of control, quickly get beyond their powers.

One who is in a position to view the raid as a whole and who has access to all the records, realises that the National Fire Service were here faced with a very big task, one which necessitated calling on very considerable reinforcements.

REPORT ON THE DAMAGE CAUSED BY FIRE AND FIRE BOMBS TO EXETER BY THE RAID ON MONDAY 4TH MAY 1942

Area No. 1

Springfield Rd - Small number fell. Fire Guard party responded immediately. Confined fires to three houses - two of which were badly damaged and one slightly.

Victoria St - Small number fell, but were successfully dealt with by street party. Assistance was then sent to help in Springfield Road.

Devonshire Place - Small number fell mostly in open spaces. These were promptly dealt with by Street Party.

Edgerton Park Road - Several fell on Edgerton Laundry and these were promptly dealt with by their fire guards backed up by Victoria Road. [Headwell Terr.] Party. No serious damage.

Lions Halt - Several dropped in roads and yards - promptly dealt with by street party.

Waverley Ave - Small number fell - two entering houses - fires confined to one room by street party assisted by several of Thornton Hill party.

Hillside Avenue - ditto

Blackall Rd - A number fell - so may fires resulted that it was impossible to control them. Army assisted. 2 houses burnt out - 2 partly.

Elm Grove Rd - A large number fell on roadway, on hedge and several entered houses. Fire guards prevented the bombs from doing more than a small amount of damage in one of the houses.

Pinhoe Rd - A small number fell at the top of this road on [Lanherne School] private premises and these were dealt with by street party and damage was restricted to roof damage.

Bath Rd - The parties in this road were not completely organised and the houses are high [3 storeyed] which should have had special attention and needed larger apparatus. A large number of I.B.s fell in roadway and on private property, the number of fires were so great that it was impossible to deal successfully with them, but a few of the fires were controlled. [15 houses affected badly by fire]. A.R.P. Wardens and fire guards did excellent work in saving some of the furniture.

Elmside - A small number fell on private houses. The street fire party responded promptly.

Salisbury Rd - A small number fell - dealt with immediately by fire guards and Wardens.

Roseberry Rd - A small number fell - all but one successfully dealt with. One house gutted but the combined work of Wardens and fire guards assisted by other householders with approx. 12 stirrup pumps prevented the fire spreading to other property.

New North Rd - Several incendiaries fell and many dealt with but fire at 24 got beyond control of stirrup pumps. 2 houses burnt out - 1 partly.

Iddesleigh Rd - A small number fell. 2 entered private houses but were immediately dealt with by fire guards and other residents and the fire confined to one room each.

May St - A small number fell on private houses and were dealt with by fire guards and other householders. 3 fires resulted and 1 house was gutted out. By the use of about 12 stirrup pumps up to dawn the fire was kept from spreading to adjoining houses. The house gutted was occupied by persons who, on the "alert" locked up the house and went to the shelter at the end of the road. Access was, therefore, impossible, otherwise this property could have been saved and the danger to the whole street averted. Girls worked very well in this incident.

Lucas Ave - A small number fell in the roadway and on private property and were promptly dealt with by fire guards. One house was unable to be saved although a large number of stirrup pumps were in use until dawn.

REPORT ON THE DAMAGE CAUSED BY FIRE & FIRE BOMBS AT EXETER ON MONDAY 4TH MAY 1942

Area No. 3

Acland Terrace - Several houses here were destroyed through the fire spreading from Sidwell Street and this area was not well covered with fire guards.

Baring Crescent - Several houses caught alight from a concentration of Incendiary Bombs, 8 houses being saved by the fire guards and the fires put out, but 3 houses completely burnt out through lack of water.

Belgrave Rd - This area was near to the Shopping locality and was badly burnt. Blast from H.E. made the fire risk exceptional and the fires were too big to be tackled by stirrup pump party. The Senior Fire Guard had resigned recently and the position was aggravated through the fire guard being without adequate leadership.

Cheeke St - Near the same area with no organised fire guard party and all the houses in this street were completely destroyed.

Crescent Row, Summerland Crescent - Here again all the properties were destroyed as the result of an I.B. attack and there was no effective fire guard organisation.

Spicer Rd - St. Matthews Vicarage here was completely destroyed. This being one of the diffficult residential areas where the forming of teams was hard.

Heavitree Rd - Many I.B.s fell in this locality but the fire guard parties worked well and saved several houses including 2 large private houses. The shortage of water, however, finally defeated their efforts and considerable damage to this area resulted. The general opinion here was that if large static water tanks had been available for the fire guard, many more houses would have been saved.

Higher Summerlands - This area has been burnt out. Fire guard parties operated well in previous raid and saved many premises, but they became disorganised afterwards and lacked leadership. Therefore, during this second attack the personnel were insufficient and not well led.

Lower Summerlands - I.B.s fell thickly in this locality, but Mr. Davis, the leader did good work with his parties and much property was saved.

Matford Ave - Several large detached houses are burnt out and no fire guard organisation existed.

St. Leonard's Terr., Wonford Rd - 13 houses were burnt out here. Nos. 8, 12, 12a, 14, 16, 32, 34, 38, 11, 27, 31 and 2 cottages. There are 58 houses in the road and at one end of the road a very good fire party operated and controlled all the bombs and resulting fires. At the other end of the road, however, which was burnt out, new volunteers had not been organised partly because of the failure to find a leader and the complete "burn out" was the result.

Summerland St - Almost a total loss. This is a mixed area of about 100 houses and business premises. The business premises had been dealt with under the Order, but no efforts had been made to co-ordinate their fire prevention arrangements with the street fire guard and the entire street is burnt out.

Wonford Rd - Here I.B.s caused a bad fire in one house, but the fire guard party concentrated on the houses each side which continually caught alight and kept the fire under control. Therefore, only one house was destroyed on this side of the street, but on the other side, the party was not so strong and more property was destroyed.

Newtown Area - This is rather more difficult to report on as the damage is so intensive and so few fire guards are living there now. We have seen and talked to Wardens and the general opinion is that those fire guards who were about behaved very well. For instance, in Codrington Street four houses near Summerland Street received direct hits from many I.B.s and caught fire immediately. A Mr. Tape, Senior Fire Guard of Chute Street who is a builder came upon the scene and seems to have taken charge of the operations. Ladders were erected and stirrup pumps brought into play against the last house which was on fire adjoining the Terrace. After a time Mr. Tape was able to smash away some of the burning timber and so prevent the fire from spreading, and there is no doubt this man's efforts saved that side of Codrington Street from being completely burnt out. The names mentioned in addition to Mr. Tape as worthy of special notice are Mr. A.F. Bolt [Senior Fire Guard of Codrington Street], Mr. S.F. Woodland 4, Codrington Street, Mr. F. Ford 19, Chute Street, Mr. Herrington and Mr. F.B. Becker 9, Chute Street [not enrolled fire guards] who all worked so well and afterwards helped the N.F.S. with the fires. This area had been bombed in a previous raid and the people had gone, leaving the fire guard short and the depleted numbers suffered badly from lack of water and machine gunning. The first arrival of the N.F.S. in this district is reported at 6 a.m. and this did not help the general situation. Larger apparatus on the spot and more water would have minimised this tremendous damage and the destruction of 600/700 houses.

Parr St and *Belmont St* - The fires caused by I.B.s and reported oil bombs were so numerous and fierce that it was impossible to attack them with stirrup pumps, and a larger type of apparatus was badly wanted here as the fire guard party, although small, appeared to be quite good and could have been better.

Sandford St, East John St, Portland St, Clifton St - This is the same sad tale. The fire guards in these streets did good work at the start and many I.B.s were successfully dealt with and the fires extinguished, but owing to lack of water and the extensive fires raging, it was impossible to do anything further. Three fire guards were injured in Sandford St: Mr. W.F. Coles and Mr. J. Webber, Mr. F.H. Lamacraft. These men were actually fighting a fire from a ladder on the roof of a house when blast from an H.E. knocked them over, fortunately without very serious damage. In Albert St, the fire guards turned out very well and did all they could to prevent fires spreading. A few houses were

saved as the result of their efforts, lack of water made the fighting of fires impossible after a time.

Clifton Place - The corner house was completely burnt out, but the Wardens in the neighbourhood speak very well of the efforts of the fire guard in combatting this fire and together they were able to confine the fire to the one property and save 5 other houses.

Heavitree Park - Several I.B.s fell here and were all successfully dealt with by the fire guards. Small fires were started, but all were dealt with promptly. I.B.s also fell in the road along Cross Park Terrace. These were extinguished with the sand bags by fire guards. One woman, Mrs. Medland, was injured whilst doing this. The blast from the bomb which fell in Mowbray House Nursing Home knocked her over, injuring her knee. Referring to Roseland Avenue, there used to be quite a good fire guard party here, but since the death in December of the Senior Fire Guard, Mr. Winter, we could not find a successor in spite of a house to house canvass. From reports it appears that the two houses, which were completely burnt out, might have been saved if fire guards had been on the spot to deal promptly with the fires started by I.B.s. The Wardens, with the help available, tackled these fires, but were handicapped by lack of water.

Salutary Mount - I.B.s fell in the road and these were dealt with promptly by the Wardens ably assisted by the girls from the A.T.S. Hostel. The fire guards in this party do not appear to have assisted. The Senior Fire Guard of Salutary Mount, Mr. Alford, was no doubt on duty with the F.A.P. and the remainder of his party were mostly elderly women. In Group "L" no fires are reported although hundreds of I.B.s fell in around Chestnut Avenue. Those that fell in the road and near the houses were promptly dealt with by sandbags and earth: those that fell in the field behind, were left to burn out harmlessly.

REPORT ON THE DAMAGE CAUSED BY FIRE AND FIRE BOMBS TO EXETER ON MONDAY 4TH MAY 1942

Area No. 4

Roseland Ave - From the fire guard point of view this street has been difficult.

Roseland Crescent - Remarkably fine work was done by some of the fire guards in this area, particularly by the Senior Fire Guard of Newcombe Terrace Mr. S.H. Stevens and Miss Davey 4, Roseland Crescent. These two with other street helpers successfully tackled a fire at 6 Newcombe Terrace caused by I.B.s and after twenty minutes work with the stirrup pump the fire was completely out; they had been able to confine the fire to the upper bedroom. This team then tackled a fire in West Terrace but unfortunately by then two houses were alight; water was running low and some time elapsed before a ladder was available. However, it is evident that by the efforts of the fire guards they were able to keep the flames from spreading to the adjoining houses. Water was the main problem in this Crescent and the premises were saved where the water was adequate. It is reported that this young girl, Miss Davey, also went to Roseland Avenue to assist in the fire fighting there.

South Lawn Terr., Stuart Rd, Anthony Rd, Hanover Rd - It seems fair to say that a good percentage of fire guards turned out on the alert and did good work. In South Lawn Terrace many incendiaries fell and one house was seen to be on fire immediately after. Available stirrup pump teams tackled this fire and eventually fifteen stirrup pumps were being used on this fire and by

their prompt and successful action the fire was confined to this one house and so saving the rest of these terrace houses. In addition, I.B.s which fell in the road and in the playground of Heavitree Junior Mixed Infants' School were put out with sandbags and the stirrup pumps. Unfortunately, one of the fire guards who did such valiant work, Mr. W.H. Gray, was killed by machine gunning. In Anthony Road the Senior Fire Guard, Mr. E.G. Parr, reports that 50% of his street party turned out on the alert. It is estimated that about three dozen I.B.s fell in this road and several fires were started in the houses. These were all dealt with by the fire guards with stirrup pumps and so prevented from spreading. Mr. Parr states that members of his party with the help of fire guards from adjoining streets got on the roofs of houses each side of the burning building to stop it from spreading and were able to confine the fires to the houses in which the I.B.s had fallen. There appears to be no doubt that Mr. Parr and his Party did admirable work and special praise should be given to the women of this street for their timely help. Many I.B.s fell in the cemetery near Hanover Road also in the road. These were all dealt with promptly and effectively by the fire guards in the adjacent streets. In Stuart Road I.B.s fell, but fortunately most of them in the road and gardens. One house was hit and caught fire immediately [reported oil bomb as the flare was almost instantaneous]. This house was almost burnt out in spite of the efforts of the fire guards with stirrup pumps. They were, however, able to prevent the fire from spreading. Leadership was given and the use of reinforcements was due to a Mr. Fenning and a Police Sergeant and it is due to their action and the methods used that the remainder of the Terrace was saved.

Ladysmith Rd, First, Second and Third Ave, Wyndham Ave, LowerAve, Bonnington Grove, Park Rd - This area was more fortunate as the only report of I.B.s is in Ladysmith Road. The school apparently was hit by several of these and as you know very severely damaged. From enquiries I made it appears that very few bombs pitched on the school buildings and it is generally stated that these could have been dealt with by the excellent apparatus available had the fire guards been in organised teams. As it is, 2 main school buildings are very badly damaged and a member of the street party stated that if he could have obtained access and used a sprinkler apparatus he was certain that the premises could have been saved. Two houses, Nos. 69 and 97 were completely burnt out, but the adjoining houses were saved as the result of the efforts of the fire guards with stirrup pumps ably lead by the Senior Fire Guard, Mr Lock, his son Mr Lock, and Mr Champion. Mr Lock reports the street party turned out very well. Special mention should be made of Mr and Mrs Norris of 145 who are both about 65 years of age who fought an IB which fell in their house. These two people without any outside help put out the bomb and consequent fire.

Old Tiverton Rd - A number fell on private and business premises - all were dealt with by fire parties and other residents. Little damage resulted.

Dinham Rd - A number fell - some on unoccupied property on the Iron Bridge - these resulted in a fire which was unable to be controlled and about three houses in Dinham Road were gutted.

Albion Place - A small number fell - mostly in the roadway - those that fell on private houses were dealt with promptly by fire guards and no serious damage resulted.

Toronto Rd - A number fell on private houses, but the combined work of fire guards and residents restricted damage in most cases to one room each.

Oxford Rd - A small number fell, but were dealt with promptly by fire guards, damage was restricted to one room each.

St James Rd - Parish Church gutted, [Home Guard Quarters], fire was of such large proportions that it was impossible to successfully deal with it with stirrup pumps.

Velwell Rd - Two houses here were bombed, but the fire guard party extinguished the bombs and fires and both houses were saved. These houses were unoccupied at the time, but the fire guards had keys and immediate access was possible.

BRIEF SUMMARY OF AIR RAID DAMAGE – CITY OF EXETER

Devastated - City centre - Sidwell St., High St. and City Library. (Main shopping and business centre.) South St. shopping area and poor residential area. Magdalen Rd; Mount Radford area shopping and business premises. Paris St. part shopping and poor residential area. Bedford Circus, Southernhay, Dix's Field (professional business area. Georgian Buildings).
Historical Buildings Devastated - Hall of Vicars Choral, Bampfield House Norman House King St.
Churches Devastated - St. Sidwell's, St. James, Bedford Church, Southernhay Congregational, St. Stephens.
Churches Extensively Damaged -Cathedral - considerable internal damage. South aisle, Choir, and Organ. Emanuel Church Heavitree R.C. Church South St. R.C. Church Heavitree Congregational Church
Schools and Colleges Devastated - St. Luke's Diocesan College, Cathedral Chorister's School.
Schools Extensively Damaged - St. Sidwell's School, Ladysmith School, Maynard School, Egerton Park School, St. Hilda's School, Deaf and Dumb Institution, Dr. Barnado's Homes.

Hospitals Damaged - City Hospital (extensively), Orthopaedic Hospital (partially).

Railways Extensively Damaged - Southern Railway Goods Yard, G.W.R. Main line damaged.

Utilities Extensive Damage - Gasworks.

Partial Damage - Water, Sewers, Electricity, Telephones.

Residential Areas Devastated - Major portion Newtown and Summerland St. areas West Avenue, Pennsylvania District. Major portion Baring Crescent, Okehampton St. and St. Thomas District, Pinhoe Road district, Portions of St. James district. Culverland Road; Prospect Park; Higher Kings Avenue. Mount Radford and St. Leonards District. Mowbray Avenue.

General - All residential areas have suffered in varying degree from the effects of the four raids between 24th April and 4th May. Casualties Deaths to date 4 raids 223. Seriously injured and in hospital 95. Slightly injured and in hospital 114. Slightly injured and sent home 374.

Casualties, Police during air raid, 4th May.

Killed:	Special Constable Luxton.
Seriously Injured:	Police-sergeant Harris. Retired. Police-constable Weeks. Pensioned. Police War Constable Hancocks.
Slightly Injured:	Police-sergeant Murray. Police-constable Dean. Police-constable Brenchley. Police War Constable Doige. Police War Constable Lee (176).Div:Commander Simey. Special Constable Foote. Special Constable Garnham. P.A.M.S. Reynolds.

Civil Defence Personnel -

Killed:	Two Wardens.
Seriously Injured:	One Warden.
Slightly Injured:	Thirteen Wardens.

For Civilian casualties see "Air Raids".

Licensed Premises - damaged

"On" licenses destroyed -
1. Globe Hotel, Cathedral Yard.
2. Exonia Vaults, South Street.
3. Grapes Inn, South Street.
4. Chevalier Inn, Fore Street.
5. Old Golden Lion Inn, Market Street.
6. New Golden Lion Inn, Guinea Street.
7. Country House Inn, Catherine Street.
8. Castle Hotel, Castle Street.
9. Bristol Inn, Sidwell Street.
10. White Lion Hotel, Sidwell Street.
11. Greyhound Inn, Paris Street.
12. Acland Hotel, Sidwell Street.
13. New Coach & Horses Inn, Sidwell St.
14. Old Coach & Horses Inn, Sidwell St.
15. King's Head Inn, Sidwell Street.
16. Red Lion Inn, Sidwell Street.
17. Royal Oak Inn, Heavitree.
18. Rising Sun Inn, Russell Street.
19. Summerland Inn, Summerland Street.
20. Elephant & Castle Inn, Summerland St.
21. Crown & Anchor Inn, Clifton Road.
22. Seven Stars Hotel, Okehampton Street.
23. Deller's Cafe, Bedford Street.
24. 74 South Street, (Messrs. Lawless).
25. Co-operative, Eastgate (Caunters).
26. No. 1. South Street.

'On' licenses - severely damaged 12, slightly or undamaged 83.

Licensed Clubs - destroyed 5, severely damaged 1, slightly or undamaged 18.

"Off licences" - destroyed 9, severely damaged 2, slightly or undamaged 19.

Raid on 4th May, 1942. Persons treated - No. 1 Post 69, No.2 Post 110, No. 4 Post 42, No. 5 Post 18, Total 239.

Fractures or suspected fractures	21
Other serious injuries	20
Burns	15
Eye cases	73
Slight injuries	99
Mainly shock	11

NOTE:- The above are in addition to casualties sent direct to hospital from the street. The burns treated and the eye cases treated are related to the prevalence of fire. The latter were mostly due to smoke, dust, grit and other foreign bodies.

Damage to Property beyond Local Repair

Grp	Houses	Shops	Dw. shops	Hses	Shps	Dw.shps
	May 4th			Prior to May 4th		
"A"	351	121	15	50	20	9
"B"	115	140	120	12	3	3
"C"	107	7	4	1	—	—
"D"	13	—	13	26	—	—
"E"	177	8	40	3	—	—
"F"	335	5	19	20	7	3
"G"	31	2	—	—	—	—
"H"	92	2	—	45	—	—
"J"	6	—	—	62	5	—
"K"	12	—	—	19	2	7
"L"	21	—	—	3	—	—
	1260	285	211	241	37	22

LOCAL AUTHORITY AREA - EXETER LIST OF PROPERTIES PROVISIONALLY CLASSIFIED BY THE WAR DAMAGE COMMISSION AS TOTAL LOSSES

Albany Place, 2, 4, 1.
Albert St, 5, 6, 7, 8, 9, 10, 11, 12, 21, 22.
Alexandra Place, Cheeke St, 1, 2, 3.
Alma Cottages, Parr St, 1, 2, 3, 4, 5, 6.
Alpha St, 1, 28.
Alphington St, Anchor Inn, 33, 34, 35, 35A, 35B, 36, 37, 39.
Anthony Road, 61.
Bampfylde Street, 5.
Baring Crescent, 2, 3, 5, The Lodge.
Barnfield Road, 37.
Barton Rd, 88, 89, 90, Geievesdon 91, 111, 113, 114, 115, 116.
Bath Road, 36, 37, 70.
Belmont Rd, 2, 4, 6, 8, 10, 12, 16, 18, 20, 22, 24, 26, 27, 29, 30.
Belgrave Rd, 1, 3, 4 Haymans Building, 1A, 2, 3, 4, 5, 6, Adjoining 7, 7, 12, 13, 14, 15, 16, 17, 23, 24, 26, 27, 28, 29.
Bedford Mews & Catherine Street Garage.
Beford Circus, 2, 3, 4, 12, 15.
Belmont Road, 28, 20, 22, 23, 24.
Belmont Villas, 1, 2.
Bidwell Street, 53.
Bishops Buildings, Summerland Street, 8.
Blackall Road, 6, 7.
Blackboy Rd, 3 Salem Place, 26, 38, 45, 43, 44,

69, 71, 72, 73, 74, 76, 109, 110, 111A, 112.
Brides Place, Paris Street, 1.
Brunswick Place, Paris Street, 3, 5, 6, 7, 7A.
Castle Street, 3, 4.
Catherine Street, Bedford Garage.
Codrington Street, 20, 21,
Catherine Street, 32, 38 41.
Chamberlain Road, 2, 4, 6, 8, 10.
Cheeke St, 9, 10, 10a, 11, 12a, 13, 15, 16, 17.
Church Lane, 6.
Clarendon Pl, Bartholomew St East, 1 - 5.
Clifton Cottages, St. Matthews, 5, 6.
Clifton Road, 15, 16, 31, 32, 46, 47, 48, 51, 52, 53, 59, 65, 67.
Clifton St, 1, 2, 10, 16, 16a, 18, 33, 40, 42, 43, 44, 55, 56, 58, 60, 61, 63 to 72, 74 to 85, 87, 91, 93, 95, 97.
Close, The, Abbots Lodge.
Codrington Street, 17, 18, 19.
Cumberland Terrace. 4, 5, 6.
Dinham Road, 1, 2, 3.
Dix's Field, 5, 10, 11, 12, 16, 19, 20, 22, 25, 26.
Cummins Cottages, 1, 2.
Ebenezer Place, Paris Street, 1, 2.
East John Street, 19, 20, 22, 42, 44, 52, 60, 61, 63 to 71, 74, 76, 82, 86, 50, 95, 102 to 104, 107, 111.
Elmside (St. James), 14.
Fore St, Heavitree, 21, 22, 23, 24, 25, 26, 1, 2 Prospect Villas.
Fore Street, Exeter, 164, 179.
Fore Street, Stafford Lodge.
Friars Walk, 22.
Gatteys Court, 24, 26.
George Street, 9, 10.
Gills Court, Cheeke Street, 8, 9.
Gladstone Road, 2, 5.
Grosvenor Place, Laburnum Cottage.
Guinea St, 7, 8, 9, 13, 14, 15, 12, 9 Milk Street (corner property).
Heavitree Rd, 47, 49, 51, 53, 55, 57, 59, Conington 95.
High Street, 257, 258.
Higher Brunswick Terr, Paris St, 1, 2, 3, 4, 5.
Holloway Street, 14, 15, 16, 17, 65.
Homefield Road, 8.
Iron Bridge, 9, 10, 11.

Longbrook Street, 4.
Lower Albert Street, 1 Cottage, 2, 3, 4, 6.
Lower Summerlands, 6, 5.
Magdalen Rd, 5, 7, 10, 22, 24, 26, 28, 30, 32, 34, 49, 61, 63, 65.
Market St, 9, 10, 12, 13, 14, 15, 20, 21, 16A, 19, 23, 24, 25.
St. Mary Arches Street, 45, 46.
Milk Street, 1, 2, 4, 5, 6, 7.
Monks Rd, 157, 161, 163, 165, 167, 169, 171, 173, 174, 175, 180.
Morgans Square, 3, 4, 5.
Paris Street, 84, 85, 95, 96, 97, 98, 100, 101
Parr St, Jarmans Cotts 2, 3, Lethbridge Cotts 1 to 6, Victoria Cotts 3, 4, 5, 2, 6; Parr St 1, la to 10, 35 to 41, 49, 50, 59 to 67, Salutation Cotts 1, Sagona Terr 3.
Pennsylvania, Maryfield House.
Pinhoe Rd, 132, 134, 136, 138, 140, 142, 144, 156, 158, 160, 176, 178, 180.
Polsloe Road, 38.
Poltimore Square, 22A.
Paris St, Morgan's Square, Nos. 6 - 14.
Mowbray Avenue, 1, 2.
Stover Place, 1.
North Street, (Iron Bridge), 7, 8.
Northernhay Place, 8.
Okehampton St, 3, 7, 8, 19, 28, 5, 21, 31, 9, 32, 33, 34.
Palace Gate, 4.
Park Place (Wonford Road), 2.
Park Street, 8.
Paris Street, Fords Court 3; 2, 3, 6, 7, 8, 9, 11, 24, 26, 27, 28, 29, 31, 32, 33, 39, 39A, 40, 41, 42, 44, 45, 45A, 48, 49, 50, 52, 62, 63, 64, 65, 66, 79, 80, 23, 81, 82, 83.
Portland Place, 8, 9.
Portland Street, 1, ?, ?, 21, 40, 66, 77, 78, 79, 80, 81, 82, 83, 84, 86, 88.
Premier Place, "Lynwood", Mount Cotts, Myrtle Cotts, 2, 3, 4, 5.
Prince of Wales Road, Swiss Cottage.
Prospect Park, 2, 3, 4.
Queen's Crescent, 5, 6.
Queen's Road, 12, 14, 16, 18.
Regent Square, 38.
Regent Street, 8, 9, 10, 11.

Roseland Avenue, 46.
Russell Street, 3, 4, 10, 15, 16, 18, 21, 22, 23, 24, 26, 27, 29, 30, 31, 32, 33, 44, 45, 46, 55, 56.
Salem Place, Blackboy Road, 4, 6.
Salem Place, St. Sidwell, 5.
Salem Place, 7.
Salutary Mount, 7.
Sandford Street, St. Matthews 3, 5, 3, 1A.
Sandford St, adjoining Golden Lion, 4.
Sandford St, 1, 5, 6, 7, 8, 10 Newtown, 37, 45 Newtown, 47, 51 Newtown, 53 Newtown, 55, 57 Newtown, 59, 61, 76 Newtown, St. Sidwells, 78 Newtown, 80 Newtown, 91, 102, 104 Newtown, 106 St. Sidwells, 110 Newtown, 111.
St. Sidwells Avenue, 1 St. Sidwells, 2 St. James, 3 St. Sidwells, 4 St. James, 5 St. Sidwells, 6, 7, 8, 9 St. James, 10 St. Sidwells, 11, 12 St. James, 14, 15, 16, 17, 18.
Sidwell Street, 17A.
St. Sidwells Street 19A, 23A.
Sidwell Street, 35, 37, 38, 39, 41A, 42; Goulds Cotts 1, 2; 141A, 46; Parsonage Ct 1, 2, 3, 45A, 46A; 47, 50 St. Sidwells, 51 St. Sidwells, 54 St. Sidwells, 87A, 88, 88A, 101A, 102 107, 108, 112 St. James, 113 St. James, 114, 115, 116, 119, 121, 122, 123, 135, Grants Cotts 10, 9; 137A, 138, 139, 140, 141, 142, 144, 147, 149, 150A, 151, 154, 155, 157 (Corner of Sidwell St and Cheeke St), 157A, 159 St. Sidwell, 62, 164 and cottage at rear, 164A, 165, 3 Southards Ct and Sheds, 9, 10 Townsends Ct and Annexe, 5 Union Terr.
Silver Place, Paris Street, 1, 2, 3, 5, 6, 7, 8.
Sivell Place, Fore Street, Heavitree, 1, 2, 3, 4, 5.
South Avenue, 22, 28.
South Avenue, Heavitree, 24, 30.
South Avenue, Polsloe, 26, 26A.
South Street, 7, 83, 13, 3 South St, St. Mary Major, 15, 79, 80, 16, 17, 98, 18, 97, 19, 78, 20, 21, 22, 32, 98, 35, 33, 33A, 36 36A, 34, 71 - 73
Southards Court, 1, 2; 121A, Sidwell Street.
Southernhay East, 7, 14; 1 Dix's Field.
Southernhay West, 43, 28, 38, 29, 25A, 41, 30, 44 St. Davids, 45, 42.
Spicer Road, Rackfield, Leebourne.

Summerland Crescent, St. Sidwells, 1 - 9.
Summerland Row, 10, 11.
Summerland Street, 4, 5, 6, 6a, 7, 8, 9 St. Sidwells, 10, 11, 13, 17, 21 to 29, 32, 33, 34, 37, 46 to 51, 54, 56 to 63, 65 to 75, 77, 78, 78A, 76 St. Sidwells, 80, 87, 88, 88A, 89 to 94, 94A, 95; 1 to 4 Snells Buildings; 5, Triangle; 6, 7, 8, Wrights Cottages.
Summerland Terrace, Newtown, 2, 4, 3; 5, 6.
Sun St, St. Mary Major, 5, 6, 7, 8, 9, 19, 25.
Sun Street, 16, 17, 18, 1, 2, 3; 82 South Street, 20, 21, 22, 23, 24.
St. Andrews Road, Exwick, 8, 10, 12'.
St. Davids Hill, 89, 91 "Nuttaberry".
St. Kerrians Place, North Street, 3, 4, 5, 6, 7.
St. Leonards Rd, 8, 11, 12, 14, 27, 31, 32, 34, 38.
St. Leonards Terr, 1, 2, 3 Wonford, 4 - 8.
The Triangle, St. Matthews, 2 Newtown, 3, 7, 8 Clifton Road.
Tudor Street, St. Edmunds, 8, 9, 10.
Union Road, 2 Marlpool Cottage.
Union Terrace, Cheeke St, St. Sidwells. 30, 4, 17, 18, 19, 20, 21.
Verney Place, St. Sidwells, 1, 2.
Verney Place, 3 to 18.
Waterloo Pl, Belgrave Rd, 1, 2, 3, 4, 5, 7, ?, ?.
Well Street, 27, 28; 1, 2, Clarence Place, adjoining; 29, 20A, 30, 30A.
Wesleyan Court, 1 - 9 (inc.).
Weir Barton Farm, Glasshouse Lane, 3, Cottages adj.
Windsor Terrace, 1, 2, 3, 4, 5, 6, 7, 8.
Wonford Rd, 1 Park Pl, 15, 26, 27, 33 - 36.
Wonford Street, 31, 33, 35.
Wood Vale Cottages, 1-6.
York Road, 18A, 8 "Kenilworth", 9, 10, 11.
Church Lane, 22, 23, 24, 25, 26.
Clifton Street, 53, 73, 89.
Coombe Street, 60, 61, 62.
Dix's Field. 23, 24.
Fore Street, 180.
George Street, 2, 3, 8.
Guinea Street, 16, 17, 18 and *South Street,* 94.
Summerland St or *Paris St,* 7 Alma Cottages.
Clifton Street, 99.
East John Street, 62.

Tudor Street, 5.
Topsham Road, Parkers Well House.
St. Leonards Road, 16.
South Street, 34A The Cottage.
South Street, 30.
Snells Cottages, 1A, 2A.

CHIEF CONSTABLES REPORT 4TH MAY 1942 – FIRE PREVENTION OFFICER

Organisation of Fire Guard
The organisation of the fire guard in Exeter had made considerable progress and was approaching a state of completeness. The "Circus" which visited the City from Regional Headquarters quite recently made suggestions of a minor character but did not suggest any radical changes. It was thought, however, that as the centre of Exeter was a very high fire risk, it might be considered that the minimum standard of cover which had been taken as the general standard here, was not sufficiently high and that steps should be taken, where possible, to improve it by increasing the number of fire watchers, particularly in business premises groups, and also, when necessary, increasing the equipment. Some increase had been made since the visit of the "Circus" but the fundamental difficulty of lack of manpower prevented much being done. It will be remembered that one of the features on which Regional Headquarters commented, was the unusually high percentage of volunteers who had been enroled in the Exeter Fire Guard.

Training a Fire Guard
Training was proceeding and although much remained to be done, yet very considerable process had been achieved. A high percentage of the fire guard personnel had undergone Part I Training, i.e. the theory of fire bomb control. A good number had been through Part II Training, consisting of the practical work of tackling a practice bomb and drill in the smoke chamber, together with dry and wet drill

with the stirrup pump. Little progress had been made with Part III Training i.e. the training of fire bomb parties to work as teams in their business premises groups and street parties. I feel that had this part of their training made further progress, in some cases the results of their efforts, which would have been co-ordinated by the training, would have been more effective.

THE RAID

The raid consisted of a violent attack on the City, with concentration on the shopping centre. The raid was a mixed one, incendiary bombs, high explosive of large calibre and machine gunning being intermingled. A strong wind was blowing and this undoubtedly had a very considerable effect on the spread of the fires which broke out.

EQUIPMENT

The reports I have received show that difficulty was experienced in some of the residential areas through lack of water. Reports say "We continued until the water gave out" and this would appear to demand that more static water is available in the residential areas, not merely in large tanks in districts, but at each house. The stirrup pump is, in Exeter, now looked upon as a most effective instrument and I have heard of no cases where it failed to function, or where difficulty was experienced with it.

Some reports indicate that ladders were not readily available and delay was caused in getting access to roofs in dwelling houses. The training which has been given to fire guards has, I think, been rather misleading. Most have been told that it is best to wait 2 minutes before the bomb is tackled, unless there is some exceptional reason to the contrary. This has rather led to the feeling that the tackling of incendiary bombs is somewhat of a leisurely matter and fire guards were inclined to the view

that the ladder available at the bottom of the street is near enough to enable the bomb which falls on the roof to be tackled in time. Experience here has demonstrated that the 2 minutes mentioned in instructions passes very quickly and that generally the bomb cannot be tackled as quickly as is desirable. Ladders, to be of use, must be dispersed so that no fire guard has far to go to get one when the emergency arises.

ACCESS TO PREMISES

I have received complaints from different sources of the difficulty experienced by fire guards in obtaining access to premises, and my attention has been directed to instances where houses had been destroyed by incendiary bombs through ready access not being available. My opinion is that generally, any system of leaving the key of premises with next door neighbours is ineffective unless the key holder is instructed on the alert to unlock the premises. All premises, whether they are private dwelling houses or business premises, should be unlocked, from the back as soon as the alert sounds. Fire guards had been issued with written authority for them to break into premises where necessary in the course of their duty, but the inherent dislike of damaging other person's property seems to have prevented the rapid and forcible entry which the circumstances demanded, and I feel that difficulty will the encountered in overcoming this natural reticence.

INCENDIARY BOMBS

You are aware that a new type of incendiary bomb was used in Exeter. I have made careful enquiries about its action and have communicated the result of my enquiries to Major Ollis at Falfield. There was a persistent story in Exeter that this new type of bomb jumped about and difficulty was experienced in putting a sandbag on it when it fell in the street. Major Ollis conducted experiments, as indeed have I, and the result has been that the alleged jumping seems to be entirely absent. My view is that the new bomb comes into operation more suddenly and more violently then the ordinary German 1 K.GT., but have been unable to make it jump about in the manner described by quite reliable observers. It is noteworthy that we had no experience of incendiary bombs in Exeter before the recent raids and my view is that the "jumping bomb" was in fact the ordinary German 1 K.G. with an explosive charge.

STREET FIRE PARTIES

The reports which I have received indicate that generally throughout the City, street fire parties came into action with the police and wardens at the commencement of the raid and functioned throughout. A number of properties in the residential areas were gutted by fire, but apart from the Newtown area there was no general conflagration in the residential parts of the town. I have on record many instances where houses were saved by the prompt and effective action of the street fire parties. In a number of cases the fire guards did very fine work in preventing the spread of fires. Where a house became involved, all the fire guards in the district assembled and set up a concentration of stirrup pumps and there are definite instances where this action prevented the spread of the fire.

It seems to have been clearly recognised among the fire guards, no doubt as a result of their training, that they could rely only on their own resources. They appear generally not to have expected any response to their call to the National Fire Service for aid, and they appear generally to have received none, all the services being required in the centre of the City.

CONCLUSION

As a result of my investigations into the work of the fire guard in this raid I am of the opinion that the fire guard in residential areas is unquestionably necessary and well conceived. I feel that more training is required, particularly in team work, but I am already faced with a new problem which will take a few weeks to overcome. I find that the fire guards who took part in the raid, particularly those who actually tackled a bomb, now feel that they know all there is to know about the matter and I think they will not take kindly to the suggestion that they should undertake further training. This, however, can undoubtedly soon be rectified.

I recommend that attention should be given to the distribution of the National Fire Service on target areas where raids may occur at short notice. Experience in Exeter has demonstrated that it is necessary to have the fire guards at the premises ready for action. The raid was on them almost at a moment's notice and the fires which broke out assumed considerable proportions in a very short time. I feel that it is equally important that the professional fire services should be on the spot with their equipment ready to go into action immediately the bombs fall. The progress of the raid demands that they should be in action as quickly as the fire guard. This would probably provide much moral support for the amateur fire guard and would certainly overcome the criticism which one hears from the fire guard, that the fire service was not on the spot to help them when their help was needed. Most of the fire guard realises that it was impossible for the fire service to get to their premises, but it is difficult to provide an adequate rejoinder to the statement that "they should have been here before it started". Where the National Fire Service got into action they did a very fine job of work, but the fact remains that a very considerable portion of the City of Exeter is now a mass of ruins.

LIST OF DEMOLISHED PROPERTIES NOT INCLUDED IN WAR DAMAGE COMMISSION'S LIST DATED 2ND JUNE 1944

Area A - Howell Road, Danes Castle Cottage, Lodge Hill, Upper Lodge, Highroyd, St. David's Place, Red Cow, 11 to 17, West Avenue, 14, 16, 18, 22, 24.

Area B - Blackboy Road, 27/28. Culverland Road, 41, 43, 45, 47, 49, 51, 53, 55. ????de Close, 5. Higher Kings Avenue, Trevone, Chilbury, Monks Road, 159, 176, 178, 182. Pennsylvania Road, The Croft, Pinhoe Road, 162. St. Sidwell's Cottages, 1, 2. Sidwell Street, 85/86. Springfield Road, 7, 18. St. Sidwell's Avenue, 13. York Road, 12, 13.

Area C - North Street, Heavitree, Orchard View, Pinhoe Road, 127, 129. Pamela Road, 4, 6, 8, 10, 12. RoselandAvenue, 51, 53, 55, 57. Tarbet Avenue, 13, 15, 17, 19, 22, 24, 26, 28. West Terrace, 11, 12.

Area D - Burns Avenue, 2, 4. Briar Crescent, 140, 142, 144, 146, 148. Fore Street, Heavitree, 27, 27A. Hoker Road, 41, 43. Hill Barton Road, Harlyn, Daneham, Wychbury, Laburnum Road, 76, 78, 80. Shakespeare Road, 54, 56, 58, 60. Salutary Mount, 6.

Area E - Bagshot Avenue, 17 to 22. Egham Avenue, 20. Feltrim Avenue, 34, 36, 38, 40.

Area E - Matford Avenue, Deepdene, Matford Road, Lahill, Magdalen Road, Dane End, Marlborough Road, 1, 3, 5, 7. Penleonard Close, 9 ("Westhorpe"), Premier Place, 1. Rivermead Road, 2, 4, 6, 8. Topsham Road, Feltrim House, Feltrim Lodge.

Area F.G.H. - Alphington Street, 2 Cottages r/o, 30/31. BartonRoad, 112. Dunsford Gardens, 25, 26, 49, 51, 53. Kerswill Road,

3, 4, 5, 6. Okehampton Road, 23, 26, 30, 34. Okehampton Street, 6, 34, 61. Seven Stars Inn, Queens Road, 8, 10. Redhills, 9. Southport Avenue, 2. Willeys Avenue, 1.

Area J.K - Bartholomew Street, East, 12, 12A, 13, 14, 15, 16. Chapel Court, 1, 2, 4, 5/6. Fore Street, (Exeter), 78/79 (Chevalier), Market House, 166. Guinea Street, 6 (Old Golden Lion), King Street, 20, 21, 22, 23, 24, 25, 26, "Reglia" "Sidwell", Market Street, 11 (GoldenLion), 17. Milk Street, 3, 8. Mary Arches Street, 33, 34, 34A. North Steet (Exeter), 17, 18, 21A. Preston Street, 26. Smythen Street, 17. South Street, 76, 77, 84, 86, 89, 90, 90A, 91, 92, 93, 95, 96, 101, 102/3 Inn,104. Tudor Street, 9A.

Area L - Adelaide Court (Sidwell Street), Cottage, Barnfield Road, 31, 33, 35. Belgrave Road, 25. Brunswick Place, (Paris Steet), 4, 8, 9, 10. Bedford Circus, 1, 5, 7, 8, 10, 13, 14, 16, 17, 20, 24. Bedford Street, 2. Bakers Court, (Sidwell Street), 6, 7. Bampfylde Street, Bampfylde House, Cosway Court, (Sidwell Street), 1. Cheeke Street, Alexandra Cottage, 2, 3, 4, 12, 14, 27, 28. Church Lane (Sidwell Street), 5. Castle Street, 5, 19 (Castle Hotel), 20, 21, 1 Easton's Buildings, Catherine Street, 23, 26, 36, 37. Cathdral Yard, Globe Hotel, Denmark Road, 1, Dix's Field, 2, 3, 4, 6, 17, 18, 21, 27. Eastgate, 1. Fords Place (Paris Street), 2.

Form No. 61.

EXETER CITY POLICE (Enquiry by Caller).
Name - Leslie John Vickery.
Address - No. 64 Newman Rd, Exeter.
Time - 10.45pm   Date - 19.5.42.
Subject - Deceased- Robert Denning.
Officer - P.S. Norden.

Particulars of Business and Action Taken
Caller states that on the night of the blitz he was one of twelve including the deceased who were sheltering in a

Morrison at 31 Summerland Street. When the house became on fire the occupants of the shelter were able to get out, but the deceased was killed by shock and his body left in the Morrison shelter. He and a friend have been digging at the scene tonight and have found the remains of the deceased. Caller produced a handkerchief in which he had wrapped burned bones and portions of burned watch, coins, braces, chain and ring. Caller asked where he could leave these remains and where he could obtain a death certificate. He did not desire a private burial.

2. Advised accordingly and as the Rack Street mortuary was closed the remains were placed in the Police Mortuary pending removal to Rack Street Mortuary on the 20th. Caller was allowed to retain the articles, the property of the deceased.

3. Miss Denning. I am speaking from the N.F.S. The Elms, Wonford, where I am employed. I have seen a Mr Vickery this morning and he was telling me that he has found my father's remains and has handed them to the Police. Will you please tell me what the position is as after the fire, my brother went to the house, and found that there was a large part of my father's corpse left in the shelter. When we visited the scene later the remains had been removed, and we were informed at the Mortuary that they were buried most probably as a person unknown. What Vickery has found may be a small part of the remains which were left behind. The matter is in the hands of my solicitor who is obtaining for me a death certificate. Will you please tell me who I should see, as it appears the finding of these remains will re-open the matter concerning my fathers death. This I do not desire, except that no certificate has been granted to me yet, and it may mean that the remains will be listed as two persons instead of one.

Informed that the remains brought to the Police Station were so small that they were contained in a large handkerchief, and would be passed to the Mortuary, Rack Street, this afternoon. She was advised to call and see the Casualty Officer at No. 5, Southernhay West. This she stated she would do.

Taken to Rack Street Mortuary at 4pm on 20.5.42 by P.C. 28 and left with explanatory note.

18 St. Loyes Terrace.
10.30am 4th June, 1942.
Statement of Mrs Annie VEAL, age 32, residing at 18 St. Loyes Terrace, Exeter, who saith:

"Prior to the air raid on the 4th May, 1942, I was employed as a waitress at The Bude, Paris Street, and I knew Mrs Eva Vaughan of 48 Paris Street, through having worked with her sister-in-law, Mrs Mary White, who also resided at 48 Paris Street. I also knew Mrs Vaughan's two sons David and Terry.

On the evening of Friday, 24th April last, I went to the Odeon Cinema with Mrs White and another friend, Miss Richards of 9 Coleridge Road, Exeter. We left the Cinema at about 11pm and left Miss Richards at the top of Paris Street, and went to purchase some fish and chips. Mrs White and I arrived at 48 Paris Street, about 11.15pm and Mrs Vaughan was at home waiting for us, and her two children I presumed were in bed as they were in the habit of going to bed early. I did not see them, but I saw them about 6pm when David was feeling rather poorly as he had previously had six or seven teeth extracted. Terry was then in his usual spirits.

I stopped there and had my fish and chips, and Mrs Vaughan pressed me to stop for the night, as my husband was away from home. She also suggested that I should sleep there on the Saturday night, as we had arranged to go to Torquay together on the Sunday. I practically made up my mind to stay the night, but changed it in the last moment and decided that I would go home, as I was expecting a letter from my husband.

I left 48 Paris Street, at about 12 midnight, when Mrs Vaughan and Mrs White stated that they were going to bed. Mrs Vaughan was in her usual spirits when I left her and since then I have not seen her or received any information which would suggest that she is still alive.

Mrs Vaughan had told me on the Friday evening, before I went to the Cinema, that they always stayed indoors when the "alert" sounded. They had no shelter, and usually remained in the kitchen or in a sort of wash house just outside the back door.

This statement has been read over to me and is true." (Signed) A. VEAL.

9 Coleridge Road, Exeter.
12 noon. 4th June, 1942.
Statement of Miss Maud Lavinia May PRIDDLE, munition worker, age 24, residing at 9 Coleridge Road, who saith:

"I was employed as a waitress at The Bude, Paris Street, until last Christmas, and I know Mrs Eva Vaughan of 48 Paris Street, through her sister-in-law Mrs May White, who lived with her and who also worked at The Bude. I was known by the staff at The Bude as Miss Richards in order to distinguish me from my sister who also worked there.

On the evening of Friday, 24th April last, I had arranged to go to the Odeon Cinema with Mrs White and a friend, Mrs Veal of 18 St. Loyes Terrace, I called at 48 Paris Street, at about 6.15pm and Mrs Veal, Mrs White and Mrs Vaughan were there. I cannot remember whether Mrs Vaughan's two sons were there then. I left with Mrs White and Mrs Veal about half an hour later, and Mrs Vaughan was then in her usual spirits. I did not return to 48 Paris Street, after we had left the cinema, but I

parted from Mrs White and Mrs Veal at the top of Paris Street.

This statement has been read over to me and is true."   (Signed)   L. PRIDDLE.
Statements taken and signatures witnessed by me: (Signed) John A. Berry Detective Constable.

81 East John Street.
6.45pm 11.7.42.
Statement of Margaret Wallace, a widow, residing at 81 East John Street, Exeter, who saith:

"I am the daughter-in-law of William Thomas John Wallace, age 61 years, and Mrs. Kate Wallace, age 63 years, who resided at 15 High Street, Exeter where they were employed as caretakers by the Pearl Assurance Company. I am also the cousin of Frederick Ernest Orville Labbett, age 17 years, who was a student at Haileybury College and whose parents, Captain Ernest Labbett and Mrs Labbett, reside at Malta.

Mr and Mrs Wallace have resided at 15,High Street for about 13 years and occupied rooms on the top floor of the premises. Labbett had spent his Easter vacation of one month with them and intended to return to College on Monday, 4th May.

I last saw Mr and Mrs Wallace at tea time on Saturday 2nd May last when I visited them at their address and they were then in their usual state of health. I last saw Labbett at about 9pm on Sunday, 3rd May when he called at my house on his bicycle to wish us good bye before returning to College. He only remained for a few minutes and on leaving he said that he was going back to 15 High Street.

I know that in the early morning of Monday, 4th May the premises were totally destroyed by enemy action and since that date I have not seen Mr and Mrs Wallace or the boy Labbett and I have received no information which would suggest that they are still alive.

I know that Mr and Mrs Wallace were never away from their place of residence at night except when they had a holiday and then my husband and I had to go there to relieve them. Until recently they were not in the habit of going to the basement under Messrs. Randals when the siren sounded but they told me that they went there when the City was raided on the 25th April and I am of the opinion that they would almost certainly have gone there on the night of the 3rd-4th May.

About a fortnight ago I went to St. Nicholas Priory, The Mint, where I received from the salvage authorities a metal cash box which was identical with the one which Mr Wallace possessed and in which he kept some of his valuables. I was told that the cash box had been recovered from the site of 16 High Street, but only a few coins remained intact in it. Mr Wallace always kept this cash box handy and I am sure that if he had left the premises he would have taken it with him.

This statement has been read over to me and is true." (Signed) M. Wallace.

Criminal Investigation Department, Exeter City Police. 4 pm 25th July, 1942. *Statement of George Sidney TRIST, age 34, a temporary relayer, Southern Railway, residing at 17 Brooke Avenue, Exeter, who saith:*

"I am the nephew of Mr William Thomas John Wallace and Mrs Kate Wallace, who resided at 15 High Street, Exeter, prior to the 4th May last, and a cousin of Frederick E. O. Labbett, who was residing with them for his Easter vacation. Mr and Mrs Wallace brought me up from the time when I was a baby and I lived with them until six years ago when I was married, which meant that I lived with them at 15 High Street for about seven years.

The premises of the Singer Sewing Machine Company, Limited, were at 14 High Street and the premises at 16 High Street were occupied by Messrs. H.E. Randall, Limited, both these firms having the ground floor and basement. The offices of the Pearl Assurance Company were situated across both these shops and was known as 15 High Street, as access to these premises was obtained through a passage between Singers and Randalls. Mr & Mrs Wallace's quarters were situated on the second floor above No. 14, the kitchen being situated at the back of the premises, overlooking Bedford Circus and the bedroom at the front, overlooking High Street. At the side of the bedroom, above the passage between the two shops, was a sitting room. The premises on the second floor above Randalls were occupied by Mr Melhuish, an accountant. Immediately above Mr and Mrs Wallace's quarters were two more bedrooms, one at the front and one at the back, the latter being occupied by Labbett. The rooms on the same floor above No. 16 (Randalls) were unoccupied.

In order to get to Mr and Mrs Wallace's quarters it was necessary to enter by a door in the passage and through the Pearl Assurance offices. There was only one flight of stairs and no fire escape. In order to get to the basement under Randalls it was necessary to come down the stairs into the passage between Randalls and Singers, then through two doors and down some steps.

I last saw Mr and Mrs Wallace on Saturday, 2 May, last, when I went to visit them at 15 High Street with my wife and Mrs Margaret Wallace. We were there all the afternoon and left at about 6.30pm and while I was there Mr Wallace took me down and showed me the basement under Randalls.

About two weeks after the raid I went to the site of 15 High Street, where I saw three bicycles on the debris, one of which was a carrier cycle belonging to Randalls. Of the other two, one was a

Hercules single speed sports model with cable brakes, and I could identify this one quite definitely as being the property of Labbett. The other was a Raleigh 3-speed model with upturned handlebars and cable brakes and also had a gear case. This cycle was also badly burnt but I could easily recognise it as being the one which Bartlett possessed. I know Bartlett's cycle because I used to frequently visit High Street and often saw him with the cycle or saw it standing in the passage. I also knew Ryan's cycle but I did not see it there at that time.

I know that Mr and Mrs Wallace kept regular hours and were usually in bed by 11pm. They were never away at night, except when they had a holiday, and then their son and Mrs Wallace went there to relieve them. From my experience of the building I am of the opinion that it would take me at least 7 or 8 minutes to get out of bed and dress roughly and get to the basement under Randalls. I consider that it would have taken Mr Wallace, who was not in very good health, at least 15 minutes.

I did see Labbett at about 11am on Sunday, 3rd May, when he came to wish us goodbye and I saw him again at Livery Dole at about 8.30pm the same evening. He was on his bicycle and said that he was going to 81 East John Street to see Mrs Wallace to wish her goodbye.

This statement has been read over to me and is true." (Signed) G.S. TRIST
Statement taken and signature witnessed by me. (Signed) JOHN A. BERRY. Detective Constable.

48, Victoria Street, Exeter.
11am 28th May, 1942.
Statement of Frederick James Bartlett, employed as a supervisory foreman, Great Western Railway, residing at 48 Victoria Street, Exeter, who saith:

"My son Geoffrey Francis George Bartlett, age 18 (20.7.41), was employed as a porter mechanic by the Singer Sewing Machine Co., in High Street and resided at home.

He was on duty for firewatching at his place of employment on every eighth night and it was his turn for duty on the night of Sunday, 3rd May, 1942 from 9pm until 7am. He left home at about 8.55pm on his pedal cycle, a gents 3 speed model, and since then I have not seen him or received any information which would suggest that he is still alive. He was in very good health and was quite his normal self when I last saw him. When my son left home that evening he was wearing a light blue suit, blue shirt, grey socks and black boots, no hat.

About ten days after the raid I went to High Street where the soldiers were digging among the wreckage of Singers and one of them showed me the toe piece of a boot which they dug out. This boot had a rubber sole nailed on to it and it was the same pattern as those which I had nailed to my son's boots. I formed the opinion that this was part of my son's boots on account of the manner in which the nails were placed as I always put in two extra ones by the toes to help keep the rubber fixed.

This statement has been read over to me and is true." (Signed) F.J. Bartlett.

51 Longbrook Street, Exeter.
11.50am 28th May, 1942.
Statement of Miss Rosina Caroline Shobbrook, 1 Manor Road, Exeter, who saith:

"I am employed as saleswoman by the Singer Sewing Machine Company Ltd., late of 14 High Street and now at 51 Longbrook Street, Exeter.

I knew Mr and Mrs Wallace who were caretakers of the Pearl Assurance Co. whose premises were situated above my place of employment and whose living rooms were situated at the top of the building. I sometimes used to visit them and I last did so on Sunday, 3rd May, 1942 when I went there to tea. I stayed with them until about 8pm when I left by the front gate and Mrs Wallace came down to let me out.

Mrs Wallace told me that her nephew, a college student whose parents were in Malta, was staying with her but he was not at home when I called on the Sunday. This nephew I had always known as Feo Labbett and he was due to return to College on Monday, 4th May and he was going to leave Exeter on the morning of that day.

I know that Mrs Wallace enjoyed good health but Mr Wallace was not very strong and when I last saw them they were in their usual state of health. I have never known them sleep away from the premises at all and Mr Wallace would be unable to do so in any case as, in addition to being the caretaker, he was also a firewatcher and had to be there every night.

This statement has been read over to me and is true." (Signed)   R.C. Shobbrook.

Devon & Somerset Stores,
65 Fore Street, Heavitree.
3pm 14.7.42.
Statement of Thomas Henry Matthews, age 48, a stock keeper, residing at 22 St. Sidwells Avenue, Exeter, who saith:

"On the night of 3rd-4th May last I was the senior fire guard on duty at the Devon and Somerset Stores whose premises were then situated at 245 High Street, opposite Bedford Circus.

When the Alert sounded at about 1.50pm I went on the roof at the rear of the Stores and after I had been there for eight or nine minutes I heard several bombs, about seven, fall in the higher part of the City but none of these fell in the neigh-

bourhood of Bedford Circus. Soon afterwards fires broke out in the Sidwell Street area but High Street was unaffected.

A few minutes later I heard a number of high explosive bombs fall in the neighbourhood followed by the crashing of glass and a shower of incendiaries then fell. The premises of Messrs. Wippell Bros. and Row caught fire and for some considerable time I was engaged with others in attempting to keep the fire from spreading to our premises.

It was about 20 minutes before the Raiders Passed that I looked across the road and saw that a high explosive bomb had fallen directly outside the premises of Messrs. Singers and Messrs. Randalls. Both these buildings were still standing but were extensively damaged and parts of the frontages were destroyed and the broken rafters were exposed. A gas main appeared to have been fractured as gas was burning on the surface of the road but the buildings were not alight at that time. When I last saw Singer's and Randall's premises at about 3.40am it was still not burning.

During the period in which I was on duty I did not see any person come out from Singers or Randalls and I did not hear any shouts or cries for help.

This statement has been read over to me and is true."   (Signed)   T. Matthews.

Barclays Bank, High Street.
5.30pm 14.7.42.
Statement of Richard Joseph Gliddon, age 59, residing at 126 Magdalen Road, who saith:

"Prior to the 4th May last I was resident caretaker and messenger of Barclays Bank, 17 & 18 High Street and when the siren sounded at about 1.45am on the 4th May I dressed and got my family from our quarters at the top of the building to the basement.

About 15 minutes after the Alert sounded I was outside our door in Bedford

Street dealing with an incendiary bomb when I heard the sound of a bomb explode apparently somewhere at the back of the bank. On going into the bank I saw that a considerable part of Messrs. Randall's premises at 16 High Street had crashed into the area and typists' room of the bank which are situated at the rear and adjoin the side and back of Randalls. At this time the building was not burning and I took my family to a shelter in Bedford Circus and returned several times to the bank. The last time that I returned was about 2.30am and Randalls and Singers were still not ablaze although there were a few minor fires at the rear.

I did not see Mr and Mrs Wallace all day Sunday and I heard no shouts or cries for help after the bomb had fallen. It was the habit of Mr and Mrs Wallace to go down to the Catherine Street end of the passage at the back of Randalls when the siren sounded and I usually heard them talking there when I was on the roof, but things happened so quickly that night that I heard nothing of them.

This statement has been read over to me and is true."   (Signed)   J. Gliddon.

51 Longbrook Street, Exeter.
10.15am 6.6.42.
Statement of Percy Ernest Beale, residing at 1 Springfields, Alphington, who saith:

"I am the manager of the Singer Sewing Machine Co., Ltd., who were in business at 14 High Street until the 4th May last. Our premises were on the ground floor and cellar and Messrs. Randalls adjoined us. The offices of the Pearl Assurance Co. were situated over the two shops and two offices over the Pearl Assurance were occupied by Mr Melhuish, an accountant. At the top of the premises resided the caretakers, Mr and Mrs Wallace.

On the night of the 3rd-4th May last two of my employees, Geoffrey Bartlett and Joseph Ryan were on firewatching duty from 9pm until 6am Mr Wallace, the caretaker, was also a firewatcher and had to be on the premises each night. The firewatchers' room was situated on the first floor and a reinforced basement was provided under Randall's shop.

The whole premises were destroyed during the air raid on the 4th May, a high explosive bomb having exploded immediately in front of the shop. I know that the remains of Ryan have been identified but since the air raid I have not seen Bartlett or received any information which would suggest that he is still alive.

About one week after the raid I went to the site of 15 High Street where I saw four pedal cycles which had been dug out of the debris. One of these was a carrier cycle belonging to Messrs. Randalls and the remaining three were gents bicycles. They were all buckled and burnt but I could identify one as being the property of Joseph Ryan as there were remains of red paint on it and because it was a racing model with dropped handlebars. The other two cycles were almost unidentifiable but they were undoubtedly the property of Frederick Labbett and Geoffrey Bartlett as I know that they both had pedal cycles and Bartlett always rode his to business. There were no other persons who would leave pedal cycles on the premises during the night and Mr Wallace did not possess one.

This statement has been read over to me and is true."   (Signed)   P.E. Beale.

Criminal Investigation Dept.
3.30pm 2nd July 1942.
Statement of Charles Alfred Bungey, residing at 20 Elm Grove Road, Topsham, who saith:

"I am the staff officer of the Exeter City A.R.P. Rescue Parties and I was in charge of the party which searched the debris at

Messrs. Randalls, High Street. The whole of the debris was searched from back to front and was cleared right down to the floor of the basement shelter which is on foundation level.

Some remains, which consisted of bones, were recovered and sent to the Public Mortuary and the search is now completed. This statement has been read over to me and is true."
(Signed) C.A. Bungey. Statements taken and signatures witnessed by me.
(Signed) John A. Berry Det. Constable.

30th July, 1942.
Sir,
re Alice Maud ELLERY, 4 Summerland Crescent, Exeter - believed killed.

I beg to report that at 4pm on Wednesday, 8th July, 1942, in consequence of a telephone message from Mr. Howells, I went to the Casualty Bureau where I saw Mrs Alice M.M. Westcott of 78 Hawthorn Road. This lady stated that she was the sister-in-law of Mrs Alice Maud Ellery, a widow, aged 48-50, who resided in the basement of 4 Summerland Crescent, and who had not been seen since the 4th May last, when the house in which she lived was totally destroyed by fire. She had not communicated with any other member of the family since the blitz but this was not of much significance as she was not in the habit of writing to them, the reason being that she drank heavily and was also slightly mental, with the result that she was shunned by her relatives.

As a result of this information I went to Newtown Post Offfice, where Mrs. Ellery drew her widow's pension, and I was informed that she had not been there since the blitz. On making enquiries in Russell Street I found that everybody understood that she had been killed but I could find no one who had seen her body and her name was not on the official casualty list. There was a vague rumour in the Russell Street district to the effect that her body had been recovered from the basement of 4 Summerland Crescent during the morning of Monday, 4th May last, but none of the persons who mentioned this rumour had seen the body taken out and were only repeating what they had heard other people saying.

The official records showed that the only persons to have been killed in Summerland Crescent were Mrs. Helina Davey and Miss Day, who both resided at No. 5. There were no other unidentified bodies or unidentified remains taken to the Public Mortuary from Summerland Crescent.

I afterwards traced the whereabouts of Mr. Charles Sampson, the former tenant of 4 Summerland Crescent, and I was informed by his wife that after the raiders passed had sounded Mrs. Ellery was still in the basement of No. 4 with her dog and stubbornly refused to come out, despite the fact that the buildings all round were on fire. Mr. and Mrs. Sampson, together with other people, decided to leave the area before it was too late and Mrs. Ellery remained in her basement.

In view of this information I contacted Mr. Bungey of the Surveyor's Department and explained the facts to him and it was arranged that the site of 4 Summerland Crescent should be searched. This was a fairly big job as the walls had been knocked down by the demolition workers and the cellar was filled with bricks, but the work was completed at 16.00 hours on 25th July, 1942. Some human bones were recovered and taken to the mortuary.

In view of the fact that some identifiable remains might have been found I did not take any statements as I can easily obtain them if an enquiry is necessary.
John G. Berry, Detective Constable. Examined & submitted: R.P. Rowlands, Detective Inspector.

City Hospital, Heavitree Road, Exeter.
12 noon, 20th May, 1942.
Statement of William Charles WOOD, who saith:

"I am the Master of the City Hospital, Heavitree Road, Exeter. On the early morning of Monday, 4th May, 1942, a number of incendiary bombs were dropped on the City Hospital in the course of the air raid, with the result that a large part of the premises were destroyed by fire.

On this night there were 193 patients, males and females, on the premises, and 175 of these were safely rescued by the staff. Of the 18 who could not be rescued, 9 were men who were detained in Block A Sick Ward, and 9 females who were detained in Block B Sick Ward. In each case these patients were situated on the first floor and it was impossible to rescue them owing to the intensity of the fire, and both blocks were burnt out.

Following is the list of males who were in Block A Sick Ward on the night of the 3rd-4th May: William Gray; Phillip Freeman; Frederick Brown; Frederick Taylor; William Northcott; Albert Batten; Harry Victor Mathews; William Henry Mock; John Holman.

The following is the list of females who were in Block B Sick Ward: Phoebe Whitfield; Annie Reid; Mary Dymond; Rhoda Rowe; Emily Byrne; Mary Ann White; ? Veale; Ellen Selley; Mary Cummings.

I am unable to give any more detailed information respecting these people, as all my records were destroyed in the fire.

All the 18 missing persons were bedridden cases and practically helpless, and I am of the opinion that they must have perished in the flames. Since the raid I know that nine skulls and other bones were found in the ruins of Block B Sick Ward which are no doubt those of the nine missing females.

In Block A Sick Ward some bones were dug out, and also some pieces of skulls, but it was not possible to tell whether it comprised the remains of the nine male persons.

This statement has been read over to me and is true."   (Signed) W.C. WOOD. Statement taken and signature witnessed by me:(Signed) JOHN BERRY. Detective Constable.

City Hospital,Heavitree Road.
8 pm 26th May, 1942.
Statement of Mrs. Emily Alberta Mardon KNEE, residing at 14 Merrivale Road, Exeter, who saith:

"I am employed as a night nurse at the City Hospital, Heavitree Road, Exeter, and I was on duty in "A" Block Sick Ward from 8pm to 8am on the night of the 3rd-4th May, 1942, when the Hospital was extensively damaged by fire during an air raid.

"A" Block Sick Ward was situated on the first floor, and the following patients were in the ward on the night of the raid:
(1) William Gray, age about 64, who was suffering from paralysis of the legs, and could not walk.
(2) Philip Freeman, age 64, who was suffering from severe heart trouble. He was on the danger list and was not expected to live.
(3) Frederick Brown, age 85, who was suffering from general senility and could not walk.
(4) Frederick Taylor, age 38, who was suffering from Parkinson's disease. He could not walk and was quite helpless.
(5) William Northcott, age 56, who was suffering from cerebral tumour and paraplegia and was paralysed from the waist downwards.
(6) Albert Batten, age 82, who was suffering from arterial sclerosis, and was quite helpless.
(7) Harry Victor Mathews, age 60, who was very ill with pneumonia, and was on the danger list.

(8) William Henry Mock, age 89, who was suffering from senile decay, but was able to walk.

(9) John Holman, age 87, who was suffering from senile decay, and who died a few moments before the Alert sounded, when I was sitting beside him. He had been dangerously ill for some time and he was expected to die that night.

When the incendiary bombs began to fall I went to the top of the building, with others, to try and put them out, but fire broke out and we began to evacuate the patients. We succeeded in getting many of the patients out, but when we came to rescue those in Block "A" Sick Ward the fire was raging and the stairs were ablaze, and we could not get to them.

In view of the condition of the men in Block "A" Sick Ward, I am of the opinion that they must certainly have perished in the fire, as they could not get out without some assistance.

This statement has been read over to me and is true." (Signed) E.A. KNEE. Statement taken and signature witnessed by me: (Signed) JOHN A. BERRY. Detective Constable.

City Hospital, Heavitree Road.
8.30pm 26th May, 1942.
Statement of Mrs. Florence Elizabeth Cartwright, residing at 107 Merrivale Road, Exeter, who saith:

"I am employed as a night nurse at the City Hospital, Heavitree Road, Exeter, and I was on duty in Block "A" Sick Ward with Nurse Knee from 8pm to 8am on the night of the 3rd-4th May, 1942.

I have read the statement made by Nurse Knee respecting the nine male patients who were killed in Block "A" Sick Ward and I agree entirely with all which she said. This statement has been read over to me and is true."
(Signed) F.E. CARTWRIGHT.

Statement taken and signature witnessed by me: (Signed) JOHN A. BERRY. Detective Constable.

Nellie Augusta MEAD

"On Sunday 3rd May, 1942, at 9.45pm my husband left home to go on night shift - 10pm to 6am - at St. David's. He left the house in his usual spirits and appeared to be his usual self and in good health.

This was the last I saw of him and the air raid on Exeter started about 2 hours after he had left. After the raid, at about 5.30am 4th May, I walked down to St. David's Station with his Mother, who was staying with me at the time. The officials at the Station told me that a shelter, in which my husband had been, had received a direct hit. I could get no more information until 10.30am that morning when two Railway offcials came to my house and told me that my husband was killed in this shelter during the raid.

On Wednesday 6th May the Stationmaster at St. David's handed me a purse and two handkerchiefs, which I identified as definitely the property of my husband, also his Identity Card. The following Friday week, the 15th, he handed me a wallet containing my husband's Armed Forces Registration Card; Civil Defence Registration Card, also photos etc., which I identified as the property of my husband. Also in the wallet was his Union Card and Station Club Card.

The N.U.R. Official later took charge of the Identity Card, Union Book and Station Club Book. I was not actually told where all these articles had been found but I understood that it was near the shelter which had been hit, on the Railway premises."

Statement of William Robert SLUMAN

"I am employed by the Great Western Railway as a goods yard inspector at St.

David's and on the night of the 3rd-4th May, 1942, I was on duty from 10 pm to 6am. My staff consisted of three shunters, one of whom was Cyril Mead, who resided at 34 Chamberlain Road and who also commenced work at 10pm on that night. Mead was employed that night at the east end of the shunting yard with another shunter named Ridgeway, and I remember seeing him last at about 12.30am before I returned to my office.

When the Alert sounded at 1.42am I went outside my office and I could hear that shunting was still in progress. I later heard the sound of bombs falling in the distance and the shunting ceased and I presumed that the staff had taken cover in the underground shelter at the east end of the yard at the side of the river. This shelter provided for the shunting staff and I know that the men always went there when danger appeared to be imminent.

After the raid was over I was informed by the signalman at the east box that the shelter had received a direct hit and I therefore went to St. David's Station and summoned a rescue party. I know that a number of bodies were afterwards recovered from the shelter and since the night of the raid I have not seen Mead or received any information which would suggest that he was still alive."

Statement of Henry Collins HUGHES

"Shunter C.K. Mead reported on duty at St. David's Goods Yard at 10pm on Sunday 3rd May, 1942. His booked duty was until 6am the following morning but he did not sign off duty and it appears that he was killed when a high explosive bomb scored a direct hit on the shelter at the east end of the shunting yard.

I know that seven other bodies were taken from the remains of the shelter and were identified, but no body was recovered which could be identified as Mead,

although pieces of flesh were found.

During rescue and demolition work a wallet was found among the debris. This wallet, which I later returned to the widow, contained a National Union of Railwaymen Contribution Card and a Railway Men's Mutual Aid Society Contribution Card in the name of Mead and also a photograph of his wife and other personal belongings which Mrs. Mead identified as belonging to her husband."

Statement of John GREEN

"On Monday, 4th May, 1942, after the air raid, I was present at the scene of the railway shelter at the east end of St. David's Goods Yard, this shelter having been destroyed by a high explosive bomb. I saw the bodies of Greaser-boy Jordan, Shunter Ridgway, Engineman Shapley and Fireman Gregory removed from the debris and I know that their legs had not been severed from their bodies. I also saw Shunter Ham taken out still alive and his legs were still attached to his body, but he has since died.

Further rescue took place and we recovered two legs which were attached at the pelvis, two more left legs and one right leg. Two of the left legs must have belonged to Examiner Webber and Telephonist Bird, parts of whose bodies were recovered, and the remaining left leg would appear to be that of Shunter Mead, who was the only person believed to have been in the shelter and who was not accounted for. Further pieces of flesh have been recovered but could not be identified as being parts of any particular person."

20th June, 1942.
Sir,
Re. Sarah Jane Balsom - Deceased.

I beg to report that I have made enquiries respecting the above named woman who was killed during the air raid on Monday, 4th May last but who is not officially recorded as having been killed and whose body cannot be accounted for.

Mrs. Balsom, aged 55 years, was the wife of the licensee of the Red Lion Inn, 117 Sidwell Street and Mr. Balsom states that they were obliged to leave the premises during the raid on account of fire. They went to the garden at the back of the inn, together with their daughter and the barmaid and lay down beside a wall. Mrs. Balsom was killed by a bomb which fell nearby and demolished the wall under which they were taking shelter. The daughter sustained a fractured leg and the barmaid was also injured but Balsom escaped with only slight injury and later made his way to the Triangle where he contacted Divisional Commander Wippell of the Special Constabulary who sent for an ambulance and a rescue party. These arrived about 5am and it was found that the body and the injured persons would have to be brought into Parr Street as Red Lion Court was blazing. This operation was carried out and the daughter and barmaid were carried away in an ambulance. Mrs. Balsom was wrapped in two rugs and was last seen by her husband lying in Chute Street near its junction with Parr Street. He then went back to the garden to collect a case and when he returned he saw that the body had gone and assumed that it had been removed to the mortuary. He therefore proceeded to the hospital to receive attention to his eyes which had been scorched.

Balsom says that he went to the mortuary on the Monday and Tuesday but was not allowed to see all the bodies. He called again on the Wednesday evening and identified a body as being that of his wife despite the fact that this body had already been identified as another person. He was not sure of himself, however, and returned on Thursday to make a further

examination and then found that the body which he had identified had some of its own teeth whereas his wife had none. It was obvious therefore that he had made a mistake and his excuse was that he was not given sufficient time when he identified the body. Balsom stated that his wife was not disfigured and in addition to the rugs which had been wrapped around her she was wearing a man's green and white dressing gown but he has not been able to discover what happened to this garment.

I have been in touch with P.C. 21 Dean, who saw the body in Parr Street where it was in danger of being burned. He moved it temporarily to the top of Chute Street, where it was last seen by Mr. Balsom, and shortly afterwards moved it again into Belmont Road where it would be out of the danger area. P.C. Dean, who was not aware of the identity of the body, went to the incident post at St. Annes and requested that Control Centre be informed that there was a body to be collected in Belmont Road. He assumed that the corpse would be collected and went on with his duties and Divisional Commander Wippell, who became aware of the action taken, also considered the matter closed.

During the afternoon of the same day however, Mr. Whittaker, Head Warden, Group "F", Clifton Hill, saw that the body was still lying in Belmont Road opposite Parr Street. He therefore moved it into the front garden of a house where he placed it behind a hedge and sent for a mortuary van. The van, a Council refuse vehicle, arrived soon afterwards and took away the body at about 4.30pm. Mr. Whittaker was not aware of the identity of the body and only knew that it was a female. It was wrapped in rugs and he did not see the clothing.

In view of this information I contacted Mrs Caddy at the Town Clerk's office and the copies of the mortuary records were searched but these contained no trace of any body, identified or unidentified, having been brought in from Belmont Road.

After some difficulty I have traced the driver of the mortuary van xxxxx H. Darke who is employed by the Cleansing Department of the City Council. He stated that he went to Belmont Road at the time in question and recovered the body from the front garden of the house and loaded it on to the refuse vehicle. He did not examine the face or the clothing but labelled it as an unknown female from Belmont Road. This was the only body which Darke collected on that journey and he took it to Rack Street mortuary where he placed it in the yard beside the bodies of some Home Guardsmen. He told the Mortuary Superintendent that it was the body of an unknown female and that he had brought it from Belmont Road. He also gave his name and Mr. Wise entered the particulars in a book after which Darke returned to his depot. I have interviewed Mr Wise, the Mortuary Superintendent, respecting the matter and the mortuary records have been carefully checked but no trace could be found of any body at all having been brought in from Belmont Road and there is no record of any body having been brought in by Darke at the time in question. Mr Wise could not remember the body and the dressing gown was not among any property at the mortuary.

I afterwards interviewed Mr Arnold of 14 Herschell Road, who is a mortuary attendant and he remembered the body being brought in and remembered seeing it lying in the yard at the side of some Home Guardsmen or Artillerymen. He could not say that it was wrapped in two rugs but was able to recall the green and white dressing gown.

It was Arnold's duty to strip and wash this body and he stated that the dressing gown was soaked in blood and he was obliged to cut it off and it was put aside to be burnt as was the rest of the clothing. Arnold stated that there was a severe cut in the abdomen of this body and it appeared to him that the ribs and pelvis were fractured. In addition there was a wound at the back of the head which may have been caused by a brick and which had bled freely and the face was similar to a person who had suffered from severe concussion. He also stated that whereas the face was not actually mutilated it was not pleasant to look at as the eyes were red and bulging and it was generally distorted. Arnold knew Mrs Balsom but did not recognise the body which had no property on it. In his opinion it would probably be classed as unidentifiable which probably explains why it was not photographed unless of course it was wrongly identified by some other person. It is apparent that Balsom would not be able to tell to what extent his wife had been mutilated when he saw her body in the darkness.

Unfortunately, Mr Arnold does not know the mortuary number of the body and can give no additional information with the result that the matter still remains unsolved. The only body which may be connected with the matter is mortuary number 134 which is described as an unidentifiable female and according to the records it was brought in from Pinhoe Road at 4.5pm on 4.5.42. No further particulars about the body are available and the name of the driver who brought it in is not shown. Also there was no property found on the body. The fact that it is shown as having been brought in from Pinhoe Road may be an error and it appears that there is a slight possibility that No. 134 may be the body of Mrs. Balsom. Apart from this I know of no other solution.

With regard to Balsom's statement that he was not given sufficient time when he wrongly identified a body, I do not think that this is true as I am informed by Mr Wise that, in addition to showing the body to Balsom, he had it turned over to see if there

was a mole on the back, which there was, but I am quite satisfied that the body which he did wrongly identify has no connection with this matter.
John A. Berry. Detective Constable. Examined and submitted Detective Inspector.

Statement of Mrs Gladys Louisa HEYBURN

"Prior to the air raid on the 4th May, 1942, I resided at 9 Strongs Court, Sidwell Street, and I knew Mr Clarke of 14 Strongs Court quite well through having resided near him.

When the alert sounded in the early morning of Monday, 4th May, I went to the archway at the top of Strongs Court and stood there with other neighbours. I remained there for about a quarter of an hour when buildings began to catch alight and I decided to go to one of the surface shelters further down Sidwell Street.

As I was passing Verney Place I saw Mr Clarke standing there and he called out to me 'What is the Court like?' I told him that it was sourrounded by fire and he said 'Is Mrs Clarke out?' I told him that I believed she had got out the bottom end of the Court into Parr Street.

I then went on my way towards the shelter and I have not seen Mr Clarke since or received any information which would suggest that he is still alive.

I am unable to recall what Mr Clarke was wearing when I last seen him."

Statement of Mrs Florence Elizabeth FROST

"On Monday, 4th May, 1942, at about 1.40am I was in bed when the alert sounded. I got out and dressed and put a coat on each of my three children and went out into Sidwell Street. A number of premises were burning and I started to walk down Sidwell Street when Mr Clarke walked over to me from the middle of the road. He told me who he was and asked me to come to the shelter in the basement of the Co-op at the corner of Verney Place.

While Mr Clarke was conducting us down the stairs a bomb exploded nearby and blew us down into the basement shelter. Mr Clarke was not hurt and immediately afterwards he went outside again and I heard more bombs falling very close.

I remained in this shelter until the building caught fire and I then went to the Methodist Chapel in Sidwell Street, but I saw nothing of Mr Clarke and I have not seen him since."

Statement of Mrs. Emelia CLARKE

"I am the wife of Walter Henry Clarke, who was employed as a brick setter at the Rougemont Tileries, Monks Road, Exeter, having worked there for nearly 21 years. We resided at 14 Strongs Court, Sidwell Street, for four years and three months and my husband did his weekly turn of fire-watching on Thursday nights and reported when the sirens sounded on Tuesdays and Sundays. The premises for which he was responsible were 112-116 Sidwell Street and 1 and 2 Verney Place, and on Sundays he was on duty with a Mr Wright and a Mr Hoare.

At about 1.40am on Monday, 4th May, 1942, my husband and I were in bed when the alert sounded. Mr Clarke dressed and went out to take up his fire-watching duties and since that time I have not seen him or received any information which would suggest that he is still alive.

When my husband went out he was wearing a blue pin-stripe coat, grey flannel trousers, blue overcoat, black shoes, khaki shirt, no tie and he was also wearing his steel helmet. He was normally in good health and was quite well on the night of the blitz.

I know that Mr Wright, who was one of the firewatchers with my husband, was killed in the raid."

Statement of Stanley Andrews HOARE

"Prior to the Air Raid on Monday, 4th May last, I resided at 112 Sidwell Street, Exeter, which is at the corner of Verney Place, and I was one of the firewatchers who were allocated to the group which comprised Nos. 112-117, Sidwell Street and Nos. 1 and 2 Verney Place, but it was not my turn on the night of the 3rd-4th May. The firewatcher who was on duty all that night was Mr Wright, of the City Cycle Works and in addition Mr Northeast, of 115 Sidwell Street and Mr Walter Henry Clarke of 14 Strongs Cottages, reported when the alert sounded.

When the alert sounded that morning I dressed and went outside my house where the other three firewatchers were standing. We all remained together for a few minutes and then Mr Wright and Mr Northeast left to see to their own premises and I know that in the course of the raid they were both killed.

I remained in my doorway with Mr Clarke for a further few minutes and during that time two high explosive bombs dropped somewhere nearby and we both ducked. Fires were burning by then and Mr Clarke said: 'I am going to see where the missus is' and I said to him: 'Alright, look out for yourself'. He then left me and went towards his home and I remained in my porch.

Some minutes after Mr Clarke left me a bomb fell somewhere very near and I ducked but the blast of it blew off my spectacles and steel helmet and ripped my over-coat right up the back and wrenched out the buttons. I am of the opinion that this was the bomb which demolished the surface shelter in Sidwell Street as I noticed shortly afterwards that the shelter had been destroyed and I consider that possibly it was the one which killed Mr Clarke. I cannot say just how soon it was that this bomb fell after Mr Clarke left me but it was

a matter of a few minutes.

I did not see Clarke again during the raid and I have not seen him since or received any information which would suggest that he is still alive."

Statement of Reginald Richard CORNISH:

"On Monday, 4th May, 1942, during the air raid I had been fighting fires in the Lions Holt district and at about the time when the 'raiders passed' sounded, some-one called me by name and asked me to come to St. Sidwells Avenue and help with the rescue work.

On going there I commenced helping with the rescue work when somebody told me that there was a body on the footpath. This body was covered up and was on the edge of the footpath outside some demolished houses about four or five houses down on the left hand side.

I uncovered the body and saw it consisted only of the head and torso, the arms and legs being missing. The head was intact except that it was dirty and by the light of my torch I immediately recognised it as that of Monty Scobie, a greengrocer, who resided at St. Sidwells Avenue. I have known Scobie for several years, having met him in the course of business on many occasions and I was on friendly terms with him. I knew that his teeth, all of which were his own, were rather large and I opened the mouth of the body and looked at the teeth and saw that they were identical with Scobie's. I also put my pencil in the mouth and found that there was no false teeth in the mouth. The hair on the body was dark and identical with Scobie but I was quite positive without having to look at the teeth or hair that the head was that of Scobie and I was so certain that when I returned home I told my wife and other people that he had been killed.

After I had examined the body I put some bricks around it and some boards across the top in order to protect it and it was still there when dawn was breaking and when a squad of soldiers arrived to take charge."

Statement of Frank Stephen BELCHER:

"On Monday, 4th May last during the air raid I was at home with my wife who was ill in bed, and when the 'Raiders Passed' sounded I went to St. Sidwells Avenue to notify my son-in-law and daughter that we were alright. They resided at No. 7 St. Sidwells Avenue and when I arrived there I saw that a bomb had dropped in the middle of the road and had demolished three or four houses on each side. My son-in-law's house was one of those which had been demolished and Mr Scobie's house, No. 9 St. Sidwells Avenue, was another.

I succeeded in rescuing my daughter and grand-daughter from a Morrison shelter at the rear and then endeavoured to extricate my son-in-law who was pinned by the legs in the front passage. In doing this I knelt on what I thought to be sandbags but when dawn arose I saw that it was the head and torso of a man's body. When I looked at the face I saw that that it appeared to be intact but was covered with mortar dust. It struck me then that it was the face of Monty Scobie of 9 St. Sidwells Avenue, who was well known to me. On examining the top of the head I saw that there was a hole in it and the contents appeared to have been blown out. There was some clothing adhering to the body and it was of a fairly light colour.

Shortly afterwards I found a foot which had been severed below the ankle and also the charred remains of the tibia and fibula bones of the leg. On the remains of the foot was the remains of a light blue sock and it was partly contained in a slipper. I cannot describe the slipper as it was covered with dirt and fell off when I picked up the foot.

The head and torso were outside No. 7 St. Sidwells Avenue, which is on the left hand side going down, and was on the pavement. The other remains were about five yards above on the same side. Later that morning I saw some soldiers removing the head and trunk but I know that the foot and leg bones were not taken away until some days later as they had been placed in a small iron bath in the wreckage and forgotten.

At about mid-day on the following day I went to the public Mortuary at Rack Street to identify the body of my son-in-law. I told the Superintendent where he was killed and he told me that he had got some remains from St. Sidwells Avenue in a sack. I did not see these remains as I knew that my son-in-law's body was intact but I am of the opinion that it consisted of the head and torso which I saw in St. Sidwell's Avenue.

I am certain in my own mind that the head and torso on which I had knelt were that of Mr Scobie. I knew all the other firewatchers and I am sure that the face did not belong to any of them."

Cornwall Constabulary.
Mrs Edith Mona Scobie, age 35 years, now residing at "Penrowan" New Road, Boscastle, Cornwall, states:
"On the night of the 3rd/4th May, 1942, I was in my house at 9 St. Sidwells Avenue, Exeter. The following named persons were also in my house that night. My husband, greengrocer; my son; my brother-in-law and his wife, and their daughter; my sister and her husband; and a Mrs Holden who was privately evacuated with me making a total of nine persons in all.

We had all gone to bed when at about 2.30am 4th May, 1942, the Air Raid Warning sounded. I awoke and awakened my husband. While I was dressing my husband awakened the rest of the household. The women and children including myself went into a Morrison shelter in a down stairs room. My husband, as he always did on receipt of the Air Raid Warning, went down the Avenue to assist a Mr Hodge who is an invalid into his shelter. Mr Hodge, who is a newspaper haulage contractor, is now residing at East Grove Road, Exeter. Mr Hodge would not allow my husband to put him into his shelter because he did not think the raid would be very serious. My husband then left Mr Hodge. Mr Hodge personally told me this.

Meanwhile my brother and brother-in-law went out to the front of our house, where they saw that the house of Mr West, No. 5 St. Sidwells Avenue, was on fire. They returned to the room where we were in the shelter and asked me where the stirrup pump was kept. Just as I told them where the pump was kept the bomb dropped right out-side our front door. That bomb killed my brother and brother-in-law, and my sister Ivy who was in the shelter with me. It injured my sister Muriel and Mrs Holden, the two children and myself were the only persons un-injured.

Living next door to us were the relatives of a Mr Belcher of 45 Well Street, Exeter. After the raid was over Mr Belcher came down to see how his relatives were. He saw that the houses were down. He located his son-in-law buried under some debris. While Mr Belcher was kneeling down trying to release his son-in-law, he thought at first that he was kneeling on some sandbags but as daylight came in he saw that he was kneeling on the trunk and head of a dismembered man who he now swears was my husband. Later the same day, the 4th May, 1942, Mr Belcher was offered these same remains at the mortuary at Rack Street, Exeter, as the remains of his son-in-law. Belcher knew that the remains were not of his son-in-law and consequently refused them. Mr Belcher later at the same mortuary recovered the body of his son-in-law.

The same day, 4th May, 1942, my brother-in-law, Walter John Scobie, who was on leave from the Army, and whose home address is at 10 Leighton Terrace, Exeter, picked up a piece of check suiting just outside our house. I have that piece of suiting and it is identical with that worn by my husband on the night of the raid.

Mr William Doble of 5 St. Sidwells Ave, Mr Edward West of 8 St. Sidwells Ave, Mr Smale of 14 St. Sidwells Ave, Mr Eric Walters of St. Sidwells Ave and my husband always on hearing the air raid warning met outside our house and stayed there until the all clear, in order that could assist in fire fighting or in any other way. The remains of these other men were found in the immediate vicinity of our house, and as they were always together there is no doubt in my mind that the remains which Mr Belcher knelt on and had offered to him in the mortuary, were the remains of my husband."   (Signed) Mrs E.M. Scobie.

Witness - Henry R. Morcumb P.C.

Extracts from letter sent by Mr Belcher

"I arrived on the scene a few minutes after the All Clear went. I know you are prepared to be told anything, however gruesome, to be satisfied respecting what happened to your husband. Well, in the dark I was kneeling on what I thought was sandbags but when dawn arose I saw to my horror that it was the trunk and head of a dismembered body, and later I saw a foot with a piece of sock attached of a light bluey colour and a slipper on it, also the bones of the leg, skin bones with flesh burnt or blasted clean off, also when they were removing it one of them showed me a piece of check pattern cloth which they picked up beside it, and knowing that we were in a quandary as to who it was, they said if anybody knew the pattern of suit they would know who it is, and the information you gave me on your letter makes me feel positive that it was Monty, and my memory of the face that I saw makes me feel sure it was him. At first I queried if it was Brian, but positive proof is abundant that Brian was in or near your doorway when the bomb exploded, whereas the body that I knelt on, and which I think was Monty, was up a little above E's doorway. It certainly wasn't Mr W., as he had a small shallow head. My view of what really took place as the bomb was whistling down was this:

Monty was standing along the pavement outside the houses and was outside Mr W.'s bay window. He made a dive for safety and just failed to reach it and got the full blast of the bomb. The remains were removed by some soldiers and put in a bag, and that was the unidentified remains that were at Rack Street School from St Sidwells Avenue which was offered to me by Ex-Sgt. Wise, a Police pensioner who was in charge of the bodies."

Signed by Mr & Mrs Belcher.

Statement of Albert William LAMACRAFT:

"Prior to the air raid on the morning of Monday, 4th May last I resided at No. 11 St. Sidwells Avenue, Exeter, and when the 'Alert' sounded that night I went out into the street to firewatch with Mr Monty Scobie of 9 St. Sidwells Avenue; two male relations of his; Mr Doble of 7 St. Sidwells Avenue; Mr West of No. 5 and Mr Smale of No. 16.

We all remained in the street for about half an hour and sheltered as far as possible in the doorways, most of us in the doorways of our own homes.

I then went indoors to see if my wife and daughter were alright in the Morrison shelter and my wife asked to go into the shelter. I remarked that I should go out with the men again when my wife shouted that a bomb was coming. I clambered into

the shelter and had only just done so when there was an explosion and the house fell in on top of us. This bomb must have fallen in less than a minute after I had left the street to go and see my wife and daughter.

When I got outside I saw that there was a crater in the middle of the road about 10 yards above my house and Nos. 5, 7, 9 and 11, St. Sidwells Avenue were completely demolished. I afterwards learned that I was the only one of the six fire watchers to be left alive.

General Office. 19th May, 1942.
To the Chief Constable:
Sir,

Police Constables James DRAPER No. 51, Norman TARR No. 80, and Police War Reserve SPROSEN No. 164.
I have been instructed by Detective Inspector Rowland to submit a report on the fire in Dinham Road in which P.C. Tarr and myself were engaged in the early hours of Monday, 4th May, 1942. As I have explained to Mr Rowland, whatever duty was performed at that fire by P.C. Tarr and myself it was after the raid, and I feel that the excellent conduct of the above named men in fighting fires in Paris Street during the raid should be brought to your notice.

On the night of the 3rd/4th May, 1942, I was on duty in Paris Street at the Incident Post, and the above named men and P.W.R. Dyer were stationed at various points. When the alert sounded Dyer, who was just finishing supper, resumed his point at Eaton Place and I did not see him again during the night, my duties keeping me at the top of Paris Street.

P.W.R. Sprosen came into the post for his tin hat and was quickly followed by P.C.s Draper and Tarr. By this time we could hear machine gunning overhead and we went into the street and stood under buildings. Within a few minutes we could hear the sickly swish of incendiaries falling, and looking towards Newtown we saw numerous fires and could hear the reports of incendiaries bursting. Within a moment the bombs were falling near us and fires commenced in Drake's, Freeth's and Parker's shops.

P.C.s Draper, Tarr and P.W.R. Sprosen formed themselves into a stirrup pump team and immediately commenced work on Freeth's front. The bomb had lodged behind the facia board on top of the front window, and the facia board was soon well alight, and was only extinguished by hard fighting over a period of about five minutes. During this period the bomb burst and sprayed molten metal down on the fighters, fortunately without injury. By this time H.E.s were falling in the locality and I was amazed at the pluck with which they stuck to their job.

When this fire was extinguished they commenced work on Drake's shop front, and by this time enemy planes overhead could be heard diving; at this time I was getting out a bath of water in Thompson's restaurant and after the bomb explosions, which did not seem far away, I was surprised to see these fellows still fighting the fire, which they quite successfully put out. I had sandbagged the bomb in Parker's shop window and beat out some curtains which had caught alight. There was an explosion shortly afterwards, and the sandbag was blown out and the shop front was in danger of becoming ignited again when they finished this off with the stirrup pump.

The fire immediately around us had been successfully dealt with, and by this time we could hear more incendiaries falling and exploding in the locality. We saw a number of bombs in Eastgate and immediately ran there. Outside Fearis' store there were quite half a dozen burning fiercely and throwing up the surrounding buildings in bold relief. These men, armed with sandbags, set about extinguishing the bombs, and as each bomb exploded and skidded along the road, it was amazing that there were no injuries. During the fighting of these bombs enemy planes were overhead, and one which was heard diving sent everyone face downwards under the canopy outside the store. The extinguishing of these bombs was resumed immediately afterwards.

These bombs extinguished, Tarr and Sprosen accompanied me up Sidwell Street towards a huge fire which was blazing near St. Sidwell's Church (Hunt's bakeries). However, we were only about 100 yards up Sidwell Street when we were driven into Hammett's passageway by the sound of another plane diving, and this was followed by H.E.s falling nearby. I decided at this point that the Fire Brigade should be informed of this fire, and turned about to return to the Incident Post. However, near the top of Paris Street, another plane was heard diving and we ran for cover and got separated. After these H.E.s had fallen I got back to the Incident Post, only to find that all communication was out.

Draper had left me at the top of Paris Street to investigate a fire at the back of Freeth's shop with a firewatcher named Joe Leat, Friar's Walk. We had been separated about fifteen minutes when I was relieved to see him come down Paris Street. He reported a huge fire in the Gas Company's Office, which was now being attacked by the Fire Brigade. He and Joe Leat had been throwing buckets of water over the wall until it appeared useless. I have verified this with Leat.

The bombing about this time became very intense, and each time that we intended to scout around we were compelled to take cover; during a quiet period we were about to remove our gear from the Post when the all clear sounded.

There was no fire in the immediate vicinity. In the circumstances I decided to leave the Incident Post and find more pressing duty. In London Inn Square there were some tremendous fires by this time, but the Fire Brigade were at work. I decided to leave Draper in Northernhay Place, where there was a huge crowd of people, and after we had marshalled everybody into the car park I left him on duty making sure there was no one in the houses. When I left he was trying to get the Brigade to play hoses on Northernhay Place and save that block of buildings which was in danger of being caught alight by the Plaza.

I made contact with Headquarters, where I found P.C. Tarr, and he assured me Sprosen was alright. We left Headquarters and went into North Street, where we saw a huge fire in Dinham Road, and seeing it was dwelling houses on fire we immediately went there. Occupiers were pulling out their furniture and after making sure that all were out of the buildings we turned our attention to organising a fire party. S.C. Bowden was on the Iron Bridge keeping back the crowd. On our arrival a stand-pipe had been obtained from St. Annes' Brewery, and this was connected with the main water supply from a hydrant.

About eight men volunteered to help, including a soldier and an R.A.F. man whose names I did not take. We were able to get two more stand-pipes and about six lengths of hose from the Blind Institution, and soon we had three jets of water on the blaze. Our efforts were concentrated on saving a block of dwelling houses which were in grave danger from the fire in the first six houses in Dinham Road, and also from the fire burning in Wippell's Yard at the rear. Hoses were played continually on all wood parts and at times fire did break out in windows and eaves of the property we were trying to save, but through the untiring work of the team who seemed to have unbounded energy and courage, the main block of houses was saved.

P.C. Tarr and I left there about 6 a.m., when it was obvious the fire would not spread any further and was damped down.

It was about this time that Tarr heard that his own home had been demolished by a direct hit. I told him to go home at once and see if there was anything he could do, but only after considerable persuasion could I get him to go home.

May I say in conclusion that the men I have mentioned showed remarkable coolness and disregard for danger during the actual air raid, and I am sure that had it not been for big fires near Paris Street, their efforts in the early stage of the raid would have saved valuable property. I cannot speak too highly of their conduct under the most trying conditions.
(Signed) L.W. MOORE, Police Sergeant No. 4. Examined and submitted. (Sgd.) R.P. Rowland. Detective Inspector.

Criminal Investigation Department, 21st May, 1942.
To the Superintendent
Sir,

Incendiaries dropped on City from Enemy Aircraft morning 4th May, 1942.
I was on duty in Paris Street at the time the alert sounded on the morning of 4th May, 1942. I was accompanied by P.C. Draper, P.C. Tarr and P.W.R. Sprosen.

My first recollection of incendiaries falling was when I heard a swishing sound and on looking towards Newtown and Heavitree Hill I saw numerous fires breaking out. There was a tremendous flow of magnesium light and countless explosions which were making a "Popping" sound.

My first impression was that these incendiaries were exploding in the air over the target. On recollection I felt satisfied that the bombs were igniting on contact causing the series of explosions which could be heard and which rather sounded as though the bombs were exploding in the air.

If these bombs had been exploding, or igniting as they travelled downwards, I feel sure that we should have seen the bombs earlier that fell in Paris Street, as it was we did not see the bombs which fell near us until they had made a report and burst into flame. Further, I think we should have been warned of the bombs falling in Eastgate in the same manner, but here again not until the incendiaries had actually made contact with the ground, were we aware that they had fallen.

Police-sergeant No. 4.

Exeter City Police
Time - 8am Date - 22nd May 1942
Re. Incendiary bombs

To the Chief Constable.
I beg to report that during the raid on Exeter on Monday May 4th 1942 I was at Livery Dole when a large number of incendiary bombs fell in that locality, most of which ignited.

With several wardens I gathered sandbags to smother them but on approaching the bombs there were minor explosions which caused burning fragments of the incendiary to be scattered several yards and the body of the bomb also moved several feet as a result of the explosion.

I do not know how many explosions occurred in the majority of bombs but one particular bomb which I tackled near a house exploded twice.

Several bombs which did not ignite were coloured red and green and I believe one was all green; the tail fins were of the cog-wheel pattern. Warden Huxtable of Heavitree may be able to give more information than this as he remained in that vicinity.   P.C. Evans. P.C. 43.

Statement of William Charles Sydney HILL:

"I am senior Air Raid Warden of Sector 51, Group 'E' and after the sirens had sounded on the early morning of Monday, 4th May last I went out in the lane at the back of my house. I was there when a high explosive

bomb fell further up Monks Road and on going to the scene I saw that No. 178 Monks Road, together with the house on each side, were totally destroyed and from the position of the crater it was apparent that No. 178 had received a direct hit.

I knew Mr Gale and his family and I searched for their bodies in the vicinity and also searched the bottom of the crater but I could not find any. Later however, when making a search of the district, I recovered a piece of a skull and a small portion of a Morrison shelter in the back garden of 223 Monks Road. I also recovered several small pieces of flesh from the back lane between Monks Road and Pinhoe Road.

When it was daylight a man came to me and handed me several medals which I saw bore the name of Mr Gale. I asked him where he had got them and he told me that he had found them outside his house in Pamela Road. I also know that Mr Gale's overcoat and tunic, together with some remains of furniture, were blown into Pinhoe Road.

On the same morning as the raid I found the piece of the Morrison shelter (produced) wedged against the surface shelter in the roadway one house below 178 Monks Road. The piece of the Morrison shelter which I found must have been part of Mr Gale's as this was the only shelter which was destroyed in any of the houses.

When I first went there I saw that there was nothing left at all of Mr Gale's house and I could not even find a complete piece of furniture."

Statement of Fred MILES

"Prior to the 4th May, 1942, I resided at 23 Elmside, Exeter, with my wife and my three children. My mother-in-law also resided with us. My brother-in-law, Percy Gale, resided at 178 Monks Road, together with his wife and his two children.

I am a member of the A.R.P. Rescue

Party, and I was on duty at 7pm on the night of Sunday, 3rd May, and I therefore took my wife, children and mother-in-law to spend the night with Mr. Gale at 178 Monks Road, as they were frightened of the sirens when I was away from home.

We arrived at 178 Monks Road, at about 7.15pm and Mr and Mrs Gale and their two children were at home. I then went on my way to work and returned for a few minutes at about 10pm, when all the family were in the dining room with the exception of Garry Gale who had gone to bed.

I later saw that the house had been totally destroyed in the air raid which took place in the early morning of the 4th May, and the only persons who I know to be left alive are my wife, and two of my children, Margaret and Ian. My wife told me that Margaret, Ian and herself left the house after the 'Alert' sounded. Since the air raid I have not seen or heard of my mother-in-law, my daughter, or Mr and Mrs Gale and their two children, and I have no reason to believe that they are still alive.

My mother-in-law and daughter enjoyed good health, and Mr and Mrs Gale and their two children also enjoyed good health, but Garry Gale was unable to speak in a normal manner. They were all in their usual state of health when I last saw them at 10pm on the 3rd May."

Further statement of Fred Miles:

"Since the air raid on the morning of the 4th May last my wife, who is now residing at 52 Brooke Street, Bampton, has told me that all the family were in the house when the siren sounded the 'Alert', and Mr Gale then went out in the back garden to see what was happening, as he usually did this when the sirens sounded.

My wife said she felt that she could not remain in the house, and therefore left with my two youngest children, Margaret and Ian, and went up to Stoke Hill, where I found her at about 8am the same morning.

She then told me that when she left the house the family were in the Morrison shelter, except for Garry Gale, who was in bed upstairs, and Mr Gale who was in the back garden and who told her not to go away. She had only gone a short distance beyond Cloister Road when she heard a bomb fall farther down Monks Road, but did not know that Mr Gale's house had been hit.

My wife is now seriously ill and can barely speak, and there is little hope of her recovery. In addition she has been affected mentally as a result of the shock.

I was one of the Rescue Party which was sent to Monks Road after the bombs had fallen there, and I saw that Mr Gale's house and the houses on either side were totally destroyed, and there was a large crater where 178 Monks Road, used to stand. I saw clothing which belonged to members of the family, and other articles which belonged in the house scattered about in Monks Road, and I was also handed two of Mr Gale's tunics which had been blown into the houses in Pinhoe Road.

Three or four days after the raid I found an angle iron and a large part of the top plate of a Morrison shelter in the allotments between Monks Road and the brickworks. The piece of the top plate was badly buckled and a part of the mattress was entangled in it. These parts must have belonged to Mr Gale's shelter, as the shelter in the house below was blown across the road intact and the shelter in the house above was still in the wreckage, and was still intact. It would appear, therefore, that the Morrison shelter in Mr. Gale's house must have almost received a direct hit.

This statement has been read over to me and is true." (Signed) F. MILES.
Statement taken and signatures witnessed by me: (Signed) JOHN A. BERRY. Detective Constable. Evidence also given by Emily Delia Miles.

16 St. Annes Rd, Exeter.
2.15pm 29th May, 1942.

Statement of Miss Edith Constance Dorothy BERRY:

"Until Monday, 4th May last, I resided at 16 St. Annes Road with my mother, my sister and my brother. My father died about thirteen years ago.

When the alert sounded at about 1.40am on Monday, 4th May, we were all at home and my sister and brother were in bed. Also with us was a friend of the family Mr Ernest Law of 40 Widgery Road.

We remained in the house for some time until my mother said that she felt unwell and wanted to go to the shelter near Polsloe Bridge. We agreed to go there, and went up Abbey Road and down the back lane between Pinhoe Road and Monks Road. Just as we were turning into the back lane my mother fell down, but we picked her up, and she said she was alright and could go on.

When we were part way down the lane we came to some debris which Mr Law, my brother and I climbed over, and proceeded towards Cloister Road. When we had almost reached Cloister Road I called back and told my mother and sister to come on, and my sister replied: 'I am coming but Mummy can't'. Just then I heard the sound of machine gunning followed by explosions, and we lay down beneath a wall and were partly covered by debris. We got out and went on to the shelter where my brother and I remained and Mr Law went back to try and find my mother and sister.

Since then I have not seen my mother or sister, and I have received no information which would suggest that they are still alive. My mother enjoyed fairly good health, but she was very frightened when she heard the sirens. My sister also enjoyed good health.

When we left home on the morning of the 4th May, my mother was wearing a blue fur-collar coat, navy blue spotted frock and blue suede shoes. She had a gold ring with a white stone which I believe she wore on her right hand. My sister also was wearing her pyjamas with a green dressing gown and a blue overcoat. She had a small black and white badge with 'R.C.' thereon pinned in her coat. She was also wearing a pair of high heeled white shoes and had a signet ring on one of her right fingers, and a silver ring with a blue stone on the left hand. The signet ring was stamped with the letters 'J.B.'."

Statement of Ernest Charles John LAW:

"I have read the statement made by Miss Edith Constance Berry, and I agree with and can confirm what she has said.

After we reached the shelter at Polsloe Bridge, I left Miss Berry and her brother there, and I returned to the Lane between Monks Road and Pinhoe Road to try and find Mrs Berry and her daughter Mary, but I was unable to find any trace of them.

At 5pm on Wednesday, 6th May last, I went to the public mortuary in Rack Street, and I was shown all the unidentified bodies. I was unable, however, to identify any bodies as Mrs Berry or Miss Mary Josephine Berry.

When we were walking down the back lane between Abbey Road and Cloister Road, there was a certain amount of debris there, but no houses had been knocked down in Pinhoe Road or Monks Road before the time we were buried beneath debris by a bomb or bombs which had fallen nearby. When I returned there in the daylight, I found that houses in Pinhoe Road and Monks Road had been demolished and a large amount of debris was strewn across the lane.

THE EXETER CITY & COUNTY BOMB CENSUS

Time of attack 0145-0238. Date 3-4/5/42.

A Bomb No. & Time	B Size of Crater	C Nature of Soil	D Size of Bomb	E Damage (to include distance from centre of crater)
1. 0240	41x14	Soft earth	250	Sidwell St.Bomb fell in churchyard,28' from Church Lane.119' from houses in Church Lane & 47' from Church.Fragment found.
2. 0145		Not known	UXB	Leighton St.Bomb fell 21' from corner of Leighton Rd & St James Rd.
3. 0145		Not known	UXB	Wells St.Bomb fell in garden back of Wells St/Oxford St.
4. 0200	18x4	4" conc. road	500	St. Sidwells Ave.Bomb fell in centre road,120' fromWells St.15A.2B.4C.60D.Fragment found.17 fatal casualties.
5. 0243			250	St. Sidwells Lane.Direct hit on St. Sidwell Church.Water mains gone.
6. 19x3		Soft earth	50	St James Rd.Bomb fell garden 20' frm house A0.B0.C0.Dl.
7. 0230	60x20		1000	Culverland Rd.Bomb fell 50 yds from junction of Union Rd & Culverland Rd A4.B0.C6.D40.Fragment found.
8. 0035	28x8	Soft earth	250	Prospect Pk.Bomb fell rear of houses. A0.B0.C.14.D.10. Water mains gone.
9.		Not known	UXB	Union Rd.Bomb fell in allotments, 25 yds from Union Rd. 21 yds from Culverland Rd.
10. 0230	18x4	Not known	250	Higher Kings Ave.Bomb fell in garden,20 yds from Penns Rd. A2.B0.C3.D6.
11. 0230	28x5	Soft soil	250	Penns Pk.Bomb fell 20' rear of building.40' from Kings Ave A1.B0.C0.D14, water main fractured fragment found.
12. 0200	24x6	Clay	250	County Cricket Ground.Direct hit on Lewis gun-site. A1.B0.C0.D2. 2 males killed.
13. 0215	23x5	Clay	250	West Ave.Bomb fell in garden 20' from house. A1.Bl. C0. D4.Fragment found.Water main gone.
14. 0215			250	West Ave.Direct hit on house.A2.B2.Cl.D12.4 mixed fatal casualties.
15.	17x4	Tarmac clay	250	West Ave.Bomb fell in road 20' from house.A1.B3.C2. D10.Water main fractured.
16.			250	West Ave.Direct hit on house. A2.B3.C2.D8.Water main fractured. House fell on Morrison shelter, 0 casualties.
17. 0300	2x2	Soft clay	UXB	Northernhay Pk. Bomb fell 15 yds. from New North Rd. 25 yds from 4 Main Static Tanks.
18. 0200	40x20	Clay	500	New North Rd. Direct hit on Station Yd, 36 yds from bridge & platform 10 yds from railway lines. No damage. Fragment found.
19. 0200	Filled in 40x	Hard rubble	500	Howell Rd.Direct hit on railway lines 50' of railway lines,lifted up 3 lines. 25' from Bridge Parapit. Damaged Main Sewer- burst. Fragment found.
20.		Soft soil	500 UXB	Rougemont Gdns.Fell on bank of Castle wall 150' frm County Council Offices.Bomb base found.A0.B1.C0.D0.
21.	46x8		500	Bedford Circ.Fell base of bank,completely demolishing Savings Bank,& part of Atherin Chambers. (These are 4 storey buildings). Fire, no damage to shelter 100' away.
22.			USB 250	Bedford Circ.Bomb fell back of building 100yds from junction - fire.

A	B	C	D	E
23.			500	Bedford Circ.Direct hit on Drill Hall 4th Bat.Devonshire Regt 43yds South-hay West Drill Hall destroyed, severe damages to surrounding property. Fire. Fragment found. 2 fatal male casualties.
24. 0345			250	Southernhay West.Direct hit No.31 150yds frm junction of Bedford Circ.5 storey building completely demolished, others severely damaged. Fire.Fragment found.
25. 0210			250	High St.Fell in St Johns Alley, Bedford Garage outside County Court Offices. Blast to garage, partly demol., St John Chambers demol. Fire, garage 75 yds from High St
26.			500	High St.Direct hit on Boat shop 81' from corner of Bedford St. 3 shops demol., blast damage to Bank and St. Lawrence Church Gas electric and water off. Fire.
27. 0245			250	Cathedral Yard. Direct hit on Kalend, two buildings destroyed, damage to buildings around.
28. 0330			500	Exeter Cathedral.Direct hit St James Chapel, Cathedral. Completely demol. damage to 2 flying buttresses, and damage to South Choir. Severe blast to Cathedral.
29. 0215	22x5'6"	Clay	250	Magdalen St.Fell in orchard in rear of 40 Dedmarsh Rd. 140' frm Magdalen Rd. Blast damage to surrounding property.
30. 0250			250	Magdalen Rd.Direct hit on house, demolished. Severe damage to Alms Houses and surrounding property.
31.			250	Magdalen Rd.Direct hit on Messrs. Normans Stores. 281' frm College Rd. Blast damage to surrounding property.
32.			UXB 50	65 Magdalen Rd.Bomb fell in back kitchen of shop. DISCREDITED.
33. 0245	34x6	Soft earth	PM	Rivermead Rd.Fell 20' frm roadway. Fragment found. A6.B0.C46.D50.Concrete shelter collapsed 5' crater edge.
34. 0245			UXB 500	Feltrim Ave.Bomb fell north side of No. 38. glancing No. 36, of Feltrim Ave. Water leaking.
35.			UXB	Bungalow Lane.Bomb fell on sewerage plant.
36	36xl5	Soft earth	500	Bungalow Lane. Bomb fell in Allotments. No damage.
37			250	St. Davids Hill.Direct hit on No91. Fire near railway. A1. B2. C2. D10.
38. 0230	Filled 19x 250			St. Davids Hill.Direct hit on wall & tree 75 yds Howell Rd.C damage to low building 20yds away fragment found.
39. 0230	18x4	Tarmac & clay	250	Red Cow Lane. Bomb fell in roadway, 20 yd. from level crossing in front of shop. A1. B3. C5. D5. Fragment found near Railway Station.
40. 0230	49x12	Earth	PM	Red Cow Village. Direct hit on shelter 10 yds from railway lines. Damage to signal box 30 yds away. 8 male fatal casualties.
41. 0230	39x12	Earth	PM	Red Cow Village. Bomb fell 10 yds from Railway Line, 160 yds from bomb No 40. Railway line pulled up, junction of New North Road and lower Cowley Rd. A0. B0. C to petrol stores. D37. Fragment 6und.
42. 0250	70x25	Soft earth	1000	Doctor Barnados Home.Bomb fell 15 ft. from building, 20 ft. from Road. A0.Bl.C0.D4. Brick surface shelter on edge of crater, walls cracked.
43. 0230	34x6	Clay	500	College Road.Bomb fell in centre of road, 3 trees uprooted. Blast damage to houses in College Rd.
44.			500	The Rachield Field. Spiar Rd.Direct hit on house, 402' from junction of Barnfield Hill. The Rachield demolished, blast damage to surrounding property.

A	B	C	D	E
45.	17x2'6"	Clay	250	Spicer Rd. Bomb fell on boundary wall, 321' from Barnfield Hill, severe blast damage to surroundin property.
46.	38xl2	Clay	500	Nearbourn Spiar Rd.Near miss opposite No45. Leabourn demolished. Severe blast to surrounding property. Fire.
47. 0207	36xl-	Clay	250	Maynard School Barnfield Hill. Bomb fell on tennis court, part R.C. retaining wall demolished. Blast damage to windows and roof of school.
48. 0207	13x2'6"	Clay	250	Maynard School.Bomb fell in ground in front of building. Severe blast damage to school, also slight blast damage to houses on Barnfield Hill.
49. 0207	30x9	Clay	250	Maynard School.Bomb fell on tennis court, between boarding house and kitchen garden. Severe blast to boarding house and kitchen garden, and blast damage to surrounding property.
50.			500	North St.Direct hit on Gaumont Cinema. B. damage to rear of Cinema. C. damage to School, 100' from impact.
51. 0230	56xl5	Clay	Unknown	Fore St. Direcr hit on building 30 yds. from junction of South St.
52. 0230	14x12	9' rein. con	500	Dunsford Garden. Bomb fell in centre of road-way A2.B5.C6.D26.Water leakage. Fragment found. 5 people saved by Morrison Shelter.
53.			Unknown	Fore St. Direct hit on shop, 78 yds. from junction of North St. Building gutted by fire through l.Bs.
54.			Unknown	Fore St. Direct hit on Marks & Spencer's Stores, 60 yds. from North St. junction corner. Building gutted by fire through I.Bs.
55. 0145	41xl2'6"	Clay	500	St. Lukes College. Bomb fell in Sport's field, nr Raleigh Rd. Blast damage to surrounding property.
56. 0140			500	St. Lukes College.Direct hit on Swimming Bath. Severe damage to same. Fragment found.
57.			500? UXB	St. Lukes College. Fell in Sports field, junction of College Ave. and Magdalen Rd.
58. 0140			500	St. Lukes Lodge, Heavitree Rd. Direct hit Lodge demolished. Severe damage to surrounding property.
59. 0218		Tarmac	50	Dunsford Rd.Fell side of road on pathway, 100' frm No. 60 bomb at bottom of wall.Gas telephone etc. damaged.
60. 0218	l5x8	Clay & soft earth	50	Dunsford Rd.Bomb fell 10' from Reservoir wall 100' S.E. of bomb No. 61, Damage to wall.
61.	l5x8	Clay & soft earth	50	Dunsford Rd. Bomb fell 20' from S.E. of Reservoir wall. Fragment found. Water effected.
62. 0220	40x12	Soft clay	250	Dunsford Rd & Barley Lane.Bomb fell side of house in field. 150 yds. N.W. of Dunsford Rd. Fragment found.
63. 0230	Filled in 40x	Tarmac, clay	500	Kerswell Gardens.Bomb fell centre of road. Fragment found. A0.B3.C3.D7.Gas and water effected.
64. 0243	2'6" diam	Stone & clay.	UXB 500	Buddle Lane.Bomb fell at edge of Ladies Convenience 100' N. of Dunsford Rd. Removed by B.D.S. 515142.
65. 0230	38xl0	Earth & stone	250	Chamberlain Rd/Willeys Ave.Direct hit on 2 houses. A5.Bl.C8.D30.Morrison Shelter in No.2 Chamberlain Rd. 5 people uninjured. 3 mixed fatal casualties.
66. 0230	35xl0	Earth & stone	250	Willeys Ave/Water Lane.Bomb fell on corner of junction. No damage.
67. 0235	38x7	6" con. s/s clay	500	Willeys Ave.Bomb fell in yard 27' frm rd. Gas affected. Near Railway and Gasworks. Fragment found.
68. 0230	53x20	Clay	1000	Gas Works, Willeys Ave.Bomb fell 60 yrds. from Water Lane & 70yds from Railway Fragment found. 4 trucks flung off rails.

A	B	C	D	E
69. 0230	21x5	8" con., s/s clay	500	Gas Works. Struck reinforced concrete pile on side of gasometer. Gasometer caught fire and wrecked. Fragment found.
70. 0230		Stone	500	Gas Works. Bomb fell on S. edge of canal 100 yds. from bomb No. 69. No damage.
71. 0230	34x8	Clay	250	Elmside Close.Fell in garden of No5. Static water tank completely demol. 20' frm Elmside. Severe blast surrounding buildings.A2.B0.C0.D30. Gas effected.Fragment found. Surface shelter 30yds away undamaged.
72.0230	Filled in 16x		500	Clifton Rd. Direct hit corner shop, junction of Sandford & Clifton Rd. A.7. B. fire obliterated any evidence of any blast. C & D. not known. Fire.
73.			500	Clifton St. Direct hit on 4 houses. A4.B2.C&D unknown. Fire. Fragment found. Concrete shelter 50' away D. damage.
74. 0230			500 UXB	Willeys Ave.Fell foot of roadway embankment 40yds frm end of Welcome St. 5oyds from Willeys Ave. (removed) Fin found.
75. 0230		Stones	500 UXB	Wdleys Ave.Centre of rail track on main Plymouth Line. Fragment found removed.
76. 0230	9x2 4'	concrete	500	Marsh Barton Lane.On cattle unloading platform, 30' from Lane. 40 yds from main line. Fragment found.
77. 0230	50x12	Soft garden	500	Cattle Mkt. SE corner of allotments 60 yds W of No 76.
78. 0230	40x10	8" rein. con	500	King Henry Rd.Centre and end of road. Water affected.
79. 0230	32xl0	Soft earth	250	Topsham Rd.Centre of cornfield S.E. of bomb No. 78.
80. 0230	18x4	Clay	50	Topsham Rd.Bomb fell rear of Ellards Close. 50' W. of No. 79 bomb. Concrete shelter at rear of garden blasted.
81. 0230	18x4	Clay	50	Ellards Close.Repeat No. 80. bomb.
82. 0230		Clay	UXB 50	43 East Ave.Bomb fell through front of house & buried between front room and kitchen. House 25 yds. from junction of North Ave.
83. 0230		Clay	UXB 50	East Avenue.Fell in garden 15' from back of house opp. junction of North Ave. Fragment found.
84. 0155	20x5	Clay	50	Lower Ave.Fell in gardens of No20/18 Lower Ave. 28' from house. No damage. Fragment found. Gas electric etc. affected.
85. 0230	8'		UXB 50	Ladysmith Rd.Fell through front window at top of house landed tower room floor. 45 ft. from junction of Lower Avenue.
86. 0230		Tarmac	UXB 50	77 Ladysmith Rd. Middle of road opposite house and school gates. 90 ft. from Lower Avenue.
87. 0155		9" rein. con	250	Ladysmith Infant School.Direct hit on West End. 231 ft. from Ladysmith Rd. 80 ft. to back of Lower Avenue. A. to school. B0.C0.D0. Fire. Gas Elec. etc.
88.18x3		Heavy clay	50	Ladysmith.In playing Fields. 110 ft. from Polsloe Rd - 35 ft. to unnamed lane.
89. 0230			250	Polsloe Rd.Direct on house. 71 ft. from Middle of road 280 ft to middle of Park Rd.Al.B0.C0.D3.Water & Gas affected. Killed. I female, I child.
90. 0236	27x8	Clay	250	South Avenue.Between houses 48 ft. to middle of Ave 43 ft East Av. A2.B4.C6.D40. Water, electric and gas. Fragments found.
91.	l5x6	Clay	50	South Ave. 2 ft frm No 90, as 90 fragments found.
92. 0215	30xl5	Soft earth	250	Mulberry Hse Drive, Fore Street.Bomb fell 75 yards up the drive A0.B0.C0.D2.Fragmentsfound.
93.	4' diam	Soft earth	UXB 500	Clifton Road.Bomb fell back St Matthews Church. 60 ft. from road.

A	B	C	D	E
94. 0200	Scooped	Soft earth	50	Belmont Rd.Direct hit on bank of disused brick works.
95	17x filled in	Earth	50	Belmont Road. Fell in Park 50 yds. from gates.
96. 0230			UXB 50	Belmont Rd.Direct hit on rear of house 3 Jesmond Rd.
97. 0200			50	Belmont Park. Fell 2 ft. from Brick building 70 yds. from No. 95 bomb. A0.Bl.C0.D0.
98. 0200	l5x5	Soft earth	50	Belmont Pk. Fell 2 ft from wall 12ft high badly cracked. 40 ft. from nearest building- no damage. Fragment found.
99.			Not known.	185 Sidwell St. Direct hit on shop corner of Paris St. All evidence destroyed by fire.Water, Electric etc. effected.
100.	21x6	Soft earth	250	Sidwell Street.Fell in Builders yard rear of Sidwell St. & Paris St. Severe damage to Garages and Builders property and surrounding dwelling houses. Fire. Fragment found-Anderson shelter 14 yds. away undamaged.
101. 0200	26x6	Soft earth	250	Sidwell Street. Fell in gardens, 22 yds. from Bomb No. 100. Fragment found. Fire.
102.	27x6	Soft earth	250	Sidwell Street. Fell in gardens opposite side of road from "Odeon'Cinema, 40 yds. from Bomb No. 101. No further evidence because of Fire.
103. 0200			250	Sidwell Street. Direct hit on brick shelter in middle of road (15 yds. wide) size of shelter 25 yds.x3 yds.xlO ft. high. C. damage to Odeon Cinema (Direct Action).
104. 0230	80x70	Earth	250	Blackboy Rd.Fell in garden back of Grocers shop. 30 yds. off road in Salem Place. A6.B4.C10.D20.Church 15ft. from crater. B. damage.
105. 0210	7xS	Tarmac	50	Belmont Park.Fell on path leading from Park, 56 yds. from Blackboy Rd. 2 Brick Garages (lockup) destroyed. Bus depot, D. damage. 10ft. away
106.	l0x4	Clay	50	Exeter Cemetery. Fell in graveyard. 50 yds. from Hanover Road, 25 yds. from junction of Hanover Close. Fragment found.
107.	24x6	Clay	250	Exeter Cemetery. Fell in graveyard. 70 yds. Hanover Rd, 28 yds. from bomb No. 106.
108.	73x20	Clay	500	Exeter Cemet. Fell in graveyard.75yds behindchurch in Ladysmith Road. Fragment found.
109.	28x6	Soft earth	250	Bramdean Field. - Fell in field. 72 ft. from Shelton Place (corner) and Park Place 25 ft. from Goldsmith Street. A0.B0.C4.D60. Fragment found.
110.	30xl0	Tarmac, s/s earth	500	Barrack Rd. Fell on payment against wall on corner of Wonford. Fragment found & part of fin. Water fracture.
111.	30x12	Soft earth	250	Wonford House. Fell in garden, 25 yds from house, 200 yds. from No. 110.
112.	35x15	Soft earth	500	Lahill & Matford Road.Fell in gardens rear of Lahil Road. Al.B0.C0.D5. Fire.
113. 0200			250	North Street.Direct hit on house opposite junction of Oakfield Rd. A.l. B.nil. C.nil. D.30. Small type Morrison shelter with wire netting bent in. Fragment found.
114. 0200	24x6	Clay	250	Vicarage Meadow Nth Rd.Fell in field,75yds frm school. 100 yds from North Rd. A0.B0.C0.D20. Fragment found.
115. 0200	22'x3'6"	Rock & earth	250	Homefield Road.Fell on parting wall of orchard & Home Guard H.Q. approx. 60 ft. away and 50 ft. from junction of Oakfield Rd. Water. Elec. & Gas effected. Fragment found.
116. 0200	20x6	Partly rock	250	Homefield Rd.Fell base of large tree 60 ft from Catholic Church, 70 ft frm Blessed Sacrament House. Fragment found.

A		B	C	D	E
117.		24x6	Rocky	250	Fore St. (Heavitree Rd).Fell infront garden of Vicarage, 6yds from house, 5 ft from roadway, & 57yds from Salutary Mount. Al. Bl. C0. D12. Fragment found.
118. 01.45		22x filled	Pavement	250	Fore Street, (Heavitree Rd.) Fell on pavement 16 ft. from house. 50 yards from Regent St, A0. B2. C0. D10.
119. 0230				250	Roseland Ave. Direct hit on house 50 ft. from Park wall, and 70 yds. from corner. A3. B l. C0. D12. Fragment found. Gas, water etc. affected. Morrison shelter intact flooded with water. Casualties. Killed.2M. 1 F. 2C.
120.		44x15	Soft earth	250	Stanway Road.Fell in field 20 yds. from house, 90 yds. from Heavitree Gardens, sewer effected.
121. 0215		3ft dia	Soft earth	UXB	Stanway Rd. Fell in field 70 yds. from Heavitree Pleasure Ground, 67 yds from Stanway Rd.
122. 0200		21x3	Clay	500	Burnthouse Lane. Fell 12 ft. behind houses of Briar Crescent and Laburnam Rd. A6. B4. C0.D15. Water, Gas & Electric affected. Severe blast. Killed. 1 male.
123. 0200		24x4	Clay		Burnthouse Lane. Fell behind Shakespeare Av. 12 ft from houses. A6.B2.C0.D14. Fragment found, severe blast. Killed 1 Male.
124.		3ft dia	Clay	500 UXB	Pennsylvania Rd.Fell rear garden in garden of first house in road. 7 yds. from road.
125. 0230		35x20	Clay	250	Town Barracks. Howell Rd.Fell on road in barracks, C. damage to barrack block. Fragment found.
126.		44xl8	Hard clay	250	Howell Rd. Direct hit on staff bungalow in centre of barracks. Al.B0.C0.D. to barrack block.
127.		4" tarmac		500 UXB	Howell Rd. In roadway of Barracks 120yds from No126.
128.		61x with water		250	Howell Rd.Fell in reservoir 6" concrete and brick. A0. B to Water Works Building. C. damage to surrounding property. D.nil.
129.		24x with water 6" con		250	Howell Rd.Fell on covered-in Reservoir with brick supports. Houses 50 yds. away A0. B0. C16. D0.
130.		6ft dia	Clay	USB	Prince of Wales Rd.Fell in open field. 100 yds from roadway.
131.	0230	48x15	Stone & rubble	500	Prince of Wales Rd.Fell in open field. 90 ft. from Washington Singer Laboratories. 200 yds. from road.
132.	0230	40x15	Earth & rubble	500	Prince of Wales Rd. Fell in open field 200 yds. from bend of road. Near to Washington Singer Laboratories.
133.	0225	20x12	Concrete	250	Pinhoe Rd.Fell in centre of road. 28 ft. from houses. 39 ft. from corner of Cloister Road. A0.B4.C5.D20 Gas, Water & Electric affected.
134. 0225		31x8	Concrete	250	Pamela Road. Fell on pavement. 6 yds. from house. 75 yds. from Pinhoe Road. Fragments. A.nil. B.3. C.6. D.14. Water, Gas and Electric damaged.
135.		22x6	Soft	250	Tarbert Rd.Fell front of house 18ft frm house 57yd frm Fulford Rd. Gas Elec & Water damage. Fragments fnd. Al.B5.C9.D15. Complete house on Morrison Shelter.
136.					50 Morgan Sq. Paris Street.Direct hit on house glancing outer wall. A2. Bl. C0. D0. Fire.
137.		9x4	Hard clay	250	Prince of Wales Rd. Fell in wood at rear of Mardon Hall 100 ft. away 10ft. from pathway. D. damage.
138.		18x4	Clay	50	Great Duryard.Fell in open field 1 house 200 yds. away. D. damage.
139. 0210		34x6'6"	Clay, stone	250	Topsham Rd. Barracks. Fell in entrance of barracks in centre of road. 20ft from main road. A2. B0. C0. D0.
140. 1210		32xlO	Clay, stone	250	Topsham Road Barracks. Fell south end of sports field corner of Barrack Road and Wonford Road.

A	B	C	D	E
141.		Clay, stone	UXB 500	Topsham Road, Barracks. Fell in ground E.S.E. of No. 139 a distance of 50 yds. Fragment found.
142. 0145	29x12	Soft earth	250	Monks Rd. Direct hit 56yds from junction of Cloister Rd A3. B2. C5. D25. Morrison shelter lifted from crater 37ft and 4 ft upwards, and buckled up. Water, gas and electric etc. Fragment. 5 killed (mixed, no trace).
143. 0145	38x15	Soft earth	250	Monks Rd. Direct hit back of house 60yds frm junction Cloister Rd 20yds frm centre of Pinhoe Rd. Extensive damage in conjunction with 144 & 145. Fragment found. Gas, water etc.
144. 0145	24x8	Heavy clay	250	Pinhoe Rd. Fell in garden of 158 Pinhoe Rd 25ft from junction Cloister Rd. 60ft from centre of road to crater. Fragment. Morrison shelter buried 24ft frm crater.
145. 0230	34x15	Soft earth	250	Pinhoe Rd. Direct hit 138 Pinhoe Rd. 110ft from junction Wykes Rd. 45ft from centre road to crater. Morrison shelter blown 20yds over wall 6ft high to garden of Monk St. Second Morrison shelter on edge of crater. Water, gas, elec etc. Fragment. Killed 1 male, 1 female, 2 children. (2nd Mor.) (1 c. killed 3 injured).
146. 0230	40x12	Soft earth	250	Exmouth junction (Exeter). Fell in allotments 300 yds. from Railway. 600 yUs. from Stoke House. No damage.
147. 0230	40x12	Soft earth	250	Exmouth junction. (Exeter). Fell in open field 100yds from bomb. No146. 200yds from railway. No damage.
148. 0230	30xl 1'6	Clay	250	Exmouth jctn (Exeter). Fell in railway yard. 20yds of rails points & switches lifted up. D damage rail workshops.
149.	2ft diam	Clay	500 UXB	York Rd. Roof & concrete floor of St Hilda's School.
150.		Clay	500 UXB	Sidwell St. Fell rear of shop, through tiled roof garage.
151.		Clay	500 UXB	York Road. Fell in rear garden of Cambridge Terrace.
152.		Clay	500 UXB	Barrack Road. Fell in allotments.
153.		Tarmac, clay	50 UXB	Wonford Road. Fell on path opp. No.2 Wonford.
154.		Clay	UXB	The Quadrant. Direct hit 3 storey house & penetrated to a depth of 20 ft. C. damage tO house.
156.		Clay	50 UXB	Mount Radford Cresc. Fell on tree trunk and penetrated 6 ft. into ground.
157.		Clay	UXB	Wonford Road. Fell at base of house (No37 Wonford Rd)
l55.		Clay	UXB	Fairpark Road. 10ft from 1 Hurst Flats on grass bank.
34A.	40x20	Soft earth	500	Feltrim Ave. Side of building. A3. B1. C8. D10. Fragment found.

CHIEF FIRE OFFICER'S REPORT

General Summary - Exeter on "*Red*" at 01.36 hours. First Incendiary Bombs reported from Newtown District at 01.51 hours. This is the Northern portion of the City. Total No. of Incendiary bombs dropped estimated at 7,000, Police War Dept. Total No. of High Explosives dropped estimated 150.

Location of Attack - The attack was most severe in the North East, North West, Eastern and centre portions of the City. Several incidents were reported from the West and South West, but the fire was fought back from these points. A High wind arose from the South West which increased the difficulty.

Water - The total gallonage of Static water stored in the City is 5,293,000 gallons [Tanks, Basins and Springs]. From 0500 hours many vague reports were received from Police, Wardens and Civilians stating that assistance was required most urgently. These incidents were situated all over the affected parts of the City, and in nearly all cases, when an appliance was despatched a report came back from the fire ground stating that the fire was of a very minor type.

Hose - Estimated quantity of Hose used 197,000 feet.

Foam - 150 gallons and 480lbs Foamite [see report re Gas Works].

Communications - Complete failure at 0212 hours. Sketchy communications re-established the following afternoon [See report].

Accommodation - Staplake and St. Germans Reinforcement Bases supplement by Northbrook and Danes Castle [Sub-division 1] able to cope with situation.

Catering - Approximately 9,000 meals were served.

Petrol - A stock of approximately 8,000 gallons was in hand previous to the raid.

Petroleum Board rendered excellent service, and answered calls made upon them most promptly. They delivered 1400 tins at intervals. In the early stages of the raid an acute shortage of tins was evident by the fact that numerous men were required for the collection of empty tins for replenishment. Falling debris interfered with delivery by vehicles in many instances.

APPENDIX 1

Time: Sunday 3rd May 1942
2337   Major A26   Major B26
          Light A3   Light B3
Special Appliances: 1 Turntable Ladder, 1 Foam Unit, 4 D.Ps [including Major figures above].
1-1,000 gallon dam, 3 Hose Layers.
Pump state for Division previous to attack. All appliances have returned from full-time fire at Woodbury Common. 3 Majors, 2 Light and 4 Mobile Dams. Fire reported 1732 hours - out at 2205 hours.
Time: Monday 4th May 1942.
0136 Exeter on "Red".
0137 Action Stations - Pipe Lines [2 stations responsible for manning pipelines]. All pipe lines were discharging within 10 minutes. Pipe Line No. 1 Engine Bridge to Paul Street/Queen Street was the first to be required. This line was manned and discharged within 10 minutes of receipt of the order "Action Stations". Relay Pump inserted to supply London Inn Square, distribution tank No. 69 [cap. 4,000 gallons]. No. 2 Line Edmund Street, St. Mary Well Street, manned and loaded. Major despatched to standby distribution tank No. 35 [cap. 80,000 gallons]. No. 5 Pipe Line manned and loaded. Brickworks to

Belmont Road to Sidwell Street, North end distribution tank No. 74 [cap. 7,200 gallons]. No 4 Pipe Line from Weirfield Road to College Road manned and loaded. Distribution tank No 118 [cap. 8,000 gallons].

0137 From Water Officer to Sub-Division 1 "Man pipe line at Weirfield Road, connect fire boat to Belmont Road pipe line".

0151 Pump state to Fire Force Headquarters - Major A26, Major B22, Light A13, Light B13, Special Appliances as at 2237. Report that Incendiary Bombs had been dropped in Newtown District.

0157 3 Majors ordered from Sub-Division 4 [Tiverton] to report to SubDivision 1 Station "Z".

0157 No. 6 Pipe line out of action. Fire Barge supplying No. 6 Line, sunk as result of enemy action.

0158 4 Majors from Sub-Division 2 [Exmouth] ordered to Sub-Division 1 [Danes Castle].

0159 2 Majors ordered from Sub-Division 3 [Sidmouth] to Danes Castle.

0200 Sub-Division 1. Received 19 reports of fires. 9 Majors despatched. [Newtown District - Northern portion of City.]

0205 17 additional fires reported. Several major fires. 2 majors despatched. East and South of City also under attack

0209 2 Reinforcing Companies requested from Fire Force Headquarters. Last message to be received from Divisional Headquarters, until communications re-established 0402.

0210 5 additional fires of a major type. Despatched 2 majors.

0210 Relay instituted from Tank No. 40 to Tank No. 181 [The Triangle]. Delivery 500 gallons per minutes. Tanks No. 71 and 72 out of action [cap. 7,200 gallons each]. Positioned in Sidwell Street, damaged by H.E.

0212 Telephone Exchange damaged by H.E. All communications between Fire Force Headquarters/ Division/ Sub-Divisions ceased.

0213 Despatch Riders ordered to contact all stations with instructions to Officers in Charge to attend any fires they find unattended. Must use own initiative.

0214 2 Despatch Riders sent from Headquarters to open up outside communications, with instructions to find undamaged lines in immediate district.

0214 1 Despatch Rider despatched to Fire Force Headquarters. "Many fires raging, send reinforcements. Oil fires believed burning." This originated from S/L Jay, who tried to sum up the fire situation in the City from grounds of Divisional Headquarters, approx. 1 mile distant.

1215 From Sub-Division 1. 13 additional fires reported. 3 garages involved location High St., Queen St., Sidwell St., and Fore St. 1 Major despatched to Sidwell Street. City centre now under attack. High Street [main artery] entirely blocked by fire preventing access to centre buildings. All available pumps at this stage were despatched to the fire ground. North West and North Eastern districts.

0219 From Sub-Division 1. 10 additional fires reported.

0219 From Sub-Division 1. From Divisional Headquarters per D/R "Telephone and light failed, reinforcements on the way - five positions of fires."

0221 Relay instituted from Tank No. 118 direct to pumps in Heavitree Road, several major fires in vicinity.

0223 Pumps operating from tanks No. 30 [cap. 84,000 gallons], No. 187 [cap. 100,000 gallons], No. 37 [cap. 80,000 gallons]. Many major fires in the vicinity.

0230 Further 5 fires reported including fires around Telephone Exchange, and fire at Gas Works - 5 Majors sent [3 Majors from Tiverton and 2 Majors from Sidmouth deployed to fire grounds]. 1 T.T.L. in attendance at Queen Street. Water supply good. River Exe giving ample supplies. Full priority ordered for these establishments.

0230 1 Company left Plymouth. 1 Company left Torbay.

0230 Pumps available: Major Nil. Light Nil. Special Appliances: 1 Foam Unit.

0249 Pipe-line No. 3, Customs House to Trinity Green, in operation to distribution tank No. 182 [cap 150,000 gallons]. Relay in operation to tank No. 187 [cap. 100,000 gallons] also to tanks Nos. 30 and 37.

0250 Reports that fires in City centre are spreading. A.R.P. Control, High Street, threatened. 2 Majors deployed to attend priority call.

0250 Air raid message "*White*"

0315 1 Reinforcing company left Taunton for Exeter.

0330 Relay instituted from Tank No. 36 [cap. 80,000 gallons] to High Street/ Bedford Street area.

0345 Gas Works fire spreading - 2 Majors deployed. One Foam Unit in attendance. Instruction given for the plant to be saved at the expense of surrounding property. Shortage of major appliances, necessitated withdrawal of pumps from other fires of less importance. Foam: 3 No. branches and 1 No. 10 in use, approx. 150 gallons of foam used and 480lbs Foamite.

0350 Communications re-established with Fire Force Headquarters. Route: Kennford via Middlemoor Police Station to Torquay, thence to Yelverton. Section Leader Jay took telephonist to Kennford to receive any messages which may come through to and from Fire Force Headquarters. Despatch Rider standing by at Kennford.

0358 1 Company left Plymouth also 1 Hose Layer.

0400 Southern Railway Goods Yard [New North Road side] on fire. Tanks Nos. 39 [cap. 50,000 gallons] No. 184 [cap. 126,00 gallons] pumping direct to fire, distance approx. 700ft. Private Brigade were working on this fire assisted by Military and Civilians.

0410 Timber Stores, Dinham Road, serious fire, tank No. 162 [cap. 15,000 gallons] adja-

cent to fire ground. Supplies supplemented from "Header" on pipe-line No. 1. Relay of two lines 21/2" via Engine Bridge, North Street junction of Bartholomew Street. Shortage of pumps was severely taxing pipe-lines.

0415 2 Hose layers and 1 Hose Lorry 6,000ft rolled hose left Plymouth

0427 Pumps feeding from distribution tank No. 54 [cap. 13,000 gallons] for fires in immediate vicinity. No. 2 Branchpipe line, King Street to Smythen Street in action to supply tank No. 54.

0435 1 Reinforcing Company arrived from Plymouth.

0444 Canteen left Plymouth.

0459 3 Despatch Riders [Reinforcements] left Plymouth.

0500 1 Reinforcing section arrived from Torquay.

0506 Situation report - "41 Reinforcement Pumps working in City attending 40 extensive fires." Static Water Tanks in affected areas in use as direct supplies. Water mains severely taxed. All Units instructed to use Static Tanks where possible.

0517 Fires in High Street/Fore Street spreading. High wind rising. No. 2 Line Header at John Street junction Fore Street put in operation feeding tank No. 82 [cap. 8,000] to cover these fires.

0518 Petrol situation fairly good. Petrol supplies were maintained by lorries [tins]. Pumps rented by N.F.S. were near several of the major fire grounds and operated continually. Acute shortage of tins was evident by the fact that numerous men were engaged in collecting empty tins.

0519 1 Foam Unit and 1,000 gallons of Foam left Plymouth for Exeter.

0521 1 Reinforcing Company despatched from Torquay.

0523 Pumps feeding from Tank No. 50 [cap. 15,000 gallons] relayed 3 lines 21/2" set up from Customs House via Quay Hill to Coombe Street to tank No. 50. Distance 1100ft. Further 6 lines of 21/2" were inserted at intervals as reinforcing pumps arrived. Area bounded by South Street, Market Street, Coombe Street, and Fore Street, a conflagration. High wind rising from South West. From 0505 hours reinforcements have been arriving at 5 minute intervals from Areas 15, 16, 17, 18 and 19. Total strength of these reinforcements 120 pumps. Since the fire situation at this period was at its height, reinforcing pumps were deployed to Fire Ground immediately on arrival and the usual Reception Base procedure was not allowed to operate at the situation did not merit any hesitation in throwing all available reinforcements on to the fire ground. All personnel escaped.

0529 Control Centre and Telephone Exchange surrounded by fire. Fire situation such that occupants leave building. The following approaches completely blocked - Castle Street, New Buildings, Northernhay Place.

0530 Despatch two Majors via Northernhay/Queen Street to tank 186 [cap. 75,000 gallons] 4 light pumps dismantled and taken through Rougemont grounds to tank No. 31 [cap. 300,000 gallons].

0536 Despatched from Plymouth 2 self-propelled [heavy] 1 self-propelled [extra heavy] and 1 Turntable Ladder.

0600 Tank No. 183 [cap. 112,000 gallons] as supplied for relay [2 lines] distance 850 feet to Magdalen Road. Area from Denmark Road to St. Leonards Road, well alight. Supplies supplemented by tank No. 85 [cap. 30,000 gallons] 2 lines 21/2" hose distance 650 feet manhandled because of debris.

0620 Additional Foam Van from 19 Area "A" Division left for Gas Works.

0621 Additional Hose Layer to Cathedral Close.

0630 Fore Street/Heavitree shopping centre well alight. Prevented spreading by supplies from tanks No. 52 [cap. 52,000 gallons] No. 95 [cap. 15,000 gallons] and

No. 89 [cap. 15,000 gallons].

0640 Situation Report: Estimated 92 Reinforcing pumps have arrived and operated on fire grounds. Fires gradually got under control and being held.

0637 From Fire Force Headquarters "Endeavouring to send 4 D/Rs and have request Military assistance send a number". To assist to maintain communications.

0650 One further reinforcing Company being sent from Torquay. 500 gallons Foam from Plymouth, 250 gallons from Torquay. Not used.

0650 From Fire Force Headquarters to Deputy Fire Force Commander Willey. "Urgent. Save Telephone Exchange - if Exchange breaks down try to reach Bristol by Middlemoor Police Headquarters. Every effort will be made to safeguard Telephone Exchange. The position is serious but not desperate.

0700 Fire spreading in Fore Street. Relay organised 6 lines, distance 1,750ft. via Gervase Avenue and Exe Bridge. 4 Pump relay to Company of Pumps at Market Street/Fore Street junction where further spreading was prevented.

0718 Message from Divisional Officer Willey - "situation well in hand, everything working satisfactorily - no need for alarm. Prepare to feed and relieve personnel on fire ground."

0738 Clifton Road area, bounded by Belmont Road, Parr Street, Summerland Street and Gladstone Road. Now a major fire. Relay from Clifton Road - discontinued and replaced by 3 line relay, distance 1800ft. from tank No. 118 [cap. 8,000 gallons] to tank No. 181. Supply supplemented by Swimming Baths No. 45 [cap. 135,000 gallons] 4 fires in Paris Street/Summerland Street/Belgrave Road. This relay was diverted because of the narrow thoroughfare well alight on both sides. Great danger from falling walls and intense heat.

0738 Tank No. 65 [cap. 15,000 gallons] now in action.

0738 Report per D/R from fire ground, York Road/Queens Terrace/Leighton Avenue - "fires now under control".

0740 Foam Unit returned from Gas Work.

0742 Report from Police Control following roads closed:- *High St, Queen St, Sidwell St., Blackboy Rd, New Bridge St., York Rd, Summerland St, Paris St, Southernhay* [East and West], *Cathedral Close, South St, Bartholomew St* [East and West], *Prince of Wales Rd, Union Rd, Blackall Rd, Willeys Ave, Ladysmith Rd, Jesmond Rd, Magdalen Rd, Matford Rd, Wonford Rd, St. Leonards Rd, Clifton Rd, Feltrim Ave, Fairpark Rd, Bedford Circus, Stanwey, Bungalow Lane, London Inn Square, Pinhoe, Northernhay Park.*

No. of unexploded bombs estimated - 39.

0812 Queens Crescent area bounded by Well Street, York Road. Pennsylvania Road and Powderham Crescent, have been checked and well in hand by supplies direct from tanks No. 185 [cap. 70,000] No. 55 [cap. 26,000 gallons] No. 33 [cap. 75,000 gallons].

0815 Mobile Kitchen arrived from Taunton.

0830 Fore Street/Heavitree Area, tanks No. 52, 95 & 89 reported empty. 4 pumps relay [twin line] distance 3,000ft. instituted from stream No. 26 [cap. 120,000 gallons] as replenishment. Fires in this area are now well in hand.

0923 2 light pumps lowered to replace sunken fire boat. No 6 Pipe-line delivering 200 gallons/minute to 500 gallon canvas in Polsloe Road. Fires in Polsloe Road, junction of Park Road prevented spreading.

1000 2 Major Pumps lowered 60ft. by block and tackle into Brickyard to boost No. 5 pipe-line supply.

1001 From Area Water Supply Officer to Company Officer Shepherd "4-1,000 gallon dams left "A" Division for Exeter, at 0950 hours. 2-1,000 gallon dams ordered form "C" Division to report at Exeter."

Water Situation

All pipeline deliveries were boosted as reinforcement pumps arrived. Supplies from following tanks used to fire in immediate vicinity.

No.	Capacity
106	6,400 galls
38	15,000 galls
188	105,000 galls
49	11,000 galls
86	30,000 galls
65	13,000 galls
139	11,000 galls
111	13,000 galls
153	26,000 galls
79	5,000 galls
99	76,000 galls
127	15,000 galls
70	6,400 galls

Tanks No. 71 and 72 out of action, these two tanks are adjacent, both were damaged by an H.E. which fell between them.

1010 Mobile Canteen from Bournemouth reported.

1011 From P.C. No. 11 - "Fore Street/Heavitree needs more water."

1017 Contact established with Officer in Charge of incident [above] reported situation well in hand. From 0500 hours many vague reports were received from Police, Wardens and Civilians stating that assistance was required most urgently. These incidents were situated all over the affected parts of the City, and in nearly all cases, when an appliance was despatched a report came back from the fire ground stating that the fire was of a very minor type.

1019 Appliances returned from fire at Woodhayes Nursing Home.

1021 Appliances returned from fire in Pinhoe Road.

1027 1 Mobile Dam reported back from St. Leonards Road.

1040 Petrol Tanker reported in from Weston-super-Mare.

1040 Report Dix's Field tank empty-passed to Water Officer.

1049 1 Major reported back from St. Thomas area - no assistance required.

1100 Report per D/R from Royal Devon & Exeter Hospital - "Water tank is empty [domestic tank] please send assistance" - 1 Major despatched. 1 Major Pump detailed to report to Royal Devon & Exeter Hospital. At 0900 hours and 1800 hours daily to replenish water tank for domestic purposes until further notice.

1100 From Column Officer Davis, Area Catering Office, "Canteens established at the following points - Cathedral Close, London Inn Square, Lower Summerlands and Danes Castle."

1125 6 Despatch Riders reported from East Surrey Regiment.

1136 Mobile Dam reported from Division "C". In view of the great numbers of fires reported, yet discovered to be of no importance when appliances attend, all available mobile dams were formed into small convoys of mobile scouts, with instructions to patrol areas from which reports originated.

1141 No. 5 Mobile Company - Cpl. Smith reported.

1143 1 Major reported back from Blackboy Road - FIRES OUT.

1145 1 Mobile scout reported to Sub-Division 1 - "Situation well in hand."

1157 From Fire Force Commander Drury to Fire Force Headquarters "Instruct Column Officer Monk to proceed immediately to Danes Castle to relieve".

1158 1 Despatch Rider reported from Warwickshire Regiment.

1159 2 Major pumps requested at Powderham Crescent. 2 Majors despatched.

1203 1 Major returned from St. Davids Hill - no assistance required.

Fire Ground No. 1 : Area bounded by Fore Street, South Street, West Street, Coombe Street including pumps working at fixed pumping site. No. 2 pipe-line - Control point junction Fore Street/Market Street.

Fire Ground No. 2: Area bounded by High Street, South Street, Southernhay West. - Control point Cathedral Yard.

Fire Ground No. 3: Area bounded by London Inn Square, Longbrook Street, York Road, Well Street, Sidwell Street.

Fire Ground No. 4: Area bounded by Paris Street, Clifton Road, Belmont Road and Sidwell Street.

Fire Ground No. 5: Area bounded by Heavitree Road, Polsloe Road, Blackboy Road, Belmont Road, Clifton Road.

Fire Ground No. 6: Area bounded by Magdalen Street, Heavitree Road, Barnfield Road, Southernhay East.

Fire Ground No. 7: Area bounded by Southernhay, Paris Street, Spicer Road and Barnfield Road.

1203 To Fire Force Headquarters "Send one Divisional Officer and 2 Column Officers to relieve in fire areas 4, 6 and 7.

1206 To Fire Force Commander No. 19 Area Fire Force Commander Coles and Column Officer Brown reporting to Danes Castle to relieve Column Officer Summers and Company Officer Cumbley.

1240 To Fire Force Headquarters from Divisional Officer Willey "The fire areas have been defined for cooling down and relief purposes, fire situation well under control and relief officers and crews are arranged.

1300 Petrol situation - supplied good, all pumps well supplied. A store of approx. 8,000 gallons was in hand previous to the raid. Petroleum Board rendered excellent service and answered all calls and demands made upon them most promptly, in all, they delivered 1,400 tins. Total petrol used . . . 8,000 gallons.

1300 Major Pump 2.Y [19.A] returned from Paris Street - fire out.

1308 Food Situation - Report from Column Officer Davies - "I contacted the Emergency Control Centre and Emergency

Feeding Centres at Heles School. Tea, Sugar, Margarine and Milk products have been obtained from the Exeter Food Office. Arrangements with Divisional Food Officer made, also Divisional Food Officer Asterley. Mobile Kitchen will replenish stocks at Bury Meadow near Heles School."

1310 From Fire Force Headquarters No. 18 Area- "Informed by Regional Headquarters that Divisional Officer Redmond and Column Officer Leek, also Column Officer Hastell proceeding to Exeter.

1323 1 Major returned from St. Lukes College - Fire out.

1330 From St. Germans Reinforcement Base - "5 Company Officers, 7 Section Leaders, 33 Pumps and Crews are available."

1335 Per Despatch Rider to Company Offcer Judd. "B.2.X broken down at West Coker have contacted Yeovil Maintenance - remainder of convoy proceeding to Exeter."

1345 To Fire Force Commander from Column Officer Summers No. 3 fire Ground "All fire in this area under control, general damping down in progress, pumps attending - Total 13."

1402 1 Major pump returned from Dix's Field. "Fire out."

1415 Air Raid Message "RED", 1436 Air Raid Message "White".

1504 25 Major Appliances [additional] available. 1 Hose Lorry. 1 Water Unit. 1 Canteen. 1 Turntable Ladder 19A 1Z4 left from Plymouth.

1533 1 Turntable Ladder 17C 2Z left for Bristol.

1550 3 Majors reported at Sub-Division 1 - back from fire.

1615 Divisional Offcer Redman reported at Sub-Division 1.

1620 Company Officer Hambly, Section Leader Kennedy reported to Sub-Division 1.

1632 Major trailer part-time crew, dismissed for Okehampton. Fire situation now under control. Local reinforcements from Division "B" dismissed to home Stations to increase local cover.

1659 Crediton pump dismissed for home station.

1708 Fire Force Commander sent for Turntable Ladder at corner of High Street and Paris Street.

1709 Pumps 19C 1Z reported back from Cathedral Close and dismissed for Home Stations.

1712 19A lZ1 reported back from Customs House.

1716 18A ZL returned from fire at South Street. Fire out.

1717 18 W1 returned from fire, York Road Air Training School.

1726 From Column Officer Lyne, Cathedral Close "Send Turntable Ladder immediately to Colsons - relay will be available on arrival."

1726 Pump 16C 2T returned from London Inn Square.

1727 Pump 17F 3Z returned from fire Albert Street. Fire out.

1747 Company Officer Shepherd reported water supply at Bedford Circus very poor owing to tappings being made off pipe lines.

1844 Exeter Pumps Nos. U4, U2 & W1 returned to station - now available.

1852 17C 1Z3 returned from York Road. Sent to Staplake Reception Base.

1932 From St. Germans Reception Base - Pumps 19A 2U1, 19A lY1, 19A 1Z5, 19A 1Y2, 19C 2R1, 17C 2 and 1 Hose Layer sent to Staplake Reception Base. Both Reinforcement Bases working to full capacity.

1945 Air Raid Message "RED".

1945 From Starcross Reinforcement Base. "Pumps available - Major 36, 5 S.P. Units, 4 Hose Lorries [only 5,000ft.], 2 Company Officers.

1949 Pumps state: Major 52, Light 7,

Special Appliances 1 D.P., 1 T.T.L., 2 Hose Layers, 1 Foam Unit. Relief Crews organised. Nearly all Firemen relieved.

2000 From Dock-Yard Fire Officer:- "About 100 German Incendiary Bombs are wanted by the Admiralty for investigation. Will you please endeavour to collect same and notify us when available for collection." [via Force Headquarters]

2002 Air Raid Message "WHITE".

2003 Taunton Mobile Kitchen left for Home Station.

2030 To Sub-Division 1:- "Tanks at Eye Infirmary now filled."

2044 Pumps 17d 2V1 returned from York road and 17D 2Z4 returned from High Street. Both Pumps sent to Starcross Reception Base.

2050 From Fire Force Headquarters: "All part-time personnel in the area are to be mobilised this evening to man as many pumps as possible tonight. All men to be on their toes ready for action. Please report any deficiencies in equipment. All surplus hose to be loaded on lorries ready to be despatched as required.

2050 1 Company and 1 Section reinforcements despatched to "C" Division to return to home stations.

2115 To St. Germans Reinforcement Base - Staplake Reinforcement Base now full; any further reinforcing crews reported back from fire grounds will be sent to you.

2123 To Divisional Headquarters from Sub-Division 1:- "Please ask an A.T.V. from Bristol to collect slight casualties and return tonight."

2149 To Chief Regional Fire Officer, Home Office: "All fire grounds are being patrolled. Still a fair amount of cooling down to be affected. It is not anticipated that many fires will show a light after dark. Reliefs are being affected as convenient. Static water supplies are being re-charged."

2153 To Staplake Reinforcing Base: "Send One Section to Exmouth to standby."

2157 From St. Germans reinforcement base: "5 Mobile Dams arrived."

2200 2 Major Pumps sent to Brickyard to charge Polsloe Road Pipeline.

2208 From Sub-Division 1: "14 Despatch Riders available." Note: Military reinforcements will be standing by.

2220 Column Officer Tremlett and Column Officer Potter reported from Fire Force Headquarters.

2220 From Staplake Reception Base: "Pumps available - 59 Major Units, 1 Foam Unit, 1 Hose Lorry, 5 Majors sent to Exmouth."

2230 From Sub-Division 1 to Taunton: "Has your Canteen Van arrived?" Reply: "Yes, arrived at 2220."

2254 Feeding Arrangements:
1 Mobile Kitchen left for St. Germans.
1 Mobile Canteen left for St. Germans.
1 Mobile Kitchen left for Danes Castle.
1 Mobile Kitchen left for Peamore.

2256 From Control Centre: "Thatch Cottage on Dunsford Hill still smouldering. Too much to be dealt with by stirrup pump." 1 Mobile Scout despatched.

2259 From Control Centre: "Fire broken out at 95 Heavitree Road, reaching adjoining house." 1 Major despatched.

2304 From Area Water Officer: "As many pumps as possible to be taken from the fire ground, hose lying dead to be collected."

2304 Air Raid Warning "RED".

2320 From Sub-Division 1: "One Company reported at Cathedral Close. [Incident Post] deployed to Queen Street, Triangle and Exe Bridge." Many small outbreaks reported from this area, wind rising.

2320 Air Raid Message "WHITE".

2322 1 Company ordered from Staplake as relief.

2338 To Divisional Headquarters from Sub-Division 1: Attending 7 fires - 6 Majors and 1 Light also Turntable attending.

2338 Divisional Officer Redman and Fire Force Commander Coles left for St. Germans Reception Base.

2358 1 Major despatched to ruins in

Marlborough Road. Small outbreaks still troublesome.

2358 Fire at Baring Crescent under control. 1 Major attending coke fire - no assistance required.

Tuesday, 5th May 1342

0005 17A 3X Mobile Scout from tour of fire ground.

0018 Divisional Officer Redman and Fire Force Commander Coles returned to Sub-Division 1.

0031 Turntable Ladder left for fire at St. Stephens Church, High Street. Isolated incidents; small outbreaks, periodically reported between 0005 and daybreak.

0046 2 Major appliances returned from South Street Area.

0053 1 Company reported out from Danes Castle for fire grounds.

0114 Fire under control at Marlborough Road. No further assistance required.

0205 1 Major returned from fire at Gandy Street. Fire out.

0234 1 Section arrived at Cathedral Square from Reinforcement Base. [Starcross].

0244 Divisional Officer Redman, Fire Force Commander Coles, left for fire grounds.

0250 1 Major [V3] returned from Dunsford Road. Fire out.

0255 2 casualties left for Bristol [Fireman Bowman and Fireman Pitman].

0303 From Company Officer Bowden:- *"No light showing in No. 5 area."*

0308 From Column Officer Potter:- "Re College Road incident, Council S/P just ordered - not needed."

0345 From Column Officer Potter:- "Hose Lorry with hose has been sent to Danes Castle. Petrol Lorry has supplied sufficient petrol and oil. Canteen Van not yet arrived."

0345 From Column Officer Potter at Incident Post College Road: *"Marlborough Road fire out. Magdalen Street damping down - no lights showing. St. Lukes College damping down - no lights showing, S/P Unit broken down. No further pumps needed."*

0345 Fire Force Commander Coles and Divisional Officer Redman returned to Danes Castle.

0417 By E. Tel: from Crediton - Message from Tiverton: "Despatching 2 pumps to Exeter, where shall these pumps report?" Reply: "To Column Officer Summers - Incident Post, Bedford Circus." Relief Pumps and Crews.

0417 Pump 19B U1 returned to Station from Triangle.

0556 The Staplake Reinforcement Base - "Send Reliefs as follows - 1 Section to Sidwell Street, 1 Section to Fore Street." General damping down in progress, and reliefs being arranged more frequently.

0659 Company Officer Parsons reported at Fore Street to relieve Company Officer Davies.

0701 18A SX1 left Sub-Division for Ilfracombe [Part-time men].

0708 From Staplake: "1 Section to Fish Quay left 1706. 1 Section to College Road, left 1701. " Relief Pumps and Crews.

0715 Company Officer Stanley reported with 11 pumps from 34 Area [from Divisions H, K & G]. 30 Pumps were despatched from Taunton reinforcement base. Arrived between 0715 and 0800.

0803 17B 2Z2 reported back from South Street.

0805 17E 3V3 dismissed for Salisbury.

0805 From Fire Force Commander Coles: "Send 30 reinforcing pumps from Taunton to corner of Queen Street and High Street where they will be deployed. I shall wait for them at this point."

0850 2 Majors reported back from College Road. 2 Majors reported back from Clifton Road.

0900 Pump Z24 [Slough] burnt clutch of towing vehicle - send replacement.

0914 From Staplake: "2 Majors left for Polsloe Road and Brickworks at 0905." Relief Pumps and Crews.

0930 From Station "U" to Sub-Division 1 : "Pumps available U1, U2 and U5. 14

D/Rs."

0934 To Station "V" from Sub-Division 1: "Men on day leave may go off duty. Report on Sirens. All rota leave cancelled."

0945 Plymouth Pump 2V2 dismissed to Home Station.

1040 Air Raid Warning "RED". 1051 Air Raid Warning "WHITE".

1155 From the City Surveyor: "Please despatch Turntable Ladder to Magdalen Street outside Warrens Furniture Stores to assist R.E.s take down dangerous brickwork."

1225 Column Officer Summers:- "Firemen R. J. Fordham, 82 High Street, Somerset, removed to Hospital suffering from exhaustion. Attached to 17B 3V Westbury. L/F Prior [Exmouth} suspected fractured femur."

1259 Slough B15 3X reporting Towing vehicle now in order. Returning to home station.

1304 L/F Clapp returned Turntable Ladder back from Warren Bros., Magdalen Road, not needed.

1312 By Exchange Telephone from No. 7 Region [via No. 18 Fire Force Headquarters]: "Please release Fireman Parnell No. 250394, member of crew 15B 31X. L/F Woodland in Charge. This man comes from Texwood Reinforcement Base. A telegram has been received for this Fireman as follows: "Brother killed. Funeral Wednesday - Boys from Windsor. Signed Grace". Copy sent to L/F Woodland by D/R.

1342 Issuing Depot, Swindon has issued 3 sets equipment for Dennis Trailer Pumps, also 3 large Beresford Pumps sent to Truro by arrangement. 3 sets now in Exeter. Report already sent.

1410 By Exchange Telephone No. 7 Region: "Fireman Parnell No. 250394 Crew 15B 31X has been released. Making his own way back in accordance with your message of 1300 hours."

1500 From Company Officer Parsons, Fire Ground No. 1 : "Fires in Area now well damped down. Standing by and making up spare hose. Filling static tanks by pipe line. Men enquiring for food; only canteen vans available."

1533 Two Crews [Torquay and Paignton] left to pick up hose.

1545 From Fire Force Headquarters:- "Please note Rendezvous for Torquay - if approaching from Plymouth - Grand Hotel. If approaching from Newton Abbot - Ealeys Garage, Newton Road. If approaching from Sidmouth - Merchants Garage."

1559 From Divisional Officer Willey: "The bearer of this message is to be given immediate assistance in the form of a pump to enable him to fill his tanks."

1600 From Divisional Headquarters: "Telephone communications still out of commission, please arrange for a D/R Service between us with Pump States etc. We are able to get Yelverton very faintly with spasmodic breaks - have you notified Telephone Exchange?"

1650 To Divisional Headquarters: "46 Pumps out on fire ground. Pumps available at Sub-Division 1 - 2 Majors, 1 Light, 1 Turntable Ladder and 1 Foam Unit.

1700 Mobile Canteen and Mobile Kitchen left for Bristol [Reg. Nos. FHT 668 and Gn 801].

1700 Trailer Canteen left for Plymouth from Exeter.

1803 Company Officer Stanley back to Sub-Division 1 from London Inn Square.

1835 Company Officer Parsons left for Plymouth.

1845 2 Lorries despatched to collect hose. All spare hose being made up.

1950 15B 1X3 returned from Fire Ground.

2045 L/F Isaac and 19 men returned to Plymouth.

2200 Pumps U4, V3, Y3 and X3 ["B" Division] reported at Sub-Division 1. General damping down in progress.

Wednesday 6 May 1942. 2400 - 1100 hours:

3 Reinforcing Companies engaged in damping down generally, also 4 Mobile Scouts patrolling fire grounds. There were several outbreaks of fire during this period, but the large number of pumps available prevented any of them becoming troublesome. The water supplies had considerably improved and full attention could be paid to topping up tanks immediately they were used.

Thursday, 7th May 1942
1230 *All reinforcements had left for home stations - position back to normal.* Total Reinforcing Pumps 195, Personnel 1080.

APPENDIX II

Fore Street (west side) - from opposite Market Street to North Street. Comprising 8 Large Shops (4-storey buildings), 3 Department Stores. William Brock-Furniture Manufacturers, Hill & Steele - General Store, Marks & Spencers, Rudds - Stationers, Messrs Lisles - Jewellers, Messrs Trisleys - Boot Manufactuers, The Works Stores - Gown Shop, Messrs Liptons Ltd., Stone & Sons - Chemists, Messrs Freeths - Confectioners, Messrs Jacksons - Footwear. *Destroyed by Fire and Water.* In addition to the above various Mews and Cottage property in rear were involved.

North Street - No. 21 North Street, Fruiters & Greengrocers, *flat at rear and above severely damaged by fire.* 3 storey Furniture Warehouse, *destroyed by fire.* No. 19A, 3 storey dwelling house, *destroyed by fire.* St. Mary Arches and St. Kerrians Parish Hall (at rear of above), the premises used as a Rest Centre, *damaged by fire and water.*

Dinham Road - Nos. 1, 2 and 3, *damaged by fire and water*

St Davids Hill (west side) - 5 - 4 storey shops, *completely destroyed.* Messrs. Wippell & Co., Timber Store (at rear), *destroyed.*

Queen Street (east side) - No. 95 - 4 storey shop premises - property of Messrs Johnsons, Dyers & Cleaners. Two top foors, *badly damaged by fire.* No. 96 Express & Echo - Publishers, *top floor badly damaged by fire.*

High Street (west side) - from Gandy Street to Northernhay comprising approximately 27 shop premises, 3 or 4 storey buildings: Commercial Union Assurance Co, Ltd., The Westminster Bank Chambers, Elands Library- Stationers, Wm Bruford & Sons - Jewellers, Messrs Wippell Bros. & Rowe - General Ironmongers, The Somerset Stores, Anns - Milliners, St. Lawrence's Church, Wilsons of Bournemouth - Gown Shop, McGahey - Tobacconist, Messrs Charles of Bath - Footwear, Messrs Tucker & Glenn, Messrs Collins - Gown Shop, The Waverley Hotel, *destroyed by fire and high explosives.*

Bedford Circus - Eastmans, Martins Bank, Constitutional Club, *damaged by fire and water.* 19 houses used mainly as offices and dwellings, *destroyed by fire.*

Catherine Street at rear of *High Street* (east side) - Comprising: small shop property - Garages, etc., including The Country House Inn, Oddfellows Hall, Bedford Garage, *destroyed by fire and H.E.*

Chapel Street leading off *Bedford Circus* - Garages, Stores, Church Army Hall, Bedford Church, Athenaeum Hall, 5 Houses used as offices, Dellers Cafe - corner of Bedford Circus, *all premises destroyed by fire and H.E.*

High Street (east side), *Bedford Circus* to *St Stephens Bow* - Bobby's, Drapers etc., *destroyed by fire.* St. Stephens Bow to Colsons, *damaged by fire and water.*

Workshops, etc., at rear Post Office Street leading to Bampfylde Street to Bedford Circus, *destroyed by fire.*

Southern Railway Goods Depot - Warehouses containing Tinned Food, Warehouse used for storage of School Furniture, Stationery, etc., Small Workshop adjoihing occupied by Messrs Pooleys - Scale Makers, *destroyed by fire.*

New North Road (North Side) - Nos. 23 and 24 - 4 storey dwelling houses, *damaged by fire.*

Corner of Southernhay East & Paris Street - L. H. Fearis - Grocers & Provision Merchants, Hotel Bude - 3 storey, *top floors damaged by fire.*

Southernhay East - V. R. Mitchell - Garage, 5 Shops and dwellings - Southernhay East, 3 storey burnt out, 1 3 storey house, *damaged by fire.*

Exeter Gas Light and Coke Co. - Offices - Showrooms & Works: Offices - 2 top floors, *damaged by fire.* Showrooms, *damaged.* Workshop rear, *destroyed by fire.*

Dix's Field - 1 - 3 storey house, *damaged by fire.* 7 - 3 storey house, 3 - 2-storey house, 1 - 3 storey building, 2-storey building at rear, 9 - 2-storey building at rear, used as private dwellings and offices including Ministry of Health, Woolwich Equitable, East Devon Assessment Committee; 4 houses and offices and garage; Southernhay Congregational Church, west end of Dix's Field, *damaged by fire.*

Southernhay East - Dominion Music Co., Garage and Workshops, 3 Houses including R.A.C. 3 storey, *damaged by fire.*

Barnfield Road - 4 private dwellings, 3 storey and attic *1 badly damaged, 3 destroyed by fire, 1 damaged.*

Spicer Road - St. Matthews Vicarage, *damaged by fire and H.E.* Leebourne (private dwelling), *damaged by fire.*

Paris Street (South side) - St. Johns Terrace, 2 Houses; Cox's Buildings, 4 shops and dwelling, 3 shops and dwelling; Greenslades Paint Shops; Mousells Depositories, 7 Cottages at rear; Old Palladium Building; Buildings, Shops and dwellings, Buildings at rear, *completely destroyed by fire.*

Ladysmith Road - Ladysmith Road Schools, top floors of main block comprising 4 classrooms and anti-rooms; Infants School, *damaged by fire.* Girls School - 2 small rooms, cloakroom and lavatories on top floor, *destroyed.* 69 Ladysmith Road - 2-storey dwelling house, 97 Ladysmith Road - 2 storey dwelling house, *damaged.*

London Inn Square - London Inn, Longbrook Street, part of Savoy Buildings, *damaged by fire and water.*

Clifton Street - 3 shops and dwelling house Nos. 49, 50, 51, 52 and 53 (2 storey), 3 dwelling houses Nos. 46, 47, 48 (2 storey), St. Matthews Hall (1 storey), *damaged by fire and H.E.*

Gladstone Road - 1 dwelling house, No. 5 (2 storey), *damaged by fire and H.E.*

Portland Street - 7 dwelling houses Nos. 2, 4, 7, 21, 40, 42, 66 (2 storey buildings), *damaged by fire and H.E.*

Lower Albert Street - 5 dwelling houses, *damaged by fire and H.E.*

Belmond Road - 2 dwelling houses Nos. 27 & 29, *damaged by fire and H.E.*

Blackboy Road - 3 dwelling houses Nos. 69, 70 and 71, 5 dwelling hosues Nos. 73,

74, 75, 76 and 77 (3 storey), *damaged by fire and H.E*

Polsloe Road - 1 dwelling house' 'Fairbank" (2 storey), *damaged by fire and H.E.*

Paris Street (North side) - 2 storey shop and cottage property Nos 1 to 11 comprising 7 shops and cottage property, A.E.C. Store, *destroyed by fire and H.E.*

Cheeke Street - Mission Hall, *destroyed by fire.*

Clarkes Place - Brunswick Place, Ebenezer Place, approximately 32 Cottages, *completely destroyed by fire and H.E.*

The Triangle - 7 small 2-storey shops including Kivells Yard, Stables and Stores at rear, *completely destroyed by fire and H.E.*

Russell Street - comprising: 2-storey Cottages and one small Public House 28, 29, 30, 31, 32 and 33, Nos. 44, 45 and 46, The Rising Sun Public, also A. E. Englands, Builders Yard and Workshop; Nos. 3, 4, 5, 10, 11, 12, 15 to 42, *destroyed by fire.*

Summerland Street (west side) - Comprising small shops and Cottages, property (2-storey buildings) covering an area approximately 300ft in length to rear of Russell Street - number of properties involved unknown as area is completely destroyed.

London Inn Square - Wessex Garage - 5 shops, Basements, Stores etc. Destroyed by fire London Inn Square, corner of Sidwell Street, 12-14 shops, Large Garage with flats above, *damaged by fire and H.E.*

Heavitree Road, St Lukes College - Comprising; College Chapel, Main block, 1 Wing (3 storey), 1 Wing (2 storey), 1 Wing (2 storey), 1 Wing (2 storey), College Day School adjoining (3 storey), 2 Wings (3 storey), Boys College (2 storey), approxi-

mate total area involved 27,090 sq. ft.; 1 dwelling house No. 95 (3 storey), The City Hospital - Wards etc. (2 storey), J. Parkes - 2 sheds attached to Nursery Gardens, all *damaged by fire and H.E.*

Corner of Denmark Road and South Summerlands - Warehouse (single storey), Express & Echo paper storage, *damaged by fire and H.E.*

South Summerlands - 3 Semi-detached Buildings (2 storey) Nos. 70, 78 & 80, *damaged by fire and H.E.*

Clifton Hill - 1 Dwelling House "Clifton House" (2 storey), *damaged by fire and H.E.*

Clifton Street - Dwelling houses (2-storey buildings) Nos. 2, 3, 8, 9, 14, 16, 18, 20, 22, 40, 44, 33, 43, 49, 51, 55, 57, 61, 63, 65, 67, 69, 71, 73, 75, 77, 79, 81, 83, 85, The Francis Houses (2-storey Alms Houses, St. Matthews School (1 storey), 3 shops Nos. 65A 67 Clifton Street (3 storey buildings), Crown & Anchor Inn (2 storey), *damaged by fire.*

Blackboy Road (Westside) - 36, 37 38 Blackbory Road - 3 storey dwelling houses destroyed by fire, also 43, 44, 45 opposite, *destroyed by fire.*

South Street (West side) - From Fore Street to Coombe Street. Shop property with flats above (3-4 storey buildings), *destroyed by fire.*

Market Street (Westside) - Holman Ham & Co. - Chemists, Market Buildings, St. Annes Well Brewery, Bonded Stores, *damaged by fire.*

Guinea Street (West side) - Golden Lion Public House - shop property, Cottages and Garages at rear, Messrs Pearse & Co. - Hardware stores, *destroyed by fire.*

Market Street (east side) - Brocks Stores,

destroyed by fire. Denham & Co. - Drapery Store, *badly damaged.* Druids Hall to Smythen Street, *damaged by fire and H.E.*

Coombe Street (east side) - 2 small shops and garage (3 storey), *damaged by fire and water.*
South Street (east side) - High Street to Bear Street, including St. Mary Major Church - Shop property and dwellings above, *all completely destroyed.*

Cathedral Yard - Globe Hotel, *damaged by fire.*

Palace Yard to **Magdalen Street** - 4 Shops and dwellings and small buildings at rear, *badly damaged by fire and water.*

Southernhay West - Nos. 21 and 22 (2 4-storey buildings), 25 to 36 (12 mainly offices), 37 to 44 (8 mainly offices), 45 to 46 (2 mainly offices). 24 properties, *destroyed by fire.* Nos. 21 and 22, 25 to 36, 37 to 44 including R.D. Council Food Offices, General Insurance Company, Belmont Nursing Home, Garages and Buildings at rear, Exeter Education Committee, Juvenile Employment Bureau, National Registration Office, *damaged by fire.*

High Street (east side) - Southernhay East to Bedford Circus; Part of Co-operative Society; Main G.P.O. Buildings; Arcade of shops including Barclays Bank, Lloyds Bank, Rendells, Singer Sewing Machine Co., Troulans (Opticians), *destroyed by fire.* Messrs Woodleys (Footwear); Messrs Luget (Tailors & Gents Outfitters); Messrs Cummins (Umbrellas); Messrs Smith (Jewelers); Messrs Berties (Confectioners); Messrs Johns (Tea Merchants); Messrs Miltons (Chemist); Messrs Mark Rowe (Furniture Manufacturers); Messrs Wright Jewellers); Messrs Chamberlains (Stationers); The London Rubber Co.; The Scotch Wool Shop. In addition to the above, Mews and Lock-up Garages, small

Warehouses etc., were involved. *Destroyed by fire and High Explosives.*

Northernhay (south side) Plaza Cinema; 4 storey dwelling houses, *severely damaged.*

York Road (north side) - Comprising 7 3-storey dwelling houses, including: St Hildas Private School; Messrs Pryke & Palmer (Builders Merchants). *Completely destroyed.*

Queens Crescent (south side) - 2 3-storey dwelling houses, 3 lock-up garages - Church Lane East Side, *destroyed by fire.*

St James Road (north side) - St James Church, *destroyed by fire.*

Sidwell Street (west side) - Between Old Tiverton Road and York Road 2 3-storey shop premises, *damaged by fire and high explosives.* 3 cottages at rear, *damaged by fire.* Messrs Hovis Ltd. (Van & body builders), *badly damaged by fire.* Flats above these premises Messrs L.H. Fearis (Grocers & Provisions Merchants), *destroyed by fire.*

Sidwell Street (west side) - Between York Road and Church Lane The Acland Hotel Messrs Freeths (Sweet Manufacturers), Messrs Cox Garage, comprising: 2-storey offices, 1 cottage, 6 lock-up garages with store rooms above workshop at rear. *Damaged by fire and H.E.* Approx. 20 3-storey shop premises as follows: Boot repairers; Footwear Manufacturers; Wireless & Electrical Supplies; Ladies Hairdressers; Butchers; Grocers; Fruiterers & Greengrocers; General Stores; Locomotive Institute; Printers and Stationers with workings at rear; Coach & Horses Public House; Messrs Eastmans (Butchers); Messrs Wonnecott (Gents Outfitters); Messrs Hunt (Bakers with bakery at rear); Messrs Panter (Ladies outfitters).

Summerland Street (west side) - From Summerland Crescent to Russell Street (number of properties involved unknown), *completely destroyed.* Belgrave Road to Sidwell Street, this includes Exeter Ignition Works. *Completely destroyed by fire and H.E.*

Summerland Street (east side) - Windsor Terrace (comprising 8 cottages, City Welding & Brealeys Yard, Builders Merchants). *Destroyed by fire and H.E.*

Parr Street to *Codrington Street* - Comprising 11 2-storey houses. The Elephant & Castle Inn and Clifton Inn whole of Westcotts, Austin & White's Builders Yard etc., including 2 cottages, *destroyed by fire and H.E.* 7 large 3-storey houses also, St Sidwells Institute (2 storeys), *destroyed by fire.*

Belgrave Road - Messrs Woodlands (Builders); Graftons Mineral Water Factory; 14 cottages; Coop Society Milk Factory and Bakery, *destroyed by fire and H.E.*

Sidwell Street - Comprising: 2 and 3 storey shop property approx. 25 shops in all. Also approx. 18 cottages together with Co-op bakery and shop. From Summerland Street to Motor Mac's shop property, comprising approx. 32 shops and cottages Goulds Cottages, Gatty's Court. Cheeke Street and Adelaide Court. *Completely destroyed by fire and H.E.*

East John Street (south side) - Comprising 2-storey small houses Nos. 15, 61, 53, 65, 67, 69 & 71.

East John Street (north side) - Nos. 22, 24, 42, 44, 48, 54, 58 & 80.

Sandford Street (south side) - Comprising 2-storey small houses Nos. 5, 7, 37, 45, 47, 49, 51, 53, 55, 57, 59, 61 also Hills Store (Bakers). *All badly damaged by fire and H.E.*

Sandford Street (north side) - Comprising 2-storey small houses, Nos. 2, 4, 5, 8, 10, 12, 72, 74, 76, 78.

Magdalen Road - Nos. 49, 51, 55, 57, 59, 61, 63 & 65. Comprising 2 and 3 storey shop property. Messrs Warrens Furniture Stores; Messrs Normans (Wine & Spirit, Provision Merchants); Messrs Newsagents and Tobacconists; Messrs Electrical Equipment Suppliers. *Completely destroyed by fire.* Nos. 22, 24, 26, 28, 30, 32 & 34. Comprising 2 and 3 storey dwelling houses, *destroyed by fire and H.E.*

St Leonards Road - Nos. 8, 11, 12, 14, 31 & 38 (all detached houses); Nos. 32 & 34 (semi-detached), *destroyed by fire.*

Premier Place - Comprising 3 2-storey dwelling houses: Sylvan Cottages, Myrtle Cottage and Mount Cottage, *damaged by fire.*

St Leonards Terrace - 8 3-storey dwelling houses, *damaged by fire.*

Baring Crescent - Nos. 2, 3 & 5, comprising 2-storey detached houses, *damaged by fire.*

Marlborough Road - Nos. 3, 5 & & comprising 2-storey dwelling houses, *severely damaged by fire.*

Wonford Road - Nos. 33, 34, 35, 36 & 49 comprising of 3 storey dwelling houses, *damaged by fire.* Nos. 25, 26 & 27 2-storey dwelling houses, *damaged by fire.*

Park Place - Nos. 1, 2 & 3 2-storey dwelling houses No. 6, *damaged.*

Gas Works - 1 large oil tank approx. 100' in diameter & 18' deep containing heavy oil and ammonical plant, *destroyed by fire.* Wynch House of Coke and Skip-hoist, *damaged by fire.* 100 kilo watt engine, *damaged by fire.*

Dunsford Hill - Cummins Cottages - 2-storey cottages, *destroyed by fire.*

Parr Street - Comprising 2 small storey houses from Southern Street - about 20 houses, also Victoria Cottages, Sagona Terrace, Alma Cottages, Salutation Cottages, Alma Cottages - approx. 61 properties in all. Chute Street comprising: 2 2-storey cottages, Codrington Street 16 to 23. *Destroyed by fire and H.E.*

Clifton Road - Small shop and 2-storey houses Nos. 2 & 3, 8 & 9, also Abbott & Mundy's Garage, *damaged by fire.*

Albert Street - Comprising small 2-storey houses Nos. 5, 6, 7, 8, 9, 10, 11 & 12 also Nos. 20, 21, 22 & 23. Belmont Road, comprising 2-storey small houses Nos. 2 to 30, *damaged by fire.*

Lower Summerlands - 2 2-storey houses, *damaged by fire.*

AIR RAID – 30TH DECEMBER 1942

On Wednesday 30th December 1942, at 10.04 hours the 'alert' was sounded in this City, at 10.05 hours the 'local alarm' was received, and almost simultaneously with the receipt of the 'local alarm' six 500 kg H.E. bombs were dropped from enemy aircraft in widely separated districts of the City.

It is reported from the Royal Observer Corps, that 5 FW190, Fighter Bombers took part in this raid which was made from very low level.

Incidents occurred in the following areas: Holloway Street, Isca Road, Polsloe Road, Attwyll Ave, Topsham Road and Laburnum Road. The incident at Laburnum Road was a UXB, and the necessary evacuation was carried out and the persons rendered homeless by this incident were accommodated and fed at the Boys' Brigade Hut, Burnhouse Lane.

All six incidents are detailed separately below:

Holloway St & Holloway Buildings:
This bomb fell on buildings of very old construction and five were completely demolished, these were Nos 16, 17, 18 and 19, No. 16 was a four-storey building let off in four flats, and at the time the bomb fell there were 14 people in this building, most of whom were trapped under debris, this is inclusive of the persons in the demolished house in Holloway Buildings.

All services were soon on the scene and most of the trapped casualties were quickly rescued and removed to the hospital for attention and those who were rescued unhurt were accommodated in nearby houses with friends or relatives.

No. 17 Holloway Street was a lock-up shop in the occupation of Mr Vincent, a boot and shoe repairer. Vincent was blown across the road by the force of the explosion and killed. No. 18 was in the occupation of Mr Dowling, a motor cycle dealer, he was in the shop at the time with his son and a customer, Mr Watson. Dowling Sen, and Mr Watson were killed and the son sustained serious injuries.

No. 19, Holloway Street, was a workshop in the occupation of Mr Bidgood, Undertaker, there was no one in this building at the time!

In the house in Holloway Buildings were Mrs Brown and the two children Broom, these three persons were trapped and killed and they were not taken from under the debris until the following day.

One person was killed in the Home of the Good Shepherd which is situated at the rear of Holloway Buildings.

The First Aid Post in Bull Meadow Road, was brought into operation and greatly used for casualties from this and other incidents.

The loud speaker mobile unit was used at this incident in an attempt to locate several persons who were trapped, it worked at the scene for a considerable time but no answer could be obtained from the trapped persons.

FRIDAY, 31 JULY, 1942.

THE LESSONS OF EXETER.

"We thought we had a very good Fire Guard organisation—but we know differently now." These words, taken from the striking speech of the Chief Constable of Exeter, Mr. A. E. Rowsell, to Civil Defence personnel in Oxford last week, should be taken to heart by everyone in Oxford. We in Oxford also think we have a very good Fire Guard organisation. Should we, in the event of a heavy blitz such as Exeter suffered, have to say sadly with her, "We know differently now"?

Mr. Rowsell followed a vivid description of the heavy attacks on Exeter with an analysis of the lessons learned by the civil defences of that city from their bitter experience, and how apt is the parallel between Exeter and Oxford is shown by two of his remarks: "Narrow streets, old buildings—Exeter is just like Oxford" and "Before the raids public opinion was 'They won't bomb Exeter—there's no military objective,' and 'They can't find Exeter—it's in a valley with a mist continually over the top.'" Have we not heard the same thing again and again in Oxford, and does it not show the pressing importance of Mr. Rowsell's advice?

We have found far too often in Oxford that fatal unreadiness to prepare and train in advance which has been one of our weaknesses in many fields in this and past wars. "When the raid came nearly everybody was willing to do something," said Mr. Rowsell of his experience in Exeter. The same thing would undoubtedly apply in Oxford, for we know the response in such dire need would be instantaneous. But would it be effective when the help came from the untrained?

"This fire-guard business is the biggest part of the Civil Defence duties," he said. Here is encouragement indeed—and a challenge, too—for the many who feel that their fire-guard duties are of minor importance. In Exeter the Fire Brigade had 65 fires reported in the early part of the raid, and many more followed in the later stages. How many of these could have been quelled in the first place by prompter action by men and women on the spot? Mr. Rowsell pointed out that street parties must look after their own neighbourhood; they must be ready for instant action; they must have their equipment handy; watch must be kept for burning embers blown in through windows shattered by blast, igniting curtains and furniture; and there must be an adequate number of leaders, with a direct chain of responsibility from the Fire Prevention Officer right down to the street parties. Each party must have its own officer—and Mr. Rowsell added, "Women can do it just as well as men."

In the case of business premises, he emphasised the importance of having sand-mats in every room. There must also be much more static water in the houses. People in Exeter had been asked to put water in their baths in case of emergency, but they did not do it. "They do it now" was his brief but significant comment. Ladders also must be distributed to the places where they are most likely to be needed, and premises must not be locked up. The locking up of premises was "a bugbear" in Exeter, and, as in the case of the great fire blitzes on London, many places were gutted because they had been locked up and unoccupied and it was impossible to gain access in time to check the fires. Yet in premises which were well watched scores of fire-bombs were dealt with and every fire was instantly checked.

All who heard this address were impressed by its practical value, but, unfortunately, the audience, large though it was, included only a small percentage of the members of street fire parties, upon whom the brunt of the work would clearly fall should Oxford be heavily attacked. It is in the hope of reaching them that we have here recapitulated some of Mr. Rowsell's chief points, and we suggest that wardens and others who had the privilege of hearing his comments on Exeter's ordeal should pass on to all the fire-watchers in their respective areas every point of the excellent advice which he gave. If that is done, and his advice is acted upon, and if the fire-watchers take every opportunity of practising their duties and are ready for action at a moment's notice, Oxford may be able to say if the time comes, "We thought we had a very good Fire Guard organisation. Now we have proved it."

Above: From The Oxford Times.

Right: From the Express & Echo.

EXETER AND THE BLITZ

NEVER to forgive, and never to forget; that is Exeter's resolve and answer to Hitler's terror raids.

Thrice blitzed, the City's mood is grim and resentful. Lashed by brutal blows, battered and scarred, she calls for swift and sure vengeance.

In grief her heart is bowed. In sorrow she suffers the indignity of disfigurement. Saddened she seeks consolation in the thought of how healing is the touch of Time.

Hitler, by his senseless assaults on the Cathedral Cities of Exeter, Bath, York and Norwich, has tried to deal a double blow at our morale, and at the essentials of British culture.

But in this the upstart Lord High Executioner has failed. Instead of cowing his victims he has only hardened their resolve to hasten the day of his undoing.

Out of the rubble and the ashes, and the smoke of blackened ruins will rise some day a new Exeter and a new world in which there will be no room for vandals of the Hitler breed.

Through adversity to opportunity. That must be the mood when the stunning effects are passed, and Exeter begins to plan afresh.

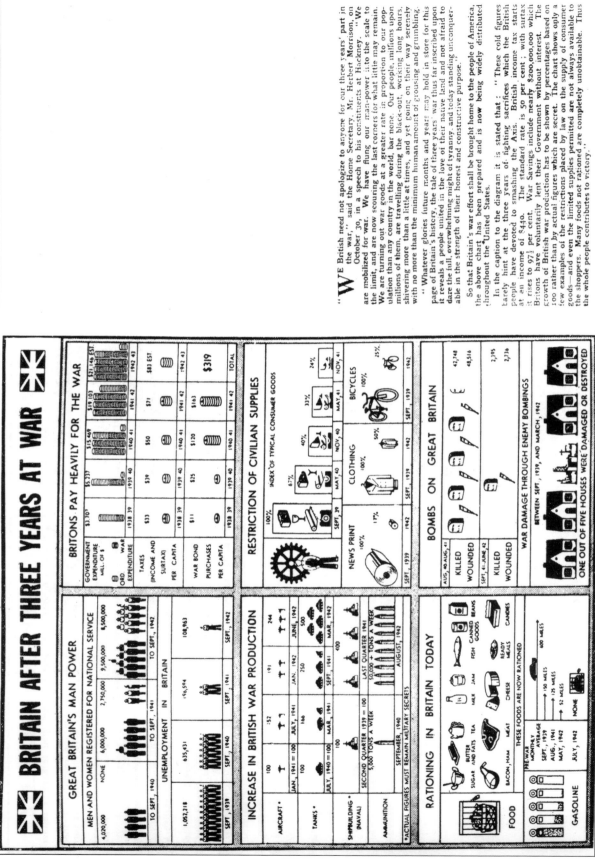

"WE British need not apologize to anyone for our three years' part in the war," said the Home Secretary, Mr. Herbert Morrison, on October 30, in a speech to his constituents at Hackney. "We are mobilized for war. We have flung our man-power into the scale to the limit, and are now scouring the last corners for what little may remain. We are turning out war goods at a greater rate in proportion to our population than any country in the world, bar none. Our people, millions upon millions of them, are travelling during the black-out, working long hours, shivering more than a little at times, and yet going on their way serenely with no more than the minimum human amount of grousing and grumbling.

"Whatever glories future months and years may hold in store for this page of Britain's history, the tale of three years' war thus far inscribed upon it reveals a people united in the love of their native land and not afraid to dare the full overwhelming might of tyranny, and today standing unconquerable in the strength of their honest and constructive purpose."

So that Britain's war effort shall be brought home to the people of America, the above chart has been prepared and is now being widely distributed throughout the United States.

In the caption to the diagram it is stated that : "These cold figures barely hint at the three years of fighting sacrifices which the British people have devoted to smashing the Axis. British income tax starts at an income of $840. The standard rate is 50 per cent ; with surtax it rises to 97½ per cent. War Savings include nearly $200,000,000 which Britons have voluntarily lent their Government without interest. The growth of British war production has to be shown by percentages based on 100 rather than by actual figures which are secret. The chart shows only a few examples of the restrictions placed by law on the supply of consumer goods—and even the limited supplies permitted are not always available to the shoppers. Many foods not rationed are completely unobtainable. Thus the whole people contributes to victory."

As war comes to a close, the citizens of Exeter celebrate, not knowing what the future may hold. Numerous street parties were to be held, much like this one on the corner of Pinhoe Road and Pamela Road. It was a VJ party in 1945.

Books by the same author

Old Exeter
The House that Moved
Aspects of Exeter
The Exe Estuary - Wildlife in Camera
Exeter in Old Postcards
Exeter in Old Photographs

Video Productions
Old Exeter
The Exeter Blitz

Further Reading

Target Exeter - Mr G. Worrall
The Baedeker Raids - Mr N. Rothnie
Exeter 1939 - 1945 - Exeter Guided Tours, Exeter City Council
The Blitz Supplement - Express & Echo 1992
The Brass Helmet - Exeter Fire Brigade
The Bombing of Exeter - J.P. Davis